Retail Marketing Plans

The Marketing Series is one of the most comprehensive collections of books in marketing and sales available from the UK today.

Published by Butterworth-Heinemann on behalf of The Chartered Institute of Marketing, the series is divided into three distinct groups: *Student* (fulfilling the needs of those taking the Institute's certificate and diploma qualifications; *Professional Development* (for those on formal or self-study vocational training programmes); and *Practitioner* (presented in a more informal, motivating and highly practical manner for personal use).

Formed in 1911, The Chartered Institute of Marketing is now the largest professional marketing management body in Europe with over 60,000 members located worldwide. Its primary objectives are focused on the development of awareness and understanding of marketing throughout UK industry and commerce and in the raising of standards of professionalism in the education, training and practice of this key business discipline.

Professional development series

How to Sell a Service
Malcolm H. B. Hibbert

International Marketing Digest
Edited by Malcolm H. B. McDonald, S. Tamer

Managing Your Marketing Career
Andrew Crofts

The Marketing Dictionary
Norman A. Hart and John Stapleton

Marketing Plans
Malcolm H. B. McDonald

Marketing to the Retail Trade
Geoffrey Randall

Professional Services Marketing
Neil Morgan

Relationship Marketing
Martin Christopher, Adrian Payne and David Ballantyne

Solving the Management Case
Angela Hatton, Paul D. B. Roberts and Mike Worsam

The Marketing Book
Edited by Michael J. Baker

The Marketing Digest
Edited by Michael J. Thomas and Norman Waite

The Marketing of Services
D. W. Cowell

The Practice of Advertising
Edited by Horman Hart

The Practice of Public Relations
Edited by Wilfred Howard

The Principles and Practice of Export Marketing
E. P. Hibbert

The Strategy of Distribution Management
Martin Christopher

Retail Marketing Plans

How to prepare them
How to use them

Malcolm H. B. McDonald

and

Christopher C. S. Tideman

Published on behalf of The Chartered Institute of Marketing

Butterworth-Heinemann
Linacre House, Jordan Hill, Oxford OX2 8DP
A division of Reed Educational and Professional Publishing Ltd

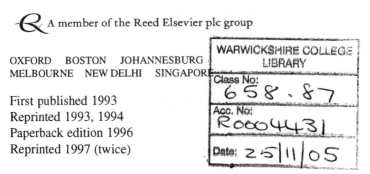 A member of the Reed Elsevier plc group

OXFORD   BOSTON   JOHANNESBURG
MELBOURNE   NEW DELHI   SINGAPORE

First published 1993
Reprinted 1993, 1994
Paperback edition 1996
Reprinted 1997 (twice)

British Library Cataloguing in Publication Data
McDonald, M. H. B.
  Retail Marketing Plans: How to Prepare
  Them, How to Use Them - (CIM
  Professional Development Series)
  I. Title   II. Tideman, Christopher C. S.
  III. Series
  658.8

ISBN 0 7506 2021 8

Composition by Scribe Design, Gillingham, Kent
Printed and bound in Great Britain by Hartnolls Ltd, Bodmin Cornwall

Contents

About the authors

Malcolm McDonald is currently Professor of Marketing Planning at Cranfield School of Management, a leading business school in the UK and a Director of a number of companies. He has extensive industrial experience, including a number of years as Marketing Director of Canada Dry. He runs a series of seminars and workshops on marketing planning in the UK, Europe, the Far East, Australia and the USA.

Christopher Tideman (BA Econ.) has over thirty years' experience in retailing. He was the first Managing Director of the Principles for Men chain, the launch of which was featured by BBC Television in its *Marketing in Action* series, and was for several years Chief Executive of the Burton Retail chain, the largest menswear multiple operation in the UK. Following this, as Chief Executive of the Retail Services and Development Sector of the Burton Group, he was in charge of the Group Marketing function and the International Development operation. He has travelled extensively in the Far East, Europe and the USA. Currently he is Chief Executive of David Jones Limited, Australia's premier upmarket department store chain, with thirty stores stretching from Cairns to Adelaide. Since joining them in 1994 he has led the successful float of the company on the Australian Stock Exchange.

Preface

Malcolm McDonald's book about marketing planning, published in 1984, proved to be a bestseller. It is now a standard text on many marketing courses in universities and in-company training programmes around the world, helping and encouraging thousands of managers with the difficult task of marketing planning. It was updated in a second edition in 1989.

Much of the book's success has been due to its practical, no-nonsense style and approach to the subject. Hundreds of letters have attested to the usefulness of the book, but among them it has been possible to detect a suggestion from those in retailing that there were areas in retailing marketing planning that differed from industrial, and general consumer/services sector marketing planning. This has encouraged us in the production of this book, a book written especially for retailers.

The purpose of the book is to explain and demonstrate how to prepare and use a retail marketing plan. It will take the reader through the process of retail marketing planning, explaining ways of implementing the various concepts and methodologies outlined. It incorporates much of the latest thinking in the field of marketing generally, and is designed to be of relevance to all types and sizes of retail businesses, since the process is universal.

Research into the marketing planning practices of many retail companies has shown it to be an area of major weakness. A brief look at strategic marketing planning in retailing over the last few decades will help to explain why this has occurred.

It was in the USA in the early 1970s that we saw the beginning of a structured approach to strategic planning. However, many retail companies tended to focus on the trappings of strategic planning rather than its substance, and, predictably, made a number of mistakes in its early use. This in turn fuelled the doubts of those retail executives who were already sceptical about new approaches to marketing. Indeed elements of this scepticism can be found in some organizations to this day.

Nevertheless the 1980s saw a burgeoning of the correct application of strategic planning in the USA and its adoption by many of Europe's leading retail groups.

Through the 1970s and most of the 1980s many retailers based their strategies on the rapid expansion of selling space with aggressive store-opening programmes. The downturn in consumer spending, high interest rates, and high inflation rates of the late 1980s brought that type of approach to a shuddering halt for all but a few.

Now, in the 1990s, far greater emphasis is being put on the more selective management of existing business operations, as retailers react to the tough trading environment. The need to achieve real competitive advantage in static or declining markets should encourage greater application of formalized, more scientific, methods of strategic marketing planning.

The emphasis is on planning because research shows that many companies that think they are planning are in fact only forecasting and budgeting, and the results can be seen in their declining relative performance. It is not that they have any philosophical problem with the importance of marketing planning, but they have difficulty in making it work effectively for them.

Partly, this difficulty is caused by the fact that most of the extant books and papers on the subject deal with the management of elements of the marketing mix rather than with the process of pulling them together into a coherent plan. Most will take you through the simple outline process – a situation review, assumptions, objectives, strategies, implementation programmes, measurement and review. However, that is not going far enough. There are a number of contextual issues that must be considered carefully if the whole exercise is not going to be sterile and fall short of its potential benefit. For instance:

When should planning be done, and how often?
Who should do it and how?
What is the role of the chief executive?
Should it be a top-down or bottom-up exercise?
Does the size of the company make a difference?
Is it different in an international company?
Is it different for a diversified company?
Should there be a separate planning department and, if so, what is its role?
What is the relationship between strategic (longer-term) and operational (one-year) planning?

A clear understanding of these issues and a sound grasp of the principles of an effective marketing planning process will be vital for success as a retailer in the highly competitive 1990s. Small wonder that there is a strong demand for a guide that strips away the mumbo-jumbo that all too often surrounds this subject, and can help retailers get to grips with it in a practical, logical, and down-to-earth manner.

This book aims to do just that. It explains what marketing is, how the planning process works, how to carry out a marketing audit, how to set objectives and construct strategies, how to schedule and cost the action plan for achieving the objectives, and how to design and implement a retail marketing planning system.

Finally, we should like to express our thanks to the many people and companies, too numerous to mention here, who, directly or indirectly, have contributed to the research and experience used in its writing. Many thanks too to John W. Leppard for his editorial assistance, which has been invaluable.

Malcolm H.B. McDonald   *Christopher C.S. Tideman*

May 1992

1

Understanding the retail marketing process

Summary

It is a sad reflection that after 50 years of formal marketing education there is still considerable confusion about what marketing is and further confusion about its terminology. This lack of understanding exists at all levels of management.

In this chapter we shall deal with the differences between the marketing concept and the marketing mix, look at the common confusions concerning what marketing is really all about, and examine the retail environment (the market place) and the variables that management can control, including the assessment of a company's own capabilities. Finally, and most importantly, we shall discuss the wants and needs of customers – what they really are – and their fundamental importance in the process of marketing.

The marketing concept

The central idea of marketing is that of a matching between a company's capabilities and the wants and needs of customers in order to achieve the objectives of both parties. This has become known as the *marketing concept*, and was described, *de facto*, as long ago as 1776 by Adam Smith, when he said that 'consumption is the sole end and purpose of production'.

The marketing mix

The *marketing mix*, on the other hand, is the term used to describe the tools and techniques used to implement the marketing concept. These are often referred to as the four Ps – Product, Price, Promotion and Place. They are also the variables in retail marketing planning over which management has direct control. It is the careful consideration of all four in relation to each other and in relation to the wants of customers, set in the context of the retail environment, that is the essence of marketing.

Common misconceptions

The most common mistake is that of thinking of, and confusing marketing with, only one of the elements of the marketing mix. Here are some examples.

Confusion with product management

There is still a widespread belief that all a retailer has to do to succeed, is to produce a good range of merchandise.

A classic example of this belief was Burton's, the UK's largest menswear retailer. In the mid-1970s, Burton's offered the best range of made-to-measure and ready-to-wear suits, at mass market prices, on Britain's high streets. The company's problem was that, by then, suits were declining rapidly as a proportion of the average man's clothing expenditure. He was spending far more on jeans and other casual clothing, which made up only a small part of Burton's range at that time. They acted quickly to redress this situation but then found that even with a balanced range of casual clothing on offer, sales did not respond adequately. The simple answer was that, firstly, they were trying to sell bright, colourful merchandise in tired, dowdy shops designed to sell tailoring, and, secondly, the bulk of their potential customers were unaware of the product changes because Burton's neglected to back up these changes with appropriate promotion. Only a crash programme of modernizations for their stores, and an aggressive advertising campaign, saved them from oblivion. Clearly, had they considered *all* the elements of marketing at the same time, much of their trauma could have been avoided.

Confusion with advertising

You cannot solve deep-rooted marketing problems purely by throwing advertising money at them. Yet it is amazing how many businesses have used this approach.

In their pre-privatization days British Airways won many awards for their advertising campaigns. They spent heavily on promotion, but still lagged behind many of their rivals in customer perception and profitability. The arrival of Sir Colin Marshall and Liam Strong led to a concentration in the late 1980s on customer service, improving operating efficiencies and reliability, and a new clear branding policy, i.e. a pulling together of all the elements of their activities within a cohesive marketing plan. The results are there to be seen. They have one of the best customer satisfaction ratings in world aviation, and a profit performance that is the envy of the bulk of their competitors.

'The Wonder of Woolworth's' campaign which hit British TV in 1975, increased spontaneous recall of their advertising from 1 per cent to 75 per cent in 1 year. From 1975 to 1982 their sales grew 128 per cent, but their margins dropped steadily, until eventually they slid into loss – all this at a time when Marks & Spencer's had increased their sales by 228 per cent. What was Woolworth's problem? Simply, that they were trying to sell higher priced, high margin merchandise to a population that neither expected nor wanted to use Woolworths for that type of product. They had thrown advertising money at a sales problem without adequately researching their customers' wants. Subsequent rationalization of the product ranges by Geoffrey Mulcahy, Mair Barnes and their teams have shown what should and could have been done.

It is naive to assume that marketing is all about advertising, since advertising is only one aspect of communication. Equally, many firms waste their advertising expenditure because they have failed to identify properly the wants and needs of their target market.

In reality many companies spend more on advertising when times are good and less when times are bad. Cutting the advertising budget is often seen as an easy way of boosting the profit and loss account when a firm is below its planned level of profit, and this tendency is encouraged by the fact that it can be done without any apparent immediate effect on sales. Unfortunately this is just another classic piece of misunderstanding about marketing and about the role of advertising in particular. The belief by the people who do this seems to be that advertising is generated by buoyant sales rather than vice versa! In addition it is very naive to assume that advertising effectiveness can be measured in terms of sales when advertising is only part of the total marketing process.

Confusion with customer service

The 'Have a nice day' syndrome is currently having its heyday in many countries, popularized, of course, by Peters and Waterman in *In Search of Excellence*.

The high street banks are types of retailer, and they have spent count-less millions training their staff to be charming. What a pity it is that it has taken until the last 2 years, and increasingly aggressive competition from building societies, to make them start revising their opening hours to suit their customers instead of themselves! Likewise, most estate agents, another form of retailer, are brilliant salespeople and could charm the birds from the trees, but seem to have a pathological fear of opening on Sundays, the only day that many of their potential customers have for house-hunting. As a final example, imagine the fate awaiting the operator of an off-licence in Glasgow who has run out of whisky on a Saturday, even if he can recite all the works of Robert Burns and is related to Billy Connolly!

We hope the message is clear. Yes, the 'sharp-end', good customer contact, is important, but it is not the only thing that matters in retail marketing. It is only one way in which one communicates with customers, and must be allied to the right product offering, correct pricing, promotion, and distribution policies to achieve the potential profit of a retail business.

Understanding the retail environment

No retailer operates in a vacuum. All his activities take place in the context of the retail environment or, as it might be better termed, the market place. His problem is to try and match the wants of his customers with the capabilities of his company within a vast market place that is subject to all manner of influences beyond his control. Here are examples of some major external factors affecting retailers.

Competition

This is perhaps the most obvious and immediately apparent factor in retailing. The arrival of Aldi, the German food giant, which has opened a trial store in the Midlands, is being watched with great care by the established major supermarket operators. The attitudes of W H Smith and the Pentos Group on book pricing will have a profound influence on the entire book retailing and publishing trade. Ratner's pricing and promotional policies have completely changed the face of mass-market jewellery retailing in the UK. The message is clear. To remain compet-itive, all retailers must monitor the actions of their competitors, and build that information into their decision-making process.

Government policies and actions

High interest rates and high inflation reduce consumers' disposable incomes, and the effects are felt very rapidly by retailers. A sudden increase in VAT rates can destroy a carefully thought out pricing structure. Switches in policy on the use of green-belt land for out-of-town shopping centres can dramatically alter the relative profitability of retail sites in the affected areas. It is important to remember that these influences, whether they are fiscal, political, economic, legal or environmental, are different for every country, and must be taken into account in the marketing planning process.

Changing social patterns and pressures

The widespread ownership of cars, refrigerators and freezers has led to a change in buying patterns from daily to weekly shopping, the growth of large supermarkets, and a decline in the number of traditional local food retailers. Television and social attitudes to drinking and driving have increased the proportion of home alcohol consumption and fuelled the growth of the Victoria Wine, Peter Dominic, Thresher, and Oddbins chains of off-licences. The pressures of the health lobby are taking their toll on the fish and chip shops, and where would one find a bank these days willing to finance a retail start-up selling fur coats?

The 'green' lobby has increased awareness and concern over environmental issues. Anita Roddick's Bodyshop chain is a prime example of a retail response to such pressures.

Changing fashions

World-wide coverage of news, sports and social events is immediate through satellite communications. People are better informed than ever before. They are stimulated by new ideas and sensations, and react more quickly and in greater volume to fashion changes. All of this puts great pressure on retailers whatever they are selling, be it toys, clothing, furniture, food, or hi-fi equipment. They must be able to spot an emerging fashion trend early to capitalize on it. Combined with the ability to recognize when a fashion is on the wane, this is a key retailing skill.

Changing technology

Products, especially those with a high technology content, can become obsolete very fast as the rate of development accelerates. Music equipment retailers will vouch for this, having seen the rapid progression from LPs to tape cassettes to compact discs in a relatively short time. The message for all retailers is that they cannot expect an indefinite demand for their current products. If they fail to keep up with the latest advances, they will very quickly find themselves at a commercial disadvantage.

Electronic point of sale systems giving up-to-the-minute stock control information, and linked into ordering systems direct to the suppliers through EDI (electronic data interchange), are changing the face of retailing across the world. Those firms who use this technology to the full, and link it into the latest 'just in time' practices, are able to gain profitable advantage. For instance, The Limited, the leading multiple fashion retailer in the USA, having invested heavily in this technology and methodology, has been able to cut the time it takes from spotting a new fashion trend to having ranges of it delivered to its 4,000 shops to under 7 weeks. What The Limited has recognized is the trend in modern retailing for the profit focus to be moving rapidly from margin management to asset management, i.e. keeping the inventory to a minimum and turning it over at a faster rate.

Cultural traditions

Of great importance to retailers seeking to expand internationally, is a clear understanding of the cultural differences that exist once you cross national boundaries. For example, a women's clothing retailer would not last long, in most Islamic countries, if it carried a stock of shortsleeved dresses and short skirts.

So far we have discussed the nature of marketing itself, and the external influences on a retailer from the market place. Now we need to move into the individual retail company, and look at the areas that it can control itself.

The controllable variables

The first thing any retail company should have is a realistic assessment of its own capabilities and skills mix. For it to succeed, it must be able to demonstrate a distinctive competence in its chosen field. Even Marks & Spencer's, with all its retailing skills and immense customer loyalty, found its attempt to enter the furniture market fraught with difficulty. It is a question of identifying strengths and playing to them, and avoiding any area where you might have weaknesses relative to the competition.

Having made an assessment of the capabilities of the company, management can then look at the opportunities to match them against the wants of the customers. There are four major variables over which the retailer has control:

- The product range – the goods or services we offer.
- The price – at which we offer those goods and services.
- Promotion – how we reach potential customers to tell them what we can offer them.
- Place – where and how we make the goods available to the customer in the most appropriate way.

The product and price are predominantly concerned with satisfying the customers' wants, whilst promotion and place are concerned with reaching potential customers.

The retail environment is the market place. It subdivides into various markets, e.g., food, clothing, electricals, furniture, etc. It is within these that the retailer operates and controls the four variables.

These markets then break down into sub-markets. For example, the clothing market consists of menswear, womenswear, and childrenswear. Menswear can then be split by price bracket, or between formal wear and casual wear, by age groupings, or by degree of fashionability.

The skill of the retailer is in putting together the optimum mix of the four variables to meet the particular wants of the customers in the targeted sub-markets. Bear in mind that retail markets are dynamic; as they change, so the skilled management of the variables presents continuing opportunities. Each variable must be reviewed, both separately and in relation to the other three. What was a satisfactory mix at planning time may well need revising later because:

- Fashions have changed, or new products have appeared, making current stocks less marketable.
- Selling prices may be undercut by competitors, or margins undermined by increases in cost prices.
- Promotional activities by competitors may demand immediate response.
- A new shopping centre, competitors opening locally, or changing traffic systems, may alter a retailer's siting plans.

We shall consider each of the controllable variables in more detail later in the book, and identify how we can best match each variable to meet customers' needs.

Understanding the customer

To complete our basic understanding of what marketing is, we must now look at the customer. It does not matter how well we understand the terminology of marketing, the retail environment, or how skilful we are in managing the components of the marketing mix, we will be lucky to survive in business, let alone be successful, if we do not devote the same, or even greater, energy to understanding the wants and needs of our customers.

In the first place, customers are powerful. If we do not provide the products they want, at a price that they find acceptable, then nothing we can do will stop them taking their money elsewhere. Certainly advertising can raise awareness of new products, but it does not, of itself, guarantee sales. There would be little point in having the best range of cheap black and white television sets in town, if all the customers want cheap colour ones.

What we must also recognize is that, more often than not, *the customer is not purchasing the product for itself, but for the benefit it brings*. Charles Revlon, the renowned American entrepreneur, put it neatly – 'People do not buy our cosmetics when they make purchases, they are buying hope!' When people buy a product, they are not motivated in the first instance by the physical attributes of the product, but by the benefits that those attributes offer. For example, men buy suits not just to clothe their bodies, but in the hope of making the right impression on business and formal social occasions. Similarly, those staggering away from health food stores under a burden of bran and high-fibre muesli have been buying the hope of a longer whirl round this mortal coil, not just breakfast cereal.

Therefore the identification and recognition of the benefits that our customers seek from our products becomes vitally important. Unless we clearly understand their needs, and translate those needs into our product offering, there is no way in which the company will reach its objectives.

Let us look at some examples.

Carnaby Street and the fashion boutiques and jeaneries of the 1960s and 1970s, were a response to the needs of the younger generation for self-expression, and a desire to distance themselves from the austerity of their parents' generation. The denim jean was not bought for its intrinsic hard-wearing, practical properties, but as a symbol of their rebellion against the established norms.

Women of all ages tend to love gold jewellery, but for most this desire was sublimated by its price. Gerald Ratner, by treating the product as a commodity, rather than a luxury, found a way of responding to the wants of a whole new raft of potential customers, and, in the process, built up one of the world's largest jewellery retail chains.

Any car dealer and service station can carry out brake and exhaust replacements, but usually only do so by making an appointment for several days ahead. Where Tom Farmer's Kwik-Fit chain achieved its success was by recognizing the underlying need of most motorists, especially business users, to save time by having such work carried out efficiently, and inexpensively, while they waited.

If we are to emulate their success, then we need to be looking all the time for the visible and latent needs that our product ranges are designed to satisfy. The real art is to get ahead of the game and to recognize real needs before our competition does.

The major food retailers have realized that an increasing proportion of their customers, in response to the pace of their lives and their desire to maximize their leisure time, are buying larger quantities of convenience foods, not just to satisfy their hunger, but to save that most precious commodity, time. Equally, they have identified the fact that, even with limited freezer space, those customers are loath to shop more than once a week, and with the help of their food technologists are producing wider ranges of long-life microwave-ready meals that can be stored in an ordinary cupboard.

This last example will also serve to illustrate another salient point that we must bear in mind when looking at the needs of our customers – that as individuals they can have different needs at different times, even within the same product group. Take food, for example. The busy professional people, who demand an ever-increasing sophistication in the range of convenience foods for use during their busy working week, tend to have a completely divergent set of food needs when it comes to entertaining their friends at the weekend.

Then the emphasis often swings to the production of more exotic menus made from scratch using carefully chosen ingredients. This need has been picked up by some operators such as Cullens, which, acknowledging that they can never match Sainsburys, etc, as high volume supermarket operators, have opted out of mainstream grocery retailing to concentrate instead on having a chain of high quality, conveniently situated, delicatessens.

Another good example can be found in the women's clothing market. Marks & Spencer's satisfy the needs of over 40 per cent of British women for bras and knickers, but have less than half that percentage of the whole womenswear market. The reason is that women have varying needs when it comes to different parts of their wardrobe. What they need from their underwear is good fit, reliable quality and washability, but as it is not generally seen by third parties, they do not have a need for it to say something about them as individuals. In fact, they regard underwear as a commodity purchase, and as classless as Nescafé or Kellogg's cornflakes.

Their buying decisions on their outer garments, on the other hand, are governed by a completely different set of needs. For the young lady executive, it may be the need to impress with her *gravitas* and good taste; for the senior director's wife, a covert desire to emphasize her social status; for the young single girl, the need to express her individuality and compete with her peers to catch the boys' eyes. Therefore, while Marks & Spencer's may satisfy their needs when it comes to underwear, it is unlikely ever to be able to meet the wide divergence of their other clothing needs.

We shall leave it to your imagination to work out the benefits sought by the men who make up a substantial proportion of the purchasers of Janet Reger's range of exotic lingerie in London, or from Fredericks of North Hollywood and Victoria's Secrets in the USA!

All these examples serve to illustrate the vital point that the retailer must get to understand the benefits his customers are seeking, not only to fine-tune his present product range, but, more importantly, to look for new lines which will deliver those benefits better. The DIY dealer who realizes that customers asking for 2mm drill bits are actually wanting 2mm holes will quickly update his range when an improved means of making holes is invented, e.g. with a pocket laser.

The retailer cannot force his customers to buy his products. Customers must want the benefits associated with these products. The difference between benefits and products is not, then, one of semantics. It is crucial for every retail company, whatever its size, to define its activities present and future, not in terms of the products and services it offers, but in terms of the benefit it provides, or problems it solves, for its customers. This is central to what retail marketing planning is all about.

As we have discussed, every individual customer has his own set of wants and needs. However, it is obviously impracticable to plan individually for the needs of so many people, so we aggregate groups of customers sharing similar needs and wants into markets and sub-markets. This process of grouping customers is known as 'market segmentation' and is an important part of marketing planning, which is why we devote much of Chapter 4 to its discussion.

Do we need a marketing department?

There is no hard and fast rule. The answer will tend to lie in the size and complexity of the company' s operations and its management style.

The important thing is not so much who is responsible for marketing in the organization, but that there is a clear understanding in the company as a whole of the structure and characteristics of the target market, and that there is a cohesive approach in pulling together the company's resources to meet that market's needs.

In a small retail company, with a handful of shops, the owner/manager will tend to be the one with the in-depth understanding of the customers and the local market. He will be the decision-maker on product, price, promotion, and place. Consciously or unconsciously, he will pull together the planning and control of the matching process between the needs and wants of the customers and the abilities of the firm to satisfy them. Patently this sort of operation neither needs, nor can afford, a formal marketing department.

As retail firms expand their number of outlets, so they start to need functional specialists such as product buyers and merchandisers, visual merchandisers, advertising management, area and regional sales executives, transport managers, etc. The role of the owner/manager becomes more complex. Ad-hoc contact between the functions becomes more difficult, because of physical separation. At this stage it is vital that there is clarity on the process and responsibilities for marketing planning and operations within the organization. Many companies tend to devolve these responsibilities to the operating functions: the product function makes the decisions on the types of merchandise, branding and pricing policies, the retail operations team on the design and siting of stores, window displays and levels of customer service, the advertising manager on promotions, etc.

There can be problems with this approach, unless all parties have a very clear understanding of the operating mores and methods of the others, and unless all subscribe to an agreed companywide marketing plan. For example, the buyers may rush in new product types that could fail without the sales team having the time to acquire the necessary fixturing and adjust the store layouts to give them appropriate exposure. Conversely, the sales team could be cutting staffing levels at a time when the buyers are introducing ranges which need a higher degree of customer service.

The answer to whether a company needs a separate marketing department rests on the ability of the chief executive to devote sufficient of his time to pulling the strands together, and on the degree to which the functional managers and their teams subjugate their parochial preferences to the common good. If they all work well enough together to achieve this in the normal course of events, then well and good. If not, then the catalyst of a formal marketing department is needed to give focus and bring cohesion to the process.

2

The marketing planning process: 1 The main steps

Summary

In Chapter 2 we discuss what marketing planning is, why it is essential, the difference between a tactical and strategic marketing plan, the marketing planning process, what a marketing audit is, why it is necessary, the form of the audit, its place in the management audit, when and by whom an audit should be carried out, what happens to the results of an audit, how marketing planning relates to corporate planning, what assumptions, marketing objectives, marketing strategies and programmes are, how plans should be used, what a budget is, what should appear in a strategic plan, and, finally, what a mission statement is.

What is marketing planning?

Any manager will readily agree that a sensible way to manage the sales and marketing function is to find a systematic way of identifying a range of options, to choose one or more of them, then to schedule and cost out what has to be done to achieve the objectives.

Marketing planning, then, is simply a logical sequence of activities leading to the setting of marketing objectives and the formulation of plans for achieving them. Companies generally go through some kind of management process in developing marketing plans. In small, undiversified companies this process is usually informal. In larger, more diversified organizations the process is often systemized. Conceptually the process is very simple, calling for a situation review, the formulation of some basic assumptions, setting objectives for what is being sold and to whom, deciding on how the objectives are to be achieved, and scheduling and costing out the actions necessary for implementation.

The problem is that as a process it is intellectually simple to understand, but in practice it is the most difficult of all marketing tasks. The reason is that it requires bringing together into one coherent plan all the elements of marketing, and in order to do this at least some degree of institutionalized procedures is necessary. It is this that seems to cause so much difficulty for companies.

Another difficulty concerns the cultural, organizational and political problems that surround the process itself. This will be dealt with in Chapter 3.

The purpose of this chapter is to explain as simply as possible what marketing planning is and how the process works, before going on to expand on the more important components of marketing planning in later chapters. There is not much guidance available to management on how the process itself might be managed, proceeding as it does from reviews to objectives, strategies, programmes, budgets and back again, until some kind of acceptable compromise is reached between what is desirable and what is practicable, given all the constraints that any company has.

In addition, a planning system itself is little more than a structured approach to the process just described. But because of the varying size, complexity, character and diversity of commercial operations, there can be no such thing as an 'off the peg' system that can be implemented without some pretty fundamental amendments to suit the situation-specific requirements of each company. The degree to which any company can develop an integrated, coordinated and consistent plan also depends on a deep understanding of the marketing planning process itself as a means of sharpening the focus within all levels of management within an organization.

Why is marketing planning essential?

There can be little doubt that marketing planning is essential when we consider the increasingly hostile and complex environment in which companies operate. Hundreds of external and internal factors interact in a bafflingly complex way to affect our ability to achieve profitable sales.

Let us consider for a moment the four typical objectives that companies set: maximizing revenue, maximizing profits, maximizing return on investment, and minimizing costs. Each one of these has its own special appeal to different managers within the company, depending on the nature of their particular function. In reality the best that can ever be achieved is a kind of 'optimum compromise', because each of these objectives could be considered to be in conflict in the terms of equivalences. Managers of a company have to have some understanding or view about how all these variables interact, and must try to be rational about their business decisions, no matter how important intuition, feel and experience are as contributory factors in this process of rationality.

Most managers accept that some kind of formalized procedure for marketing planning helps sharpen this rationality, so as to reduce the complexity of business operations and add a dimension of realism to the company's hopes for the future. Because it is so difficult, however, most companies rely only on sales forecasting and budgeting systems. It is a well-known fact that any fool can write down figures! All too frequently, however, they bear little relation to the real opportunities and problems facing a company. It is far more difficult to write down marketing objectives and strategies.

Apart from the need to cope with increasing turbulence, environmental complexity, more intense competitive pressures, and the sheer speed of technological change, a marketing plan is useful as follows:

• For you	• To help identify sources of competitive advantage
	• To force an organized approach
	• To develop specificity
	• To ensure consistent relationships
• For superiors	• To inform
• For non-marketing functions	• To get resources
• For subordinates	• To get support
	• To gain commitment
	• To set objectives and strategies

Are we talking about a tactical or a strategic marketing plan? The authors' research into the murky depths of organizational behaviour in relation to marketing planning has shown that confusion reigns supreme, and nowhere more than over the terminology of marketing. Few practising marketers understand the real significance of a strategic marketing plan as opposed to a tactical, or operational, marketing plan. Why should this be so?

For an answer we need to look at some of the changes that have taken place during the past two decades. For example, the simple environment of the 1960s and early 1970s, characterized by growth and the easy marketability of products and services, has now been replaced by an increasingly complex and abrasive environment, often made worse by static or declining markets. The days when it was only necessary to ride the tidal wave of growth have gone for most firms. There wasn't the same need in earlier days for a disciplined, systematic approach to the market. A tactical, short-term approach to marketing planning seemed to work perfectly well in such conditions. But by failing to grasp the nettle of strategic orientation in plans that identify and develop their distinctive competence, companies have become, or will increasingly become, casualties during the 1990s.

The problem is really quite simple. Most managers prefer to sell the products they find easiest to sell to those customers who offer the least line of resistance. By developing short-term, tactical marketing plans first and then extrapolating them, managers merely succeed in extrapolating their own shortcomings. It is a bit like steering from the wake – all right in calm, clear waters, but not so sensible in busy and choppy waters! Preoccupation with preparing a detailed 1-year plan first is typical of those many companies that confuse sales forecasting and budgeting with strategic marketing planning – in our experience the most common mistake of all.

This brings us to the starting point in marketing planning – an understanding of the difference between strategy and tactics and the association with the relevant adjectives, 'effective' and 'efficient'. Figure 2.1 shows a matrix in which the horizontal axis represents strategy as a continuum from ineffective to effective. The vertical axis represents tactics on a continuum from inefficient to efficient. Those firms with an effective strategy and efficient tactics continue to thrive, while those with an effective strategy but inefficient tactics have merely survived. Many

Figure 2.1

such firms have devoted much of their time and energy to shedding unnecessary and inefficient peripheral activities and are once more moving towards the top right-hand box. Many of course have gone bankrupt. Those firms to the left of the matrix are destined to die. It is in circumstances like this where the old style management fails.

Already companies led by chief executives with a proactive orientation that stretches beyond the end of the current fiscal year have begun to show results visibly better than the old reactive companies with only a short-term vision. Figure 2.2 shows the old style of company in which very little attention is paid to strategy by any level of management. It will be seen that lower levels of management do not come into it at all, while the directors spend most of their time on operational/tactical issues.

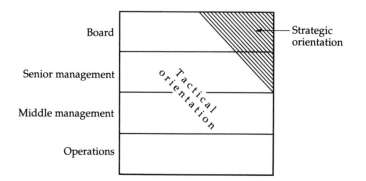

Figure 2.2

Figure 2.3 is a representation of those companies that recognize the importance of strategy and manage to bring all levels of management into strategy formulation.

The rules, then, are simple:

- Develop the strategic marketing plan first. This entails greater emphasis on scanning the external environment, the early identification of forces emanating from it, and developing appropriate strategic responses, with all levels of management taking part in the process.
- A strategic plan should cover a period of between 3 and 5 years, and only when this has been developed and agreed should the 1-year operational marketing plan be developed. Never write the 1-year plan first and extrapolate from it.

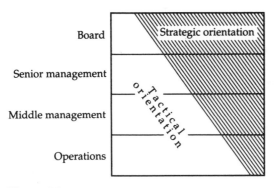

Figure 2.3

The emphasis throughout this book is on the preparation of a strategic marketing plan. The format for an operational or tactical plan is exactly the same, except for the amount of detail. This will be dealt with in Chapter 13.

The marketing planning process

Figure 2.4 illustrates the several stages that have to be gone through in order to arrive at a marketing plan.

A recent major study of leading companies carried out by the authors showed that a marketing plan should contain:

- A summary of all the principal external factors that affected the company's marketing performance during the previous year, together with a statement of the company's strengths and weaknesses *vis-à-vis* the competition. This is what we call a SWOT (i.e. strengths, weaknesses, opportunities, threats) analysis.
- Some assumptions about the key determinants of marketing success and failure.
- A list of marketing objectives and strategies.
- Programmes containing details of timing, responsibilities and costs, with sales forecasts and budgets.

Each of the stages illustrated in Figure 2.4 will be discussed in more detail later in this chapter. The dotted lines joining up steps 5, 6 and 7 are meant to indicate the reality of the planning process, in that it is

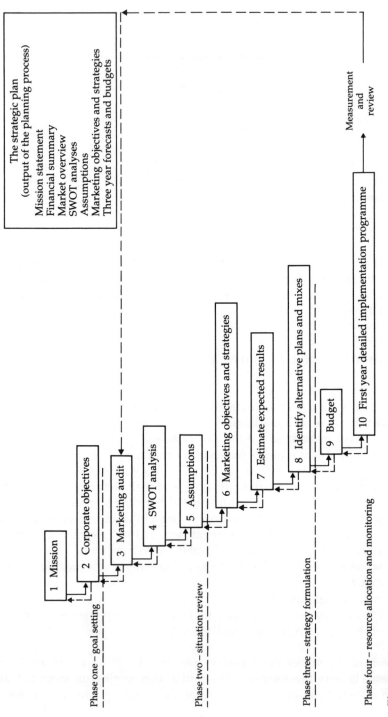

The strategic plan
(output of the planning process)

Mission statement
Financial summary
Market overview
SWOT analyses
Assumptions
Marketing objectives and strategies
Three year forecasts and budgets

Measurement and review

1 Mission

2 Corporate objectives

3 Marketing audit

4 SWOT analysis

5 Assumptions

6 Marketing objectives and strategies

7 Estimate expected results

8 Identify alternative plans and mixes

9 Budget

10 First year detailed implementation programme

Phase one – goal setting

Phase two – situation review

Phase three – strategy formulation

Phase four – resource allocation and monitoring

Figure 2.4

likely that each of these setups will have to be gone through more than once before final programmes can be written.

Although research has shown these marketing planning steps to be universally applicable, the degree to which each of the separate steps in Figure 2.4 needs to be formalized depends to a large extent on the size and nature of the company. For example, a small retail operation with a limited product range generally uses less formalized procedures, since top management tends to have greater knowledge and expertise than subordinates and because the lack of diversity of operations enables direct control to be exercised over most of the key determinants of success. Thus, situation reviews, the setting of marketing objectives, and so on, are not always made explicit in writing, although these steps still have to be gone through.

In contrast, in a diversified company, it is usually not possible for top management to have greater functional knowledge and expertise than subordinate management; hence the whole planning process tends to be more formalized in order to provide a consistent discipline for those who have to make the decisions throughout the organization. Either way, however, there is now a substantial body of evidence to show that formalized marketing planning procedures generally result in greater profitability and stability in the long term, and also help to reduce friction and operation difficulties within organizations.

Where marketing planning has failed, it has generally been because companies have placed too much emphasis on the procedures themselves and the resulting paperwork, rather than on generating information useful to and consumable by management. In addition, where companies relegate marketing planning to someone called a 'planner', it invariably fails, for the simple reason that planning for line management cannot be delegated to a third party. The real role of the 'planner' should be to help those responsible for implementation to plan. Failure to recognize this fact can be disastrous. Finally, planning failures often result from companies trying too much, too quickly, and without training staff in the use of procedures.

One Australian department store company tried unsuccessfully three times to introduce a marketing planning system, each one failing because managers throughout the organization were confused by what was being asked of them. Moreover, not only did they not understand the need for the new systems, but they were not provided with the necessary resources to make the system work effectively. Training of managers, and careful thought about resource requirements, would have largely overcome this company's planning problems.

In contrast, a major British retail company, having suffered grave profitability and operational difficulties through not having an effective marketing planning system, introduced over a 3-year period one that included a training programme in the use of the new procedures and the provision of adequate resources to make them work effectively. This company is now firmly in control of its diverse activities and has regained its confidence and its profitability.

We can now look at the marketing planning process in more detail, starting with a look at the marketing audit. So far we have looked at the need for marketing planning and outlined a series of steps that have to be gone through in order to arrive at a marketing plan. However, any plan will only be as good as the information on which it is based, and the marketing audit is the means by which information for planning is organized.

The marketing/buying audit

Auditing as a process is usually associated with the financial side of a business and is conducted according to a defined set of accounting standards, which are well documented, easily understood, and which therefore lend themselves readily to the auditing process. The total business process, although more complicated, innovative and relying more on judgement than on a set of rules, is still nevertheless capable of being audited.

Basically an audit is the means by which a company can understand how it relates to the environment in which it operates. It is the means by which a company can identify its own strengths and weaknesses as they relate to external opportunities and threats. It is thus a way of helping management to select a position in that environment based on known factors.

Expressed in its simplest form, the purpose of a corporate plan is to answer three central questions:

• Where is the company now?
• Where does the company want to go?
• How should the company organize its resources to get there?

The audit is the means by which the first of these questions is answered. An audit is a systematic, critical and unbiased review and appraisal of the environment and of the company's operations. A marketing audit is part of the larger management audit and is concerned with the marketing environment and marketing operations.

Why is there a need for an audit?

Often the need for an audit does not manifest itself until things start to go wrong for a company – declining sales, falling margins, lost market share, underutilized store capacity, and so on. At times like these management often attempts to treat the wrong symptoms. For example, introducing new products or dropping products, reducing prices, and cutting costs, are just some of the actions that could be taken. But such measures are unlikely to be effective if there are more fundamental problems that have not been identified. Of course, if the company could survive long enough, it might eventually solve its problems through a process of elimination! Essentially the argument is that problems have to be properly defined, and the audit is a means of helping to define them.

To summarize, the audit is a structured approach to the collection and analysis of information and data in the complex business environment and an essential prerequisite to problem-solving.

The form of the audit

Any company carrying out an audit will be faced with two kinds of variable. Firstly, there are variables over which the company has no direct control. These usually take the form of what can be described as environmental, market and competitive variables. Secondly, there are variables over which the company has complete control. These we can call operational variables.

This gives us a clue as to how we can structure an audit, i.e. an external audit and an internal audit. The external audit is concerned with the uncontrollable variables, while the internal audit is concerned with the controllable variables.

The external audit starts with an examination of information on the general economy and then moves on to the outlook for the health and growth of the markets served by the company. The purpose of the internal audit is to assess the organization's resources as they relate to the environment and *vis-à-vis* the resources of competitors.

The place of the marketing/buying audit in the management audit

The term management audit merely means a company wide audit that includes an assessment of all internal resources against the external environment. In practice the best way to carry out a management audit

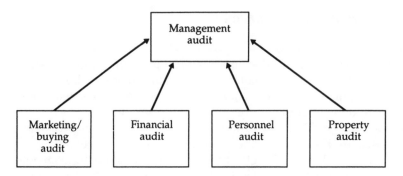

Figure 2.5   *Components of the management audit*

is to conduct a separate audit of each major management function, as indicated in Figure 2.5. Thus, the marketing/buying audit is merely part of the larger management audit. What it covers is shown in Figure 2.6. While stages 4, 5 and 6 will apply to all retailers stages 1 to 3 will affect each retailer differently.

For example, Marks & Spencer's and the Burton Group will work closely with yarn and fabric manufacturers, buying and specifying cloths for making up by their garment suppliers. The finished clothes are then delivered direct either to their warehouses or stores, missing out the wholesale stage. A small retailer, on the other hand, may well do most of his buying from wholesalers and agents, and only enter the process at stage 3. For a small food retailer, 'The Man from Del Monte' is the manager of his local cash and carry, not someone in a panama hat who leaps from a helicopter to attack helpless pineapples with a machete!

Because, as Figure 2.6 shows, the marketing/buying audit covers the whole process, from a concern with raw materials through to the provision of after-sales service, it is the collective responsibility of all the

Figure 2.6   *The marketing/buying audit*

functions taking part at any stage. For a retailer, this means the market research, buying and merchandising, advertising and sales promotion, and stores operations functions.

The following checklist should be covered in carrying out the audit. Every company should examine the external factors for the effect they might have on themselves, since not even the mightiest retailer operates in a vacuum.

MARKETING AUDIT CHECKLIST

EXTERNAL (opportunities and threats)

The business and economic environment

Economic/fiscal   Inflation and interest rates current and projected, personal taxation levels and consumers' disposable incomes, VAT rates, heat/light/power pricing forecasts, state of retail property market and rental, cost trends, minimum wage and/ or equal opportunities legislation, statutory employment costs (National Insurance, etc.), local business taxes/rates forecasts, import duty/quota forecasts, impending EEC legislation.

Political/legal   Union legislation, potential privatizations or nationalizations, environmental legislation (including any restrictions/regulations on materials used for product or packaging), national and local planning policies on shopping centres/out of town developments/shopper packing/urban public transport, advertising legislation, Sunday trading and opening hours' legislation.

Social/cultural   Demographic changes (not only age distribution, but also geographic/regional distribution); consider life-style changes (increased leisure time, longer holidays, willingness to travel, increasing concern with personal fitness/ healthy living), growing disparity between 'haves' and 'have nots' (the Henley U-curve), rising environmental awareness (the 1990s are predicted to be 'the caring decade' and see a growing awareness of individualism. This, allied to the economic pressures of the housing market, could well see a change in the way in which people apportion their disposable income, which could have a significant effect on the retail sector).

Technological   Impending or forecast changes in product or communications technology that could profoundly affect the economics and methodology of the retail sector.

Intergroup   If your company is part of a group, watch out for restrictions on capital investment, store acquisitions or disposals.

Your market
• Current size and forecast growth both by value and volume.
• Changes in sizes of sub-market groupings of customers by their tastes and attitudes

---

- Distribution of sales by product type and price level for total market, for identified sub-markets, and trends in both.
- Movements in customer purchasing patterns, e.g. changing distribution of sales between department stores and speciality shops or the penetrations of mail order, discount warehouses, and market stalls into chosen market.
- Changing product characteristics, e.g. moving from imperial to metric sizes, packaging types, methods of display and presentation.
- Supply side movements, merger/takeover activity among large suppliers, emergence of new countries as potential sources, changes in patterns of air/sea freight price/speed equations.

Your competition
- The major players in your market and those you regard as your immediate competition.
- Their likely patterns of growth/decline and the potential effect of any recent or forecast mergers/acquisitions.
- Their strengths and weaknesses *vis-à-vis* yourself, together with your assessment of their likely market positioning and stance going forward. Include in this not only estimates of sales levels and market share, but also as much as you can find out about their relative profitability, cost/margin structures, and rates of return on investment.
- Identification of any potential new entrants to your market, an assessment of the financial and other barriers to entry, and thereby a prediction of the likely stability of the sector.
- Identification of internal links by competitors that could lead to the introduction of new products or brands.
- Identification of 'partnership sourcing' agreements/opportunities. An example of these is the Argyll Group, which has joined up with two other major European food retailers to form a huge buying group to put pressure on common suppliers. Long term, this sort of arrangement could affect the margin structure of large-scale food retailing in the United Kingdom.

INTERNAL (strengths and weaknesses)

- What are the corporate objectives and are they clearly stated and understood?
- Does the management team understand the nature and process of marketing planning?
- Who is in charge of the process and what is the role of the chief executive in it?
- What are the responsibilities of each of the functions? Do they understand their relations to each other?
- What is the company's market research programme? Is it sufficiently comprehensive? How are its findings disseminated?
- Who are the company's target customers? What are their defined needs, attitudes, and characteristics? If they can be subdivided into smaller groups/sub-markets, what are the needs, attitudes, and characteristics for each?
- What are the strategies and objectives derived from these, and what is the process for having them understood by all the functions?

Product, price, and the buying function

- What is the current buying strategy, and is it consistent with the company's marketing and corporate objectives?
- Is the buying function correctly structured and resourced to meet its planned objectives?
- Which existing product lines/categories are to be carried forward and which deleted, and what new products are to be introduced?
- What are the criteria for making these decisions, and, once made, what are the control mechanisms for measuring their effectiveness against planned objectives?
- What are the pricing/margin strategies/objectives in the company, and what is the policy on supplier discounts, and how are these procedures monitored and controlled?
- What are the policies and procedures for supplier evaluation and selection? How is supplier performance measured and reviewed against the required standards? How does the company keep abreast of emerging potential supply sources?
- Does the company carry out direct product profitability analysis (DPP) to determine accurately which products are giving the best rates of return after the apportionment of their true buying, stockholding, and selling costs? If not, why not?
- What is the process for deciding on the allocation of stock to the different regions and stores? Is it effective in taking into account regional variances in demand, and ensuring balanced stock packages between different sizes of store?
- What are the procedures for deciding on frequency of delivery to the stores? Are they monitored regularly? Similarly, is there a regular review of the cost effectiveness/efficiency of existing transport methods/contractors and alternatives?
- How does the company handle quality control to minimize customer dissatisfaction and the extra margin costs caused by faulty goods?
- Do the information systems provide complete, accurate, and timely data for use in making the above decisions?

Promotion

- Are the company's advertising and promotional policies sufficiently supportive of the product range?
- On what criteria are decisions made between different types of promotion, direct offers via mailing lists, money-off offers in the windows/in-store, image adverts, prize promotions, etc?
- What have been the measured results of recent promotional activities? Were there preset objectives for each?

Place

- How do the store operations function, plan and prepare for incoming product ranges
- What are the procedures for layout planning and space allocation?
- How do stores set out to achieve uniformly high standards of window and in-store presentation across multiple outlets?
- What are the performance standards set for branch/store staff in product knowledge, customer service, complaint handling, and housekeeping/store appearance? Are the training and incentive programmes robust enough to deliver those standards?

When should the marketing audit be carried out?

A mistaken belief held by many people is that the marketing audit should be a last-ditch, end-of-the-road attempt to define a company's marketing problem, or at best something done by an independent body from time to time to ensure that a company is on the right lines. However, since marketing is such a complex function, it seems illogical not to carry out a pretty thorough situation analysis at least once a year at the beginning of the planning cycle.

There is much evidence to show that many highly successful companies, as well as using normal information and control procedures and marketing research throughout the year, also start their planning cycle each year with a formal review, through an audit-type process, of everything that has had an important influence on marketing activities. Certainly in many leading consumer goods companies the annual self-audit approach is a tried and tested discipline integrated into the management process.

Who should carry out the audit?

Occasionally it may be justified to hire outside consultants to carry out a marketing audit to check that a company is getting the most out of its resources. However, it seems an unnecessary expense to have this done every year. The answer therefore is to have an audit carried out annually by the company's own line managers on their own areas of responsibility.

Objections to this usually centre around the problems of time and objectivity. In practice these problems are overcome by institutionalizing procedures in as much detail as possible, so that all managers have to conform to a disciplined approach, and, secondly, by thorough training in the use of procedures themselves. However, even this will not result in achieving the purpose of an audit unless a rigorous discipline is applied from the highest down to the lowest levels of management taking part in the audit. Such a discipline is usually successful in helping managers to avoid the sort of tunnel vision that often results from a lack of critical appraisal.

What happens to the results of the audit?

Some companies consume valuable resources carrying out audits that bring very little by way of actionable results. Indeed, there is always the danger that at the audit stage insufficient attention is paid to the need to concentrate on analysis that determines which trends and developments will actually affect the company. While the checklist demonstrates the completeness of logic and analysis, the people carrying out the audit should discipline themselves to omit from their plans all the information that is not central to the company's marketing problems. Thus, inclusion of market research reports, or over-detailed sales performance histories by product that lead to no logical actions whatever, only serve to rob the audit of focus and reduce its relevance.

Since the objective of the audit is to indicate what a company's marketing objectives and strategies should be, it follows that it would be helpful if some format could be found for organizing the major findings. One useful way of doing this is in the form of a SWOT analysis – a summary of the audit under the headings internal Strengths and Weaknesses as they relate to external Opportunities and Threats.

This SWOT analysis should, if possible, contain not more than four or five pages of commentary focusing on key factors only. It should highlight internal differential strengths and weaknesses *vis-à-vis* competitors and key external opportunities and threats. A summary of reasons for good or bad performance should be included. It should be interesting to read, contain concise statements, include only relevant and important data, and give emphasis to creative analysis.

To summarize, carrying out a regular and thorough marketing audit in a structured manner will go a long way towards giving a company a knowledge of the business, trends in the market, and where value is added by competitors, as the basis for setting objectives and strategies.

How marketing planning relates to corporate planning

There are five steps in the corporate planning process. As can be seen from Table 2.1, the starting point is usually a statement of corporate financial objectives for the long-range planning period of the company. These are often expressed in terms of turnover, profit before tax (PBT), and return on investment (ROI). The latter is sometimes referred to as return on capital employed (ROCE).

More often than not, this long-range planning horizon is 5 years, but the precise period should be determined by the amortization period for any investment associated with entering a chosen market. If a retail company is able to achieve a business plan allowing it to depreciate its shopfitting costs over a shorter term, then it may choose to use the shorter period for its strategic planning. Ideally, to put sufficient detail into a strategic plan to make it of practical use, it is advisable to restrict the period to 3 years forward. Beyond this, detailed planning of any kind can become pointless, a waste of valuable management time, and, as a

Table 2.1 Marketing planning and its place in the corporate planning cycle

Step 1	Step 2	Step 3	Step 4	Step 5
	Management audit	Objective and strategy setting	Functional plans	Corporate plans
	Marketing/ buying audit	Marketing/ buying objectives and strategies	Marketing/ buying plan	Issue of corporate plan to include corporate objectives and strategies, marketing/ buying strategies, etc. long-range profit and loss accounts, balance sheets
Corporate financial objectives	Financial audit	Financial objectives and strategies	Financial plan	
	Personnel audit	Personnel objectives and strategies	Personnel plan	
	Property audit	Property objectives and strategies	Property plan	

result, runs the risk of devaluing the whole exercise. There can certainly be outline scenarios for 5 to 10 years, but not a plan in the sense intended by this book.

The next step is the management audit, which we have already discussed. This is an obvious activity to follow on with, since a thorough situation review, particularly in the area of marketing, should enable the company to determine whether it will be able to meet the long-range financial targets with its current range of products in its current markets. Any projected gap can be filled by the various methods of product development or market extension.

Undoubtedly the most important and difficult of all stages in the corporate planning process is the third step, objective and strategy setting. If this is not done properly, everything that follows is of little value.

Later on we shall discuss marketing objectives and strategies in more detail. For now, the important point to make is that this is the time in the planning cycle when a compromise has to be reached between what is wanted by the several functional departments and what is practicable, given all the constraints that any company has. For example, it is no good setting a marketing objective of penetrating a new market, that the company does not have the product expertise and management to cope with, and if capital is not available for whatever investment is necessary in additional selling space. At this stage objectives and strategies will be set for five years, or for whatever the planning horizon is.

Step 4 (Table 2.1) consists of producing detailed plans for 1 year, containing the responsibilities, timing and costs of carrying out the first year's objectives, and broad plans for the following years. These plans can then be incorporated in the corporate plan, which will contain long-range corporate objectives, strategies, plans, profit and loss accounts, and balance sheets.

At this point it is worth noting that one of the main purposes of a corporate plan is to provide a long-term vision of what the company is or is striving to become, taking account of shareholder expectations, environmental trends, resource market trends, consumption market trends, and the distinctive competence of the company as revealed by the management audit. What this means in practice is that the corporate plan will contain the following elements:

1 Desired level of profitability.
2 Business boundaries:

  (a) What kinds of product will be sold to what kinds of markets (marketing).
  (b) What kinds of facility will be developed (outlets and distribution).
  (c) The size and character of the labour force (personnel).
  (d) Funding (finance).

3 Other corporate objectives, such as social responsibility, corporate image, stock-market image, employer image etc.

Such a corporate plan, containing projected profit and loss accounts and balance sheets, being the result of the process described above, is more likely to provide long-term stability for a company than plans based on a more intuitive process and containing forecasts that tend to be little more than extrapolations of previous trends. This process is further summarized in Figure 2.7.

The headquarters of one large retail organization with a sophisticated budgeting system used to receive 'plans' from all its merchandising groups and coordinate them in quantitative and cross-functional terms, such as numbers of employees, units of sales, square feet, shelf space, and so on, together with the associated financial implications. The trouble was that the whole complicated edifice was built on the initial sales forecasts,

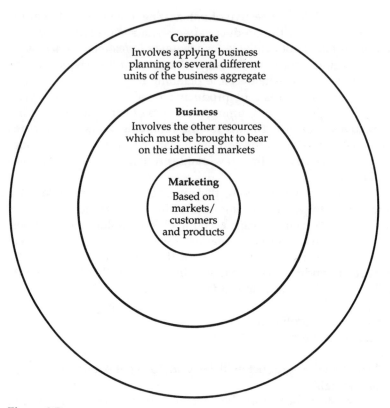

Corporate
Involves applying business
planning to several different
units of the business aggregate

Business
Involves the other resources
which must be brought to bear
on the identified markets

Marketing
Based on
markets/
customers
and products

Figure 2.7

which were themselves little more than a time-consuming numbers game. The really key strategic issues relating to products and markets were lost in all the financial activity, which eventually resulted in grave operational and profitability problems.

Assumptions

Let us now return to the preparation of the marketing plan. If we refer again to the marketing planning process, and have completed our marketing audit and SWOT analysis, assumptions now have to be written.

There are certain key determinants of success in all companies about which assumptions have to be made before the planning process can proceed. It is really a question of standardizing the planning environment. For example, it would be no good receiving plans from two product managers if one of them believed the market was going to increase by 10 per cent and the other believed the market was going to decline by 10 per cent.

Examples of assumptions might be:

1 Our store capacity (selling space) will be increased by 200 per cent over the planning period.
2 Price competition will force us to hold prices despite inflation.
3 Our two major competitors will merge within a year.

Assumptions should be few in number, and if a plan is possible irrespective of the assumptions made, then the assumptions are unnecessary.

Marketing objectives and strategies

The next step in marketing planning is the writing of marketing objectives and strategies, the key step in the whole process.

An objective is what you want to achieve. A strategy is how you plan to achieve your objectives. Thus, there can be objectives and strategies at all levels in marketing. For example, there can be advertising objectives and strategies, and pricing objectives and strategies.

However, the important point to remember about marketing objectives is that they are about products and markets only. Commonsense will confirm that it is only by selling something to someone that the company's financial goals can be achieved, and that advertising, pricing, service levels, and so on are the means (or strategies) by which we might succeed in doing this. Thus, pricing objectives, sales promotion objectives, advertising objectives and the like should not be confused with marketing objectives.

Marketing objectives are simply about one or more of the following:

• Existing products in existing markets.
• New products for existing markets.
• Existing products for new markets.
• New products for new markets.

They should be capable of measurement, otherwise they are not objectives. Directional terms such as 'maximize', 'minimize', 'penetrate', 'increase' etc. are only acceptable if quantitative measurement can be attached to them.

Measurement should be in terms of sales volume, value, market share, percentage penetration of outlets, and so on.

Marketing strategies are the means by which marketing objectives will be achieved and generally are concerned with the four Ps, as follows:

Product	The general policies for product deletions, modifications, additions, design, packaging, etc.
Price	The general pricing policies to be followed for product groups in market segments.
Place	The general policies for store siting and acquisition and customer service levels.
Promotion	The general policies for communicating with customers under the relevant headings, such as advertising, store/branch staff, sales promotion, direct mail, etc.

Once this major planning task has been completed, it is normal at this stage to employ judgement, analogous experience, field tests, and so on, to test the feasibility of the objectives and strategies in terms of market share, sales, costs, profits, and so on. It is also normally at this stage that alternative plans and mixes are delineated, if necessary.

Programmes

In a strategic marketing plan these strategies would normally be costed out approximately and, if not practicable, alternative strategies would be proposed and costed out until a satisfactory solution could be reached. This would then become the budget. In a 1-year tactical plan the general marketing strategies would be developed into specific sub-objectives, each supported by more detailed strategy and action statements.

Use of marketing plans

A written marketing plan is the backcloth against which operational decisions are taken. Consequently too much detail should not be attempted. The plan's main functions are to determine where the company is now, where it wants to go, and how to get there. It lies at the heart of a company's revenue-generating activities and from it flow all other corporate activities, such as the timing of the cash flow, the size and character of the labour force, and so on.

The marketing plan should be distributed on a 'need to know' basis only. It is important that it should be used as an aid to effective management. It cannot be a substitute for it.

The marketing budget

It will be obvious from all of this that the setting of budgets now becomes not only much easier, but the resulting budgets are more likely to be realistic and related to what the company wants to achieve rather than just one function. The problem of designing a dynamic system for budget setting rather than the 'tablets of stone' approach, which is more common, is a major challenge to the marketing and financial directors of all companies.

The most satisfactory approach would be for a marketing director to justify all his marketing expenditure from a zero base each year against the tasks he wishes to accomplish. A little thought will confirm that this is exactly the approach recommended in this chapter. If these procedures are followed, a hierarchy of objectives is built up in such a way that every item of budgeted expenditure can be related back to the initial corporate financial objectives. For example, if sales promotion is a major means of achieving an objective in a particular market, then it should be possible for each sales promotion item appearing in the programme to be related back to a major objective.

Doing it this way not only ensures that every item of expenditure is fully accounted for as part of a rational, objective, and task approach, but also that when changes have to be made during the period to which the plan relates, such changes can be made in such a way that the least damage is caused to the company's long-term objectives.

There is, of course, no textbook answer to problems relating to questions such as whether packaging development should be a marketing or a product expense, and whether some distribution costs could be considered to be marketing costs. For example, insistence on high service levels can result in high inventory-carrying costs. Only commonsense will reveal workable solutions to issues such as these.

Under price, however, any form of discounting that reduces the expected gross income, such as promotional discounts, quantity discounts, royalty rebates, and so on, as well as store-staff selling incentives should be given the most careful attention as incremental marketing expenses. Most obvious incremental marketing expenses will occur, however, under the heading of promotion in the form of advertising, sales promotional expenditure, direct mail costs, and so on.

The important point about the measurable effects of marketing activity is that anticipated levels should be the result of the most careful analysis of what is required to take the company towards its goals, while equal attention should be paid to gathering all items of expenditure under appropriate headings. The healthiest way of treating these issues is a zero-based budgeting approach.

What should appear in a strategic marketing plan?

A written strategic marketing plan should not be too detailed. What should actually be written down is shown in the following checklist. Further details and explanations about each of the components will be given in later chapters.

WHAT SHOULD APPEAR IN A STRATEGIC MARKETING PLAN?

1 Start with a mission or purpose statement.
2 Next include a financial summary that illustrates graphically revenue and profit for the full planning period.
3 Now do a market overview:

    (a) What is the market?
    (b) Has the market declined or grown?
    (c) How does it break down into segments?
    (d) What are the trends in each?

    Keep it simple. If you do not have the facts, make estimates. Use life cycles, bar charts and pie charts to make it all crystal clear.
4 Now identify the key segments and do a SWOT for each one:

    (a) Outline the major external influences and their impact on each segment.
    (b) List the key factors for success. There should be less than five.
    (c) Give an assessment of the company's differential strengths and weaknesses compared with those of its competitors. Score yourself and your competitors out of ten and then multiply each score by a weighting factor for each critical success factor, e.g. CSF 1 = 60, CSF 2 = 25, CSF 3 = 10, CSF 4 = 5.

5 Make a brief statement about the key issues that have to be addressed in the planning period.
6 Summarize the SWOTs, using a portfolio matrix in order to illustrate the important relationships between the key points of your business.
7 List your assumptions.
8 Set objectives and strategies.
9 Summarize your resource requirements for the planning period in the form of a budget

---

This checklist should be borne in mind throughout the remainder of this book.

What is a mission or purpose statement?

The checklist above shows that a strategic marketing plan should begin with a mission or purpose statement – perhaps the most difficult task in marketing planning for managers to master, largely because it is philosophical and qualitative in nature. Many organizations find their different departments, and sometimes even different groups in the same department, pulling in different directions, often with disastrous results, simply because the organization hasn't defined the boundaries of the business and the way it wishes to do business.

Take, for example, a multiple clothing company, where the product director feels the route to success is high volume at very competitive prices, while the retail operations director hankers after sophisticated store design and layout, with low stock densities on the shop floor. With such confusion at the top, it is not hard to imagine the potential for chaos among the rest of their teams further down.

A different example concerns a hosiery buyer for a department store group. She believed her mission was to maximize profit, whereas research showed that women shopped in department stores for items other than hosiery. They did, however, expect hosiery to be on sale, even though that was rarely the purpose of their visit. This buyer, in trying to maximize profit, limited the number of brands, colours and sizes on sale, with the result that many women visitors to the store were disappointed and did not return. So it can be seen that in this case by maximizing her own profit, she was suboptimizing the total profit of the group. In this case the role of her section was more of a service role than a profit-maximizing role.

Here we can see two levels of mission. One is a corporate mission statement, the other is a lower level, or purpose, statement. But there is yet another level, as shown in the following summary:

Type 1   'Motherhood'. Usually found inside annual reports and designed to 'stroke' shareholders. Otherwise of no practical use.

Type 2   *The real thing*. A meaningful statement, unique to the organization concerned, which 'impacts' on the behaviour of the executives at all levels.

Type 3   A *'purpose' statement* (or lower level mission statement). It is appropriate at the strategic business unit, departmental or product group level of the organization.

The following should appear in a mission or purpose statement, which should normally consist of no more than one page:

1 Role or contribution:

   (a) Profit (specify).
   (b) Service.
   (c) Opportunity seeker.

2 Business definition – define the business, preferably in terms of the benefits you provide or the needs you satisfy, rather than in terms of what you make.

3 Distinctive competences – these are the essential skills/capabilities/ resources that underpin whatever success has been achieved to date. It can consist of one particular item or the possession of a number of skills compared with competitors. If, however, you could equally well put a competitor's name to these distinctive competences, then they are not distinctive competences.

4 Indications for the future:

   (a) What the firm will do.
   (b) What the firm might do.
   (c) What the firm will never do

This process and its relation to the other issues discussed in this chapter, are summarized in Figure 2.8.

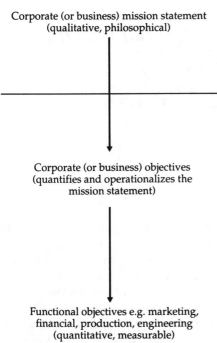

Figure 2.8

3

The marketing planning process: 2 Removing the myth

Summary

Having described the process of marketing planning and the ground to be covered in a marketing audit, our purpose now is to highlight some of the problems you are likely to encounter on the way. It is an important chapter, especially if you operate in a medium-sized or large company, as it will make you aware of some of the barriers to be overcome.

Chapter 3 has a reminder of what marketing planning is, a discussion of the naivety/ignorance surrounding the subject, and a list of the most commonly encountered marketing planning problems. These include weak support from the chief executive and top management; the lack of a plan for planning; lack of line management support; confusion over planning terms; the use of numbers in lieu of written objectives and strategies; too much detail, too far ahead; once a year ritual; the separation of operational planning from strategic planning; failure to integrate marketing planning into corporate planning; and the delegation of planning to a planner.

Finally there are some specific thoughts on the essential requisites for retail strategic marketing planning in the 1990s.

Introduction

Much of what passes for marketing planning is largely ineffective, owing to naivety and lack of understanding of the apparent simplicity and logic of the process outlined in the previous chapter. This is the conclusion drawn from 4 years' research into marketing planning in 200 British industrial goods companies carried out by Malcolm McDonald, one of the authors. There were 400 interviews with directors in these companies, and subsequent research work was with leading retail organizations. Recent studies at universities in Europe, the USA and Australia have confirmed McDonald's findings.

Let us remind ourselves that, when the business concerned is in manufacturing, distribution, or (as we are concerned with in this book) retailing, marketing's contribution to its success lies in the identification and detailed analysis of opportunities to meet the future needs of its potential customers, and a professional approach to selling to well-defined market segments those goods or services that deliver the sought-after benefits. Make no mistake, whatever the importance of pricing, discounts, advertising and promotion, the product itself is the paramount factor in the relation with a retailer's customers.

In addition, beware the trap of confusing this analytical process with budgets and forecasts. Those of course we need. Would the accountants in our midst ever let us forget it? Remember, however, that budgets and forecasts are a by-product of the marketing planning process, and a means of measuring its efficacy. They do not exist in splendid isolation, with a *raison d'être* of their own.

Another myth worth dealing with at this stage is that retailing is somehow unique and subject to a number of factors that mitigate against effective strategic marketing planning. The sort of factors quoted include:

- The speed and unpredictability of changes in retail markets.
- The fluidity of the competitive structure of retailing.
- Shortening life cycles for retail formats and propositions.
- The highly geared and rapid effect on retail sales and margins of relatively small shifts in the general economic climate.

There can be no argument that the retail environment calls for a high degree of flexibility from its decision-takers. However, in the 1990s, with a high cost of capital, a slowing down in consumer spending, and continued inflation, greater emphasis is going to be placed on the effective management of established business resources. Flexibility and speed of reaction will still be important, but they will be doubly effective if they are used in conjunction with a well-constructed marketing strategy. Distinctive competence in what will be a very tough market place will not come from thrashing about like a beast in torment. It will come from the considered application of increasingly complex competitive data analysis, and the formulation of more scientific methods of strategic marketing planning among the more forward-looking retail organizations.

Ignorance of marketing planning and associated operational problems

Let us now return to the more general issues of marketing planning. The degree to which a company is able to cope with its retailing environment is very much a function of the understanding it has of the marketing planning process as a means of sharpening the rationality and focus of all levels of management throughout the organization.

This requires further explanation. What most companies think of as planning systems are little more than forecasting and budgeting systems. These give impetus and direction to tackling the current operational problems of the business, but tend merely to protect the current business unchanged into the future – something often referred to in management literature as 'tunnel vision'.

The problem with this approach is that because companies are dynamically evolving systems within a dynamically evolving business environment, some means of evaluation of the way in which the two interact has to be found in order that there should be a better matching between them. Otherwise, because of a general unpreparedness, a company will suffer increased pressures in the short term, in trying to react and to cope with environmental factors.

Many companies, having gone through various forms of rationalization or efficiency-increasing measures, become aware of the opportunities for making profit that have been lost to them because of their unpreparedness, but are confused about how to make better use of their limited resources. This problem increases in importance in relation to the size and diversity of companies.

In other words, there is widespread awareness of lost market opportunities through unpreparedness and real confusion over what to do about it. It is hard not to conclude therefore that there is a strong relation between these two problems and the systems most widely in use at present, i.e. sales forecasting and budgeting systems.

The most frequently mentioned operating problems resulting from a reliance on traditional sales forecasting and budgeting procedures in the absence of a marketing planning system, are the following:

1   Lost opportunities for profit.
2   Meaningless numbers in long-range plans.
3   Unrealistic objectives.
4   Lack of actionable market information.
5   Interfunctional strife.
6   Management frustration.

7   Proliferation of products and markets.
8   Wasted promotional expenditure.
9   Pricing confusion.
10 Growing vulnerability to environmental change.
11 Loss of control over the business.

It is not difficult to see the connection between all these problems. However, what is perhaps not apparent from the list is that each of these operational difficulties is in fact a symptom of a much larger problem, which emanates from the way in which the objectives of a firm are set.

The meaningfulness, hence the eventual effectiveness, of any objective is heavily dependent on the quality of the informational inputs about the business environment. However, objectives also need to be realistic, and, to be realistic, they have to be closely related to the firm's particular capabilities in the form of its assets, competences and reputation, which have evolved over a number of years.

The objective-setting process of a business, then, is central to its effectiveness. What the research study demonstrated conclusively is that it is inadequacies in the objective-setting process that lie at the heart of many of the problems of British companies. Since companies are based on the existence of markets, and since a company's sole means of making a profit is to find and maintain profitable markets, then clearly setting objectives in respect of these markets is a key business function. If the process by which this key function is performed is inadequate in relation to the differing organizational settings in which it takes place, it follows that operational efficiency will be adversely affected.

Some kind of appropriate system has to be used to enable meaningful and realistic marketing objectives to be set. A frequent complaint is the preoccupation with short-term thinking and an almost total lack of what has been referred to as 'strategic thinking'. This was referred to briefly in Chapter 2. Another complaint is that plans consist largely of numbers, which are difficult to evaluate in any meaningful way, since they do not highlight and quantify opportunities, emphasize key issues, show the company's position clearly in its markets, or delineate the means of achieving the sales forecasts. Indeed very often the actual numbers that are written down bear little relation to any of these things. Sales targets are often inflated in the hope of stimulating higher achievement, and the actual budgets themselves are deflated in order to provide a safety net against shortfall. Both actions are demotivators and both lead to the frequent use of expressions such as 'ritual', 'the numbers game', 'meaningless horsetrading', and so on. It it easy to see how the problems listed above begin to manifest themselves in this sort of environment. Closely allied to this is the frequent reference to profit as being the only objective necessary to successful business performance.

This theme is frequently encountered. There is in the minds of many business people the assumption that in order to be commercially successful, all that is necessary is for 'the boss' to set profit targets, to decentralize the firm into groups of similar activities, and then to make managers accountable for achieving those profits.

However, even though a majority of British companies have made the making of 'profit' almost the sole objective, many of them have gone into decline, and, ironically, there has also been a decline in real profitability. There are countless examples of companies pursuing decentralized profit goals that have failed miserably. Why should this be so? It is largely because some top managers believe that all they have to do is to set profit targets, and somehow middle management will automatically make everything come right. Indeed there is much evidence to show that many companies believe that planning is only about setting profit goals. However, while this is an easy task for any company to do, saying exactly how these results are to be achieved is altogether a different matter.

Here it is necessary to focus attention on what so many companies appear to be bad at, namely determining strategies for matching what the firm is good at with properly researched market-centred opportunities, and then scheduling and costing out what has to be done to achieve these objectives. There is little evidence of a deep understanding of what it is that companies can do better than their competitors or of how their distinctive competence can be matched with the needs of certain customer groups. Instead, volume increases and minimum rates of return on investment are frequently applied to all products and markets, irrespective of market shares, market growth rate, or the longevity of the product life cycle. Indeed there is a lot of evidence to show that many companies are in trouble today precisely because their decentralized units manage their businesses only for the current profit and loss account, often at the expense of giving up valuable and hard-earned market share and running down the current business.

Thus, financial objectives, while being essential measures of the desired performance of a company, are of little practical help, since they say nothing about how the results are to be achieved. The same applies to sales forecasts and budgets, which are not marketing objectives and strategies. Understanding the real meaning and significance of marketing objectives helps managers to know what information they need to enable them to think through the implications of choosing one or more positions in the market. Finding the right words to describe the logic of marketing objectives and strategies is infinitely more difficult than writing down numbers on a piece of paper and leaving the strategies implicit. This lies at the heart of the problem; for clearly a numbers-orientated system will not encourage managers to think in a structured way about strategically relevant market segments, nor will it encourage the collection, analysis and synthesis of actionable market data. And in the absence of such activities within operating units, it is unlikely that headquarters will have much other than intuition and 'feel' to use as a basis for decisions about the management of scarce resources.

This raises the difficult question of how these very complex problems can be overcome, for this is what baffles those who have been forced by market pressures to consider different ways of coping with their environment. The problem is to get managers throughout an organization to think beyond the horizon of the current year's operations. This applies universally to all types and sizes of company. Even chief executives of small companies find difficulty in breaking out of the fetters of the current profit and loss account.

The successes enjoyed in the past are often the result of the easy marketability of products, and during periods of high economic prosperity there was little pressure on companies to do anything other than solve operational problems as they arose. Careful planning for the future seemed unnecessary. However, most companies today find themselves in increasingly competitive markets, and there is a growing realization that success in the future will come only from patient and meticulous planning and market preparation. This entails making a commitment to the future.

The problem is that, in large companies, managers who are evaluated and rewarded on the basis of current operations find difficulty in concerning themselves about the corporate future. This problem is exacerbated by behavioural issues, in the sense that it is safer, and more rewarding personally, for a manager to do what he knows best, which in most cases is to manage his current rate of products and customers in order to make the current year's budget.

Unfortunately long-range sales forecasting systems do not provide the answer. This kind of extrapolative approach fails to solve the problem of identifying precisely what has to be done today to ensure success in the future. Exactly the same problem exists in both large diversified companies and in small undiversified companies, except that in the former the problem is magnified and multiplied by the complexities of distance, hierarchical levels of management, and diversity of operations. Nevertheless the problem is fundamentally the same.

Events that affect economic performance in a business come from so many directions, and in so many forms, that it is impossible for any manager to be precise about how they interact in the form of problems to be overcome, and opportunities to be exploited. The best a manager can do is to form a reasoned view about how they have affected the past, and how they will develop in the future, and what action needs to be taken over a period of time to enable the company to prepare itself for the expected changes. The problem is how to get managers to formulate their thoughts about these things, for until they have, it is unlikely that any objectives that are set will have much relevance or meaning.

Einstein wrote: 'The formulation of a problem is far more essential than its solution, which may be merely a matter of mathematical or experimental skill. To raise new questions, new possibilities, to regard old problems from a new angle, requires creative imagination.'

Unfortunately such creativity is rare, especially when most managers are totally absorbed in managing today's business. Accordingly, they need some system that will help them to think in a structured way about problem formulation. It is the provision of such a rational framework to help them to make explicit their intuitive economic models of the business, that is almost totally lacking from the forecasting and budgeting systems of most companies. It is apparent that in the absence of any such synthesized and simplified views of the business, setting meaningful objectives for the future seems like an insurmountable problem, and this in turn encourages the perpetuation of systems that merely extrapolate from numbers.

There is also substantial evidence that those companies that provide procedures for this process, in the form of standardized methods of presentation, have gone some considerable way to overcoming this problem. Although the possible number of analyses of business situations is infinite, procedural approaches help managers throughout an organization at least to consider the essential elements of problem definition in a structured way. This applies even to difficult foreign markets where data and information are hard to come by, and even to markets that are being managed by agents, who find that these structured approaches, properly managed, help their businesses as well as those of their principals.

However, there are two further major advantages enjoyed by these companies. Firstly, the level of management frustration is lower and motivation is higher because the system provides a method of reaching agreement on such difficult matters as an assessment of the company's distinctive competence and the nature of the competitive environment. The internecine disputes and frustration we all experience so often in our business lives are largely the result of an almost total absence of the means of discussing these issues and of reaching agreement on them. If a manager's boss does not understand what his environmental problems are, what his strengths and weaknesses are, or what he is trying to achieve, and any structured procedure and common terminology that can be used and understood by everybody are lacking, communications will be bad and the incidence of frustration will be high. Secondly, some form of standardized approach that is understood by all considerably improves the ability of headquarters management not only to understand the problems of individual operating units, but also to react to them in a constructive and helpful way. This is because they receive information in a way that enables them to form a meaningful overview of total company activities, which provides a rational basis for resource allocation.

To summarize, a structured approach to situation analysis is necessary, irrespective of the size or complexity of the organization. Such a system should:

1 Ensure that comprehensive consideration is given to the definition of strengths and weaknesses and to problems and opportunities.
2 Ensure that a logical framework is used for the presentation of the key issues arising from this analysis.

Very few companies have planning systems that possess these characteristics. Those that do have them manage to cope with their environment more effectively than those that do not. They find it easier to set meaningful marketing objectives, are more confident about the future, enjoy greater control over the business, and react less on a piecemeal basis to daily events. In short, they suffer less operational problems and are as a result more effective organizations.

What is marketing planning?

Let us begin by reminding ourselves of what we said in Chapter 2. Marketing planning is a logical sequence of activities leading to the setting of marketing objectives and the formulation of plans for achieving them. It is a management process. Conceptually the process is very simple and, in summary, comprises the steps outlined in Figure 2.4.

This process is universally agreed by the experts. Formalized marketing planning by means of a planning system is, *per se*, little more than a structured way of identifying a range of options for the company, of making them explicit in writing, of formulating marketing objectives that are consistent with the company's objectives, and of scheduling and costing out the specific activities most likely to bring about the achievement of the objectives. It is the systematization of this process that is distinctive, and is found to lie at the heart of the theory of marketing planning.

Naivety about marketing planning

We have just rehearsed with you the notions that any textbook would offer should you care to re-read it. We have long been bemused, however, by the fact that many meticulous marketing planning companies fare badly while the sloppy and inarticulate in marketing terms do well. Is there any real relation between marketing planning and commercial success? And, if so, how does that relationship work its way through?

There are of course many studies that identify a number of benefits to be obtained from marketing planning. But there is little explanation for the commercial success of those companies that do not engage in formalized planning. Nor is there much exploration of the circumstances of those commercially unsuccessful companies that also have formalized marketing planning systems; and where the dysfunctional consequences are recognized, there is a failure to link this back to any kind of theory.

'Success' is, of course, influenced by many factors apart from just planning procedures. For example:

1   Financial performance at any one point in time is not necessarily a reflection of the inadequacy or otherwise of planning procedures (cf. the hotel industry, location, tourism etc.).
2   Some companies just happen to be in the right place at the right time(s).
3   Companies have many and varied objectives, such as, for example, stylistic objectives.
4   There is a proven relation between management style and commercial success.

In other words, marketing planning procedures alone are not enough for success.

We have said that the process of marketing planning is conceptually very simple and universally applicable. However, it is this very simplicity and universality that make it extremely complex once a number of contextual issues are added, such as (a) company size, (b) degree of internationalization, (c) management style, (d) degree of business environmental turbulence and competitive hostility, (e) market growth rate, (f) market share, (g) technological changes, and so on. It is very clear that the simplistic theories do not adequately address such contextual issues in relation to marketing planning, which may well account for the fact that so few companies actually do it.

In fact 90 per cent of industrial goods companies in the author's study did not, by their own admission, produce anything approximating to an integrated, coordinated and internally consistent plan for their marketing activities. This list included a substantial number of companies that had highly formalized procedures for marketing planning. In six other recent studies in British universities the highest estimate of companies getting marketing planning right was 25 per cent.

Certainly few of these companies enjoyed the claimed benefits of formalized marketing planning, which in summary are as follows:

1 Coordination of the activities of many individuals whose actions are interrelated over time.
2 Identification of expected developments.
3 Preparedness to meet changes when they occur.
4 Minimization of non-rational responses to the unexpected.
5 Better communication among executives.
6 Minimization of conflicts among individuals that would result in a subordination of the goals of the company to those of the individual.

Indeed many companies have a lot of the trappings of sophisticated marketing planning systems but suffer as many dysfunctional consequences as those companies that have only forecasting and budgeting systems. It is clear that for any marketing planning system to be effective, certain conditions have to be satisfied, which we shall deal with in detail shortly.

It should be pointed out, however, that it is by no means essential for any company not suffering from hostile and unstable competitive and environmental conditions to have an effective marketing planning system. Without exception, all those companies in the author's study that did not have an effective marketing planning system but were profitable were also operating in buoyant or high-growth markets. Such companies, though, were less successful than comparable companies with effective marketing planning systems. Success was considered to be not only a company's financial performance over a number of years, but also the way it coped with its environment.

What this means is that, apart from profitability, a company with an effective marketing planning system is likely to have:

• Widely understood objectives.
• Highly motivated employees.

- High levels of actionable market information.
- Greater interfunctional coordination.
- Minimum waste and duplication of resources.
- Acceptance of the need for continuous change and a clear understanding of priorities.
- Greater control over the business and less vulnerability from the unexpected.

In the case of companies without effective marketing planning systems, while it is possible to be profitable over a number of years, especially in high-growth markets, such companies will tend to be less profitable over time and to suffer problems that are the very opposite of the benefits referred to above. Furthermore, companies without effective marketing planning systems tend to suffer more serious commercial organization consequences when environmental and competitive conditions become hostile and unstable.

None of these points are new, in the sense that most of these benefits and problems are discernible to the careful observer. They are, however, actionable propositions for marketers.

Marketing planning systems: design and implementation problems

Many companies currently under siege have recognized the need for a more structured approach to planning their marketing, and have opted for the kind of standardized, formalized procedures written about so much in textbooks. These rarely bring the claimed benefits and often bring marketing planning itself into disrepute.

It is clear that any attempt at the introduction of formalized marketing planning systems has serious organizational and behavioural implications for a company, as it requires a change in its approach to managing its business. It is also clear that unless a company recognizes these implications, and plans to seek ways of coping with them, formalized marketing planning will be ineffective.

Marketing planning is in practice a complex process, proceeding as it does from reviews to objectives, strategies, programmes, budgets and back again, until some kind of acceptable compromise is reached between what is desirable and what is practicable, given all the constraints that any company has.

It has been stated that the literature underestimates the operational difficulties of designing and implementing systems and procedures for marketing planning, and that the task becomes progressively more complex as the size and diversity of a company increases. In addition, the literature is inadequate in the extent to which it provides practical guidance on design and implementation.

The authors' research included a number of examples of companies that had been forced by market pressures to initiate procedures to help top management gain better control over the business. In all such cases those responsible for designing the system found very little of practical help, either in the literature or in management courses. Enormous difficulties in system design and implementation were encountered in every instance.

The purpose of this section is to discuss these design and implementation problems. The most frequently encountered problems are the following:

1 Weak support from chief executive and top management.
2 Lack of a plan for planning.
3 Lack of line management support.
    (a) Hostility.
    (b) Lack of skills.
    (c) Lack of information.
    (d) Lack of resources.
    (e) Inadequate organization structure.
4 Confusion over planning terms.
5 Numbers in lieu of written objectives and strategies.
6 Too much detail, too far ahead.
7 Once-a-year ritual.
8 Separation of operational planning from strategic planning.
9 Failure to integrate marketing planning into a total corporate planning system.
10 Delegation of planning to a planner.

Weak support from chief executive and top management

There can be no doubt that unless the chief executive sees the need for a formalized marketing planning system, understands it, and shows an active interest in it, it is virtually impossible for a senior functional marketing executive to initiate procedures that will be used in a meaningful way. This is particularly so in companies that are organized on the basis of divisional management, for which the marketing executive has no profit responsibility and in which he has no line management authority. In such cases it is comparatively easy for senior operational managers to create political difficulties, the most serious of which is just to ignore the new procedures entirely. Usually, however, the reasons for not participating in or for only partially following instructions, centre around the issues summarized in the ten points listed above.

The vital role that the chief executive and top management must play in marketing planning underlines one of the key points in this section: that it is people who make systems work, and that system design and implementation have to take account of the 'personality' of both the organization and its people, and that these are different in all organizations. One of the most striking features we have observed is the difference in 'personalities' between companies, and the fact that within any one company there is a marked similarity between the attitudes of executives. These attitudes vary from the impersonal, autocratic kind at one extreme to the highly personal, participative kind at the other. This is discussed further in Chapter 12.

Any system therefore has to be designed around the people who have to make it work, and has to take account of the prevailing traditions, attitudes, skills, resource availability and organizational constraints. Since the chief executive and top management are the key influences of these factors, without their active support and participation any formalized marketing planning system is unlikely to work.

This fact emerged very clearly from the authors' research, the worst possible manifestation of which was the way in which chief executives and top managers ignored plans that emerged from the planning system and continued to make key decisions that appeared illogical to those who had participated in the production of the plans. This very quickly destroyed any credibility that the emerging plans might have had, and led to the demise of the procedures, and to serious levels of frustration throughout the organization. Indeed there is some evidence leading to the belief that chief executives who fail, firstly, to understand the essential role of marketing in generating profitable revenue in a business, and, secondly, to understand how marketing can be integrated into the other functional areas of the business through marketing planning procedures, are a key contributory factor in poor economic performance.

Lack of a plan for planning

The next most common cause of the failure or partial failure of marketing planning systems is the belief that, once a system is designed, it can be implemented immediately. Failure, or partial failure, then, can often be the result of not developing a sensible timetable for introducing a new system, to take account of the following:

1 The need to communicate why a marketing planning system is necessary.
2 The need to develop top management support and participation.
3 The need to test the system out on a limited basis to demonstrate its effectiveness and value.
4 The need for training programmes, or workshops, to train line management in its use.

Above all, a resolute sense of purpose and dedication is required, tempered by patience and a willingness to appreciate the inevitable problems that will be encountered in the plan's implementation. This problem is closely linked with the third major reason for planning system failure, which is lack of line management support.

Lack of line management support

Hostility, lack of skills, lack of data and information, lack of resources, and an inadequate organizational structure, all add up to a failure to obtain the willing participation of operational managers.

Hostility on the part of line managers is by far the most common reaction to the introduction of new marketing planning systems. The reasons for this are not hard to find, and are related to the system initiators' lack of a plan for planning.

New systems inevitably require considerable explanation of the new procedures, and are usually accompanied by pro formas, flow charts and the like. Often these devices are most conveniently presented in the form of a manual. When such a document arrives on the desk of a busy line manager, unheralded by previous explanation or discussion, the immediate reaction often appears to be fear of his possible inability to understand it and to comply with it, in the required time scale, followed by anger, and finally at best, grudging acquiescence and half-hearted participation. Managers begin to picture headquarters as a remote 'ivory tower', totally divorced from the reality of the market place.

This attitude is often exacerbated by their absorption in the current operating and reward system, which is geared to the achievement of current results, while the new system is geared to the future. In addition, because of the trend in recent years towards the frequent movement of executives around organizations, there is less interest in planning for future business gains from which someone else is likely to benefit. Allied to this is the fact that many line managers are ignorant of basic marketing principles, and have never been used to breaking up their markets into strategically relevant segments, or of collecting meaningful information about them.

Some kind of appropriate headquarters organization has therefore to be found for the collection and dissemination of valuable information. Training on ways of solving this managerial problem has also to be provided.

Again, these issues are complicated by the varying degrees of size and complexity of companies. It is surprising to see the extent to which organizational structures cater inadequately for marketing as a function. In small companies there is often no one other than the operations manager, who spends most of his time managing the stores. Unless the chief executive is marketing-orientated, marketing planning is just not done.

In medium-sized and large retail companies there is often no provision at board level for marketing as a discipline. Usually there is an operations or commercial director, with line management responsibility for the stores, but apart from the senior and buying merchandising executives, marketing as a function is not particularly well catered for. Where there is a marketing manager, he can often be somewhat isolated from the mainstream activities. The most successful organizations are those with a fully integrated marketing function.

It is clear that without a suitable organizational structure, any attempt to implement a marketing planning system which requires the collection, analysis and synthesis of market-related information, is unlikely to be successful.

The problem of organizing for marketing planning is discussed further in Chapter 11.

Confusion over planning terms

Confusion over planning terms is another reason for the failure of marketing planning systems. The initiators of these systems, often highly qualified, frequently use a form of planning terminology that is perceived by operational managers as meaningless jargon. One company even referred to the Ansoff matrix, and made frequent references to other forms of matrices, missions, dimensions, quadrants, and so on. Those companies with successful planning systems try to use terminology that will be familiar to operational management, and where terms such as 'objectives' and 'strategies' are used, these are clearly defined, with examples given of their practical use.

At the end of the book, p.329, there is a glossary of terms.

Numbers in lieu of written objectives and strategies

Most managers in operating units are accustomed to completing sales/margin/cost forecasts, but not as accustomed to considering underlying causal factors for past performance or expected results, or of highlight-ing opportunities, emphasizing key issues, and so on. Their outlook is often parochial and short-term, with a marked tendency to extrapolate numbers and to project the current business unchanged into the next fiscal year.

Thus, when a marketing planning system suddenly requires that they should make explicit their implicit economic model of the business, they cannot do it. So, instead of finding words to express the logic of their objectives and strategies, they repeat their past behaviour and fill in the data sheets provided without any narrative. It is the provision of data sheets, and the emphasis which the system places on the physical count-ing of things, that encourages the questionnaire-completion mentality and hinders the development of the creative analysis so essential to effec-tive strategic planning.

Those companies with successful marketing planning systems ask only for essential data and place greater emphasis on narrative to explain the underlying thinking behind the objectives and strategies.

Too much detail, too far ahead

Connected with this is the problem of over-planning, usually caused by elaborate systems that demand information and data that headquarters does not need and can never use. Systems that generate vast quantities of paper are generally demotivating for all concerned.

The biggest problem in this connection is undoubtedly the insistence on a detailed and thorough marketing audit. In itself this is not a bad discipline to impose on managers, but to do so without also providing some guidance on how it should be summarized to point up the key issues merely leads to the production of vast quantities of useless infor-mation. Its uselessness stems from the fact that it robs the ensuing plans of focus, and confuses those who read it by the amount of detail provided. The trouble is that few managers have the creative or analyti-cal ability to isolate the really key issues, with the result that far more problems and opportunities are identified than the company can ever cope with. Consequently the truly key strategic issues are buried deep in the detail and do not receive the attention they deserve until it is too late.

In a number of companies with highly detailed and institutionalized marketing planning systems the resulting plans contain so much detail that it is impossible to identify what the major objectives and strategies are. The managers in these companies are rarely able to express a simpli-fied view of the business or of the essential things that have to be done today to ensure success. Such companies are often over-extended, trying to do too many things at once.

In companies with successful planning systems there is at all levels a widespread understanding of the key objectives that have to be achieved, and of the means of achieving them. In such companies the rationale of each layer of the business is clear, and actions and decisions are disciplined by clear objectives that hang logically together as part of a rational purpose.

The clarity and cohesiveness are achieved by means of a system of 'layering'. At each successive level of management throughout the organization, lower-level analyses are synthesized into a form that ensures that only the essential information needed for decision-making and control purposes reaches the next level of management. Thus, there are hierarchies of audits, SWOT analyses, assumptions, objectives, strategies and plans. This means, for example, that at conglomerate headquarters top management has a clear understanding of the really key macro issues of companywide significance, while at the lower level of profit responsibility management also has a clear understanding of the really key micro issues of significance to the unit. It can be concluded that a good measure of the effectiveness of a company's marketing planning system is the extent to which different managers in the organization can make a clear, lucid and logical statement about the major problems and opportunities they face, how they intend to deal with these, and how what they are doing fits in with some greater purpose.

Once-a-year ritual

One of the commonest weaknesses in the marketing planning systems of those companies whose planning systems fail to bring the expected benefits is the ritualistic nature of the activity. In such cases operating managers treat the writing of the marketing plan as a thoroughly irksome and unpleasant duty. The pro formas are completed, not always very diligently, and the resulting plans are quickly filed away, never to be referred to again. They are seen as something that is required by headquarters rather than as an essential tool of management. In other words, the production of the marketing plan is seen as a once-a-year ritual, a sort of game of management bluff. It is not surprising that the resulting plans are not used.

While this is obviously closely related to the explanations already given as to why some planning systems are ineffective, a common feature of companies that treat marketing planning as a once-a-year ritual is the short lead time given for the completion of the process. The problem with this approach is that in the minds of managers it tends to be relegated to a position of secondary importance.

In companies with effective systems the planning cycle will start in month 3 or 4 and run through to month 9 or 10, with the total 12-month period being used to evaluate the progress of existing plans. Thus, by spreading the planning activity over a longer period, and by means of the active participation of all levels of management at the appropriate moment, planning becomes an accepted and integral part of management behaviour rather than an addition to it that calls for unusual behaviour. There is a much better chance that plans resulting from such a system will be formulated so that they can be converted into things that people are actually going to do.

Separation of operational planning from strategic planning

This sub-section must be seen against the background of the difficulty the majority of companies experience in carrying out any meaningful strategic planning. In the majority of cases the figures that appear in the long-term corporate plan are little more than statistical extrapolations that satisfy boards of directors. The numbers are just altered every year, and frequently the gap between where a company gets to compared with where it had planned to be in real terms grows wider over time.

Nevertheless most companies make long-term projections. Unfortunately in the majority of cases these are totally separate from the short-term planning activity that takes place largely in the form of forecasting and budgeting. The view that they should be separate is supported by means of the writers in this field, who describe strategic planning as very different, and therefore divorced, from operational planning. Indeed many stress that failure to understand the essential difference between the two leads to confusion and prevents planning from becoming an integral part of the company's management system. It is precisely this separation between short- and long-term plans that the authors' research revealed as being the major cause of the problems experienced today by many of the respondents. It is the failure of long-term plans to determine the difficult choices between the emphasis to be placed on current operations and the development of new business that leads to the failure of operating management to consider any alternatives to what it is currently doing.

The almost total separation of operational or short-term planning from strategic or long-term planning is a feature of many companies whose systems are not very effective. More often than not the long-term strategic plans tend to be straight-line extrapolations of past trends, and because different people are often engaged in this form of planning, such as corporate planners, to the exclusion of some levels of operating management, the resulting plans bear virtually no relation to the more detailed and immediate short-term plans.

This separation positively discourages operational managers from thinking strategically, with the result that detailed operational plans are completed in a vacuum. The so-called strategic plans do not provide the much-needed cohesion and logic, because they are seen as an ivory tower exercise that contains figures in which no-one really believes.

Unless strategic plans are built up from sound strategic analysis at grass-roots level by successive layers of operational management, they have little value as a basis for corporate decisions. At the same time, operational plans will become increasingly parochial in their outlook and will fail to incorporate the decisions that have to be taken today to safeguard the future.

Operational planning, then, should very much be part of the strategic planning process, and vice versa. Indeed, wherever possible, they should be completed at the same time, using the same managers and the same information streams.

The detailed operational plan should be the first year of the long-term plan, and operational managers should be encouraged to complete their long-term projections at the same time as their short-term projections. The advantage is that it encourages managers to think about what decisions have to be made in the current planning year, in order to achieve the long-term projections.

Failure to integrate marketing planning into a total corporate planning system

It is difficult to initiate an effective marketing planning system in the absence of a parallel corporate planning system. This is yet another consequence of the separation of operational planning from strategic planning; for unless similar processes and time scale to those being used in the marketing planning system are also being used by other major functions, such as financial and personnel, the sort of trade-offs and compromises that have to be made in any company between what is wanted and what is practicable and affordable will not take place in a rational way. These trade-offs have to be made on the basis of the fullest possible understanding of the reality of the company's multifunctional strengths and weaknesses, opportunities and threats.

Delegation of planning to a planner

The incidence of this is higher with corporate planning than with marketing planning, although where there is some kind of corporate planning function at headquarters, and no organizational function for marketing, whatever strategic marketing planning takes place is done by corporate planners as part of a system that is divorced from the operational planning mechanism. Not surprisingly, this exacerbates the separation of operational planning from strategic planning and encourages short-term thinking in the operational units.

Very often corporate planners are young, highly qualified people, attached to the office of the chairman or group chief executive. They appear to be widely resented and are largely ignored by the mainstream of the business. There is not much evidence that they succeed in clarifying the company's strategy, and there appears to be very little account taken of such strategies in the planning and thinking of operational units.

The literature sees the planner basically as a coordinator of the planning, not as an initiator of goals and strategies. It is clear that without the ability and the willingness of operation management to cooperate, a planner becomes little more than a kind of headquarters administrative assistant. In many large companies where there is a person at headquarters with the specific title of marketing planning manager he has usually been appointed as a result of the difficulty of controlling a business that has grown rapidly in size and diversity, and which presents a baffling array of new problems to deal with.

His tasks are essentially those of system design and coordination of inputs, although he is also expected to formulate objectives and strategies for the board. In all cases it is lack of line management skills and inadequate organizational structures that frustrate the company's marketing efforts, rather than inadequacies on the part of the planner. This puts the onus on the planner himself to do a lot of the planning, which is, not surprisingly, largely ineffective.

Two particularly interesting facts emerged from the authors' research. First, the marketing planner manager, as the designer and initiator of systems for marketing planning, is often in an impossibly delicate political position *vis-à-vis* both his superiors and the operational managers. It is clear that not too many chief executives understand the role of planning and have unrealistic expectations of the planner, whereas for his part the planner cannot operate effectively without the full understanding, cooperation and participation of top management – and this is rarely forthcoming. Often the appointment of a marketing planning manager, and sometimes of a senior marketing executive, seems to be an easier step for the chief executive and his board to take than giving serious consideration themselves to the implications of the new forces affecting the business and reformulating a strategy to take them into account.

This leads on naturally to a second point. The inevitable consequence of employing a marketing planning manager is that he will need to initiate changes in management behaviour in order to become effective. Usually these are far-reaching in their implications, affecting training, resource allocation, and organizational structures. As the catalyst for such changes, the planner, not surprisingly, comes up against enormous political barriers, with the result that he often becomes frustrated and eventually ineffective. This is without doubt a major problem, particularly for big companies. The problems raised by a marketing planning manager occur as a result of the failure of top management to give thought to the formulation of appropriate strategies. They have not done this in the past because they have not felt the need. However, when market pressures force the emerging problems of diversity and control to the surface, without a total willingness on their part to participate in far-reaching changes, there really is not much that a planner can do.

This raises the question again of the key role of the chief executive in the whole business of marketing planning. Without both his support and understanding of the very serious implications of initiating effective marketing planning procedures, whatever efforts are made, whether by a planner or a line manager, they will be largely ineffective.

Requisite marketing planning systems

The implications of all this are principally as follows:

1   Any closed-loop marketing planning system (but especially one that is essentially a forecasting and budgeting system) will lead to a gradual decline of marketing creativity. Therefore there has to be some mechanism for preventing inertia from setting in through the over-bureaucratization of the system.
2   Marketing planning undertaken at the functional level of marketing, in the absence of a means of integration with other functional areas of the business at general management level, will be largely ineffective.
3   The separation of responsibility for operational and strategic marketing planning will lead to a divergence of the short-term thrust of a business at the operational level from the long-term objectives of the enterprise as a whole. This will encourage a preoccupation with short-term results at operational level, which normally makes the firm less effective in the long term.
4   Unless the chief executive understands and takes an active role in marketing planning, it will never be an effective system.

In Chapter 12 we will explore in detail what is meant by the term requisite marketing planning' when we explain how to design and implement an effective marketing planning system. For now, we believe we have given sufficient background information about the process of marketing planning, and why this apparently simple process requires much more perception and attention than is typically accorded it. We can now go on to explore in the next few chapters, in more detail, each of the elements of this process before putting all the pieces together again in the final chapter.

The dos and don'ts of retail marketing plans

The mistakes made by many retailers in the 1980s can be summarized as follows:

- Thinking that strategic plans were extensions of financial plans.
- Confusing strategy with objectives.
- Expecting consultants to produce plans.
- Over-reliance on staff experts.
- Sole reliance on quantitative tools.
- Sacrificing the base business, while focusing on expansion or diversification.
- Taking too narrow a perspective.

For success in the 1990s, the strategic marketing planning requirements can be summarized thus:

1 There must be the backing of top management.
2 A customer/market orientation is essential.
3 Expansion or diversification should not take place at the expense of maximizing the potential of the base business.
4 The strategic marketing planning process must bring in all the administrative, as well as the trading functions in the company.
5 There must be contingency planning – the 'what if' scenarios.

Evolution in retail marketing – some hypotheses for the future

All the signs for the 1990s seem to point to:

- Continued economic volatility.
- Sustained inflationary pressure.

- Recurring capital crises.
- High interest rates.
- The saturation of major areas of retailing.
- Slow growth.
- Low productivity gains.
- Increased competition.
- Growth in costs (which can make those retailing sectors that traditionally work with thin margins particularly vulnerable).
- A growing polarization between the haves and have-nots in society and a less amorphous middle market.

The effect of these factors will lead to more consumer research, improved store positioning and focused marketing, as retailers struggle for market share. Mass merchandisers and super speciality stores should prosper, while consumers will force entirely new retailing concepts as the mass market fragments into segments, each with its own needs, tastes and way of life. The individual will be looking for 'experiences' rather than goods, and will have a higher quality of life expectation, at the same time as developing greater economy-consciousness.

Store 'positioning' (in the same view as brand positioning) will thus become crucial, as will the brands stores stock, with the result that the shift in balance of power from manufacturers to retailers will continue. In such a context better-focused concepts will lead to more efficiency as retailers become bigger buyers of a more limited number of items. Equally, stock turnover will increase because of an unambiguous store image.

The creation of sustainable competitive advantage will thus become the dominating challenge of the 1990s. Correspondingly, strategic marketing planning will become a key skill required of managers in their battle to achieve a long-run, time-phased, high return on investment and consequent growth in the capital value of shares and earnings per share.

In the process executives will have to learn how to spot opportunities and threats, to develop genuine organizational strengths and to minimize the weaknesses. Above all, they need to develop appropriate strategies – in other words, they will need to know how to prepare a strategic marketing plan.

4

Completing the marketing audit: 1 The customer and marketing audit

Summary

This chapter focuses specifically on whom we sell to, and the next chapter on what we sell to them. It describes the various approaches and methods that can be used to segment markets, including the important consideration that must be given to customer behavioural and attitudinal analysis.

Introduction

Now that we understand the process of marketing planning, we can begin to look in more detail at its principal components. We have, as it were, seen the picture on the front of the jigsaw puzzle; we can now examine the individual pieces with a better understanding of where and how they will fit together.

As we have already discussed, the framework within which any retailer operates is the market place itself. The first stage is to gain a clear understanding of the myriad ways in which that market can be subdivided/segmented by adopting a structured approach to answering three questions:

- Who are the customers?
- What is being bought?
- What are the reasons for purchase?

Following this, we can look at the second stage, which is the use of this information to define the target segment, or segments, for the individual company.

Before doing so, however, it is important to dwell for a moment on the difference between 'customers' and 'consumers'. The prime concern of the retailer is obviously with the person actually in the shop, at the check-out or cash point, i.e. the customer. In a bank, where most personal transactions require a signature, or at a men's tailor, where fittings are made, the customer is usually also the final consumer. On the other hand, the person buying breakfast cereals is more often acting as the buying agent for the end consumers, the family. Similarly, nearly half of the men's socks and underwear sold in the UK are purchased on their behalf by women. Therefore, in order to retail cereals or socks effectively, it is clearly necessary to understand what the end-consumer wants, as well as what the housewife wants. The retailer needs to be constantly alert to any changes in the consumption patterns and needs of the ultimate consumers of the products stocked by the company, as well as to the requirements of the customers who actually come through the door.

Market segmentation by customer

There are many ways of segmenting the marketing from the analysis of the characteristics or attributes of groups of customers, as follows.

Demographic segmentation – age, sex, marital status, etc.

Basic as it may seem, the simple study of how the population is split between the sexes and into age groups can have a profound effect for many types of retailing. In the UK the 15–19 age group will have fallen by over 500,000 in the 5 years to 1994, a drop that will have a potentially severe effect on the economics of any fashion clothing chains aimed at this age group. With the big players – Top Shop, Top Man, Miss Selfridge, Fosters, and River Island – battling it out for market share in a declining market, it is small wonder that some smaller companies have gone under.

Conversely, the bulge in the birth-rate from the baby boom of the 1960s is leading to an expansion in the 30–34 age group, with commensurate volume growth opportunities for those retailers targeted at them. Equally, the prosperity of the mid/late 1980s lifted the UK birth-rate during that period, giving similar chances to such as Adams, Toys R Us, and Marks & Spencer's, which are strong in the 0–9 year-olds markets.

Italy, on the other hand, has had a marked fall in the birth-rate over the same period. The prospects for children-orientated retailing are therefore less promising than those in the UK. This sort of information is obviously a key starting point for any international retailers looking at expansion options.

Socio-economic groups – social class, status, income, etc.

The influence of the customers' type of occupation, social class, and income level on their shopping behaviour patterns has been investigated extensively. In most industrial countries aspects of customer behaviour, such as payment methods and store preference, vary with social class. A full list of UK socio-economic groupings is provided in Table 4.1. As this is based on British census returns, it is obviously peculiar to the UK. However, it will be found that similar data groupings are available for most advanced economies.

This method describes people by their social status in life as represented by their jobs. Knowledge of the behavioural characteristics of these groupings is important to retailers in helping them to identify their target markets and then put together appropriate, effective marketing plans. For example, if your target market is the A, B and C1 categories, which include most of the professions and senior managers, then being

Table 4.1 Socio-economic groups

Social grade	Social status	Occupation of household head	Percentage of adults
A	Upper middle class	Higher managerial Administrative Professional	3
B	Middle class	Middle managerial Administrative Professional	10
C1	Lower middle class	Supervisory Clerical Junior managerial Administrative Professional	23
C2	Skilled working class	Skilled manual workers	33
D	Working class	Semi and unskilled manual workers	22
E	Subsistence level	Pensioners Widows Casual Lowest paid workers	9

aware that they are relatively light television viewers, and tend to read quality newspapers and magazines rather than the tabloids, will enable you to direct your promotional spend more cost-effectively. Knowing this, Harrods uses *The Times* and *Daily Telegraph* for much of its media spend, rather than the *Sun* and *Daily Mirror*, and with the exception of the annual sales, avoid television advertising.

The upper and middle groupings are more at home with bank services and use of credit cards, than the working class, which is only gradually moving away from the traditional weekly pay-packet, and is much more likely to make use of hire-purchase and store-based credit schemes. The middle classes tend to shop weekly and are prepared to make bulk buys to save money, while many of the working class still seem to shop for food on a daily basis. This latter example accounts for the continued existence of the corner shops, in spite of the proliferation of huge supermarkets.

Segmentation by lifestages – differing stages in the family cycle

Also available from the census statistics in the UK is another way of segmenting the market, namely by lifestage. Young single people, living at home, are high spenders on pop music and fashion clothing and are the target segment for the Virgin, HMV, Top Shop/Top Man, Miss Selfridge chains. Habitat, on the other hand, was conceived to aim at the young marrieds, who wanted well-designed furniture and household goods, but at budget prices. Patently, the Mothercare chain will keep a close eye on any trends in the number of families with young children. Of growing interest, as the demographic bulge moves through, will be the larger number of empty-nesters in the 45+ age group who have a big boost to their disposable income as their children finish education and leave home, and as they reach the final stages of their mortgage repayments. Equally, as more people retire early and medical advances promote longevity, the population of older, but still active, senior citizens is another market segment that mass-market retailers should not ignore in their planning process.

The high-street banks, the building societies, and insurance companies have become particularly adept at developing products and services targeted specifically at particular lifestage groups.

Geographic segmentation – country, region, urban or rural dwellers, etc.

For international retailers population sizes are a top line indicator of the scale of relative opportunities between various countries. However, that is only a first stage. What is important to them, and of course for the single country retailer, is the geographic distribution of that population between the different physical and economic regions in that country, the relative split between city/town dwellers and those living in the countryside, and the size and prosperity of the catchment areas of the major towns and cities.

In the USA there are significant differences in the product mix required for stores in New York and the surrounding states, as opposed to those on the West Coast in California. There are similar parallels in most of the large European countries. Paris is a different market from Nice, Naples from Milan, Madrid from Seville, etc.

The size of population within catchment areas is also a prime determinant of the viability and size of any retail proposition for those areas. Not only are the numbers of people in an area important, but also their predominant socio-economic characteristics. In the UK the census data provide a basis for ACORN (A Classification of Regional Neighbourhood groups), which classifies all households according to thirty-eight different neighbourhood types. Used in conjunction with market research, this is particularly useful to retailers in helping them to predict consumption patterns in specific geographical locations.

Psychological segmentation – attitudes, motivators, lifestyles, etc.

Our hidden emotions, psychological make-up, and aspirations, manifest themselves unwittingly in our shopping behaviour. Advances in market research questionnaire construction and clustering techniques now enable the segmentation of markets according to these psychological drivers. This makes a very powerful additional tool available to retailers in helping them target appropriate market segments and achieve meaningful focus in the construction of their marketing strategies.

What it does is to add a third dimension to the simplistic division of the market by Age and SEG (socio-economic group). It explains to us, for instance, why people of the same age, sex, and income, but with differing shopping attitudes, may well be members of separate market segments, and have completely different requirements from retailers.

Let us look at an example of how the market might be subdivided five ways according to customers' attitudes to fashion and modernity:

1 'The trendsetters'
The first group are those driven by the need to be first to have the latest technology or fashion. They are trendsetters and innovators, and want to be recognized as such. Depending on income, they will be the first to

have all the latest hi-fi and television equipment. Their homes will be decorated and furnished with the last word in modernity, almost irrespective of what the look is. When it comes to clothing, again they want to be noticed, and will spend heavily in time and money to stay one step ahead of their peers. They will be the first to try out the new boutique, disco, or trendy restaurant. As a group, they are supremely self-confident, they know what they want, and they will spend heavily to get it. They devour all the trendsetting magazines, and will remain loyal customers only as long as the retailer keeps a reputation for being at the leading edge of fashion.

2 'The followers of fashion'
Next comes a group, much larger in number, who believe themselves to be modern and fashionable, but who are in fact followers of fashion rather than trendsetters. Though they would not openly admit to it, they are fashion conformists. They tend to respond to peer pressure and do not adopt a fashion until it is apparent that it will have widespread acceptance. It is the young girls in this group who turn high fashion looks such as Lycra mini-skirts and torn denim jeans into a street fashion uniform. In the mid-1980s Levi's 501 jeans and Reebok trainers were high fashion. Now they are standard dress for many young football supporters. The subliminal desire to 'keep up with the Jones's' drives this group, which can range in age from schoolchildren, suffering abject deprivation if they are denied the latest video game, Sony Walkman, or mountain bike, to the 40+ age group, who feel the need to keep up with the flashy neighbour's latest microwave, satellite dish, or all-singing, all dancing lawnmower. They will never be the first to try a new product, but they are lifeblood customers for all those retailers who sell product ranges constantly updated by fashion or technological innovation.

3 'The confident classics'
The first two groups were primarily concerned with fashion and modernity. Now we come to a group of people who are more concerned with good taste and good quality than with fashion for its own sake. They are self-assured and confident in their own ability to choose for themselves rather than follow the herd. This does not mean that they ignore improving technology or fashion shifts, but more that they select from what is going on only those products or services that they feel suit them, and which meet their criteria of quality and taste. For the most part their clothing purchases will reflect an updated classicism, which will last them over a period. Their furniture and home furnishings will reflect the same attitude. The materials and styling chosen will be of a quality and taste level that will stand the test of time. They will buy new

technology for the home on a selective basis, because it improves their quality of life, not simply because it is new.

They look for retailers that carry good quality, tastefully designed merchandise, and that offer a high standard of knowledgeable customer service. Having found stores that satisfy these criteria, they tend to be loyal customers as long as the standards they require are met.

4 'The conventional replacers'
Another substantial slice of the population shares the same disinterest in fashion as those in the previous group. In this case, however, they do not have the self-assurance or, for the most part, money to express themselves, as they might wish to, through their purchases. They tend to have traditional values and a well-developed sense of quality and value for money. They are conventional in their attitude and do not experiment. They are creatures of habit, both in the stores they frequent and in the products they buy. Most of their buying is done on a replacement basis. They are most at home in the large chain stores and high-street multiples, where the amount of nearly identical products on offer gives them the comfort that they are not going to be seen as being unconventional.

5 'The price-led replacers'
Finally, we have a group who have no interest in fashion at all, only a vague idea of what is conventionally acceptable, and little money anyway. Their buying is forced by replacement needs, and price is the dominant factor. When the soles finally fall off their shoes, they replace them by the cheapest pair available, irrespective of colour or style. Clothing is bought to cover the body, and cooking equipment to heat food, and that's it. Market stalls, charity shops, jumble sales, car boot sales and discount shops make up the bulk of their shopping repertoire, with the multiples and chain stores used during offer periods.

Benefit segmentation

Another way in which emotions and psychological drivers are used to define market segments, can be seen in the growing emergence of 'contexts', such as 'wellness' and 'environmental awareness', which can span most of the socio-economic and age groups. The blossoming number of health food products clearly fall into the 'wellness' context, and Body Shop in the UK and The Nature Company in the USA would probably fall into the 'environmental awareness' context.

The common thread running through the fashion attitude and contextual examples shown above is that of segmenting the market by the psychological characteristics of groups of customers. They demonstrate the possibilities of a more meaningful segmentation of the market by looking more closely at the benefits sought by different groups of people, rather than just at their physical characteristics.

Here are two further examples of benefit segmentation.

1 Retailing watches
Obviously the common benefit sought is that of being able to tell the time, but people buy watches for many other reasons. Market surveys show that about 23 per cent of buyers look for cheapness, about 46 per cent for durability, and the remaining 31 per cent choose watches that imply status. Knowing this, a retailer in the watch market will either aim at a single segment, at the first two, or at the last two. Any attempt to target all three simultaneously in the same location could lead to a loss of credibility with one of the groups. Those looking for cheapness will be scared off if they see expensive brands on display, while those looking for a status symbol will feel the exclusiveness of their requirements undermined if they see cheap products in the same shop.

2 Retailing toothpaste
In Table 4.2 we show Russell Haley's segmentation of the toothpaste market, which uses a matrix of different customer characteristics to create a novel set of customer types or segments, in a similar way to the fashion attitude segmentation we discussed above.

What is being bought?

Total consumer spending

At top level there are copious government statistics from which a retailer can keep abreast of changes in consumer spending patterns between housing costs, cars, holidays, food, drink and tobacco, heat/light/power, clothing, consumer durables, etc. Keeping up to date with these and the state of the economy is important, because of the relatively high level of gearing of consumer spending in the high street to shifts in disposable income.

For instance, in a time of recession, a family's first priority is keeping the roof over its head, keeping warm, and having enough to eat. Outside this, spending will be prioritized on a necessity basis, with forced

Table 4.2 Toothpaste market segmentation

	Sensory segment	*Sociables*	*Worriers*	*Independent segment*
Principal benefit sought	flavour, product appearance	brightness of teeth	decay prevention	price
Demographic strengths	children	teens, young people	large families	men
Behavioural character-istics	users of spearmint flavour	smokers	heavy users	heavy users
Brands favoured	Colgate Stripe	Macleans Plus White Ultra Bright	Crest	brands on sale
Personality character-istics	High self-involvement	high sociability	high hypo-chrondriasis	high autonomy
Life style character-istics	hedonistic	active	conservative	value-orientated

From Russell Haley, 'Benefit segmentation: a decision-orientated research tool', *Journal of Marketing* Vol. 32, July 1968.

replacements of vital household items and children's clothing coming high on the list, and the new car, new lounge furniture, and father's new suit having to wait for better times.

The retailer should therefore develop a view on the elasticity of demand for his type of merchandise to shifts in the economy. This will help him to take a more considered view on forward investment planning for selling space and stock levels.

Sector-specific consumer spending

For most sectors of the retail industry there are specialist research statis-tics available on a commercial basis from companies such as AGB, Taylor-Nielson, TMS (Textile Market Studies). These companies operate large customer surveys on a perpetual basis across the whole country, using sample sizes that would be beyond the budget of all but a very few individual firms.

These surveys dissect each type of retailing in considerable detail, giving the individual company substantial information with which to monitor its own performance against its competitors', and also data from which to identify trends.

Here are some of the types of data available:

- Total market sales by month, season or year.
- Sales by age, sex, and socio-economic group.
- Sales by product category and sub-categories.

Example – Men's clothing:
   – Shirts
   – Casual shirts.
   – Knitted casual shorts.
- Sales by price points.
- Sales by size.
- Frequency of purchase.
- Sales by geographic region or area.
- Sales by type of outlet (chain store/multiple/department store/ independent/mail order/discount shop, etc.).
- Market shares of all major companies in each sector.
- Methods of payment, use of credit, store-cards, etc.

Own company consumer spending

If there are acknowledged industry sources for data, it will obviously make life easier for the individual retailer to arrange his own data in a similar format to make comparison easier. Patently, retailers will know what they are selling themselves, and they should all compare their internal data with that available in their sector, to get a firm understanding of their relative strengths and weaknesses *vis-à-vis* their competition.

What are the reasons for purchase?

As we discussed earlier, it is possible to segment the customers in the market place according to their shopping attitudes, which manifest themselves in their shopping behaviour. This is one of the most important issues for a retailer to consider in planning his marketing strategies. It is vital to know what is driving purchasing decisions, why some customers are choosing to use his store, and, conversely, why others are not. We must therefore consider the potential customers as well as the actual customers. For a retailer these will include those former customers who have stopped coming to his store, and others who have never bought there.

Remember that the whole exercise is one of meeting the wants and needs of *all* the customers in the chosen market segment. We need to get behind their overtly expressed needs in order to understand the benefits they are really looking for. As we discussed, these benefits are sometimes not so much the purchase of the product for its intrinsic value, but as a means for the customer to express himself in his working or social environment. The Trendsetters' avid pursuit of all that is new is a perfect example of this, where possession of the product can assume greater importance than the product itself.

Once the retailer has a clear grasp of the attitudes of the various shopper groups, the next stage is to be able to understand the perceptions of his customers, and potential customers, as to how his firm measures up against the criteria that they consider important. This can be accomplished by specifically commissioned market research, in the case of the larger operation, or by in-house research by the owner–manager. Wherever possible, this research should include cross comparison on the same criteria with those firms seen as being the nearest market competitors.

Here are some examples of the types of statements that might be used in such research, to establish gradings of customer perceptions of a company's image in different market segments. Against each, the respondents would be asked to – Agree strongly/Agree/Disagree/Disagree strongly.

For a firm targeting Trendsetters and/or Followers of Fashion:

- Always has the latest fashions/technology in stock.
- Catches on to new brands quickly.
- Stocks the brands I want.
- There is plenty to choose from.
- Lets me browse without being hassled.
- Has the fashionable staff I can relate to.
- The shopfit is modern and exciting.
- I like their choice of music.
- The windows displays the latest looks and pulls me in.

For a firm targeting the Confident Classics group:

- The products are always of good quality.
- They offer good value for money.
- They keep up to date without being extreme.
- They stock the most reliable brands.
- The shop is comfortable and uncluttered.
- I can find what I am looking for easily.

- The displays, packaging, and labelling are clear and informative.
- The staff are attentive, courteous, and knowledgeable.
- They handle complaints well and promptly.
- I always shop there first for this type of product.

Those are just a few examples of the areas that can be explored in such research, with the object of building a comprehensive picture of the customers' perceptions of the company, measured against their personal shopping attitudes. If a firm is unclear about the shopper groups it is attracting, it may find it best to use an amalgam of statements covering a broad span of shopper types, and, from the resulting gradings, home in on its area of relative strength.

Criteria for effective segmentation

We have now looked at who the customers are and the multi-dimensional ways in which they can be segmented, at the number of ways in which we must study what they buy, and finally at the complexities of understanding their buying behaviour. From this it is apparent that no company, not even a Marks & Spencer's or a J C Penney, can set out to be 'all things to all men'. Each undertaking needs to select the segment or segments, which will bring it the greatest chance of meeting its corporate objectives, by bringing in an income appropriate to the effort it gives to it.

The following are the major criteria on which to judge whether a market segment will be viable.

Is the market segment really distinct from other segments?

The segment must be readily identifiable from other segments and the variable(s) on which the segmentation is based should be easily measurable. The segment must stand on its own and be supported by clearly quantified sets of specific attributes for the customers it contains. Woolly thinking at this stage will court disaster later on. If you cannot separate it, lift it, and weigh it, don't touch it.

For instance, the Evans womenswear chain in the UK and the Lane Bryant chain in the USA have identified as their targets the segment of the womenswear market containing women who are UK size 16 and upwards. It is a segment not catered for by the national fashion multiple shops, which tend to major on UK sizes 10–14. The segment is easily measurable from demographic research, and its customers have clearly identifiable shopping needs, which differ from those of smaller sized ladies.

Is the segment big enough?

The segment should be of sufficient size to ensure an adequate return from any investment made in it. Care must be taken not to over-segment the market. Here, market sizes come into play.

For example, a conurbation the size of London or New York can support large numbers of highly specialized retailers because of the huge population in their catchment areas. A shop selling only men's umbrellas and walking sticks would scarcely enjoy the same success in Banbury as it does in Bloomsbury Street, London.

Niche businesses can succeed, but only if they are carefully planned in relation to the economies of this type of retailing. Sock Shop and Tie Rack were two successes of the mid-1980s which grew very fast. Their problems began when the recession of the end of that decade set in, and they found themselves with a lot of small sites that were very expensive to run, per square foot/metre, compared to the larger retail premises of the chain stores and multiple operations. At the same time the chains and the multiples put substantially more effort into these product types, giving them more footage and variety than before. The result was that Tie Rack and Sock Shop found themselves struggling for survival and growth in what is a relatively small part of the total clothing market.

We hope the message is clear. Make sure the economics of operating in the segment stack up, and be quite sure that you will not be squeezed unacceptably if others enter the market, or if you wake a sleeping tiger.

Can the segment be easily reached?

This is a variation on the previous point, but one worth considering. It is often possible to find an area for which, at face value, there would seem to be an opportunity for a successful retail operation, but which on closer examination turns out to be uneconomic, not so much from the numbers of potential customers in the segment or the dangers of competition, but from the wide variety of characteristics of those potential customers.

For example, using another clothing analogy, there are a large number of females in the UK who are over 5 feet 10 inches tall. They are not as numerous as the outsize market, but nevertheless sufficient in number, seemingly, to offer a possible opportunity for a specialist chain of shops. However, the females making up that number are a mixture of different age groups, sizes, socio-economic backgrounds and lifestages, and are geographically spread out across the country. In addition, and very importantly in this case, they are further subdivided into groups with differing fashion attitudes. It does not take a doctorate in mathematics to work out that the economics of carrying sufficient stock to meet the potential matrix of customers' needs in this market could be very tenuous. It is for this reason that a company like Long Tall Sally will limit its retail investment to big cities like London, and attempt to reach the rest of the market through a mail order offering.

Segment selection for the individual company

Much will depend on whether the company is entering the market for the first time, or is an established retailer seeking to redefine its marketing planning going forward. The potential new operator will need to conduct analysis to find areas that are currently under-exploited, and then assess the economics of entry and sustained competition in that segment. The established player, on the other hand, will be looking to the process to identify the segment or segments where it is stronger, with a view to maximizing performance, and dealing with its weaker areas either by dropping them or by identifying routes to improvement.

Here is an example of how market segmentation can be used only by a retail company as part of its total marketing planning process

Step 1
(a) Define the broad target customer in demographic/socio-economic terms, having plotted where you are currently operating, or are hoping to operate, on a matrix of the whole market for your type(s) of product.
(b) This will differ according to the type of store. For example, the Marks & Spencer chain stores will target a large number of segments of the UK clothing market compared to a single sex fashion multiple operator such as Miss Selfridge; Sainsbury's and Tesco target more segments of the food market than either Fortnum & Mason or the local convenience shop, etc.

Step 2
(a) Study the regional distribution of sales for your products to ensure that you are aware of any quirks that need taking into account.
(b) Overlay on your assessment of the demographic/socio-economic structure of your target market as much information as is available

on the shopping behaviour, psychological drivers, and benefit requirements of the potential customers in that market. This may lead you to adopt a different, and more appropriate, basis for segmentation.

For instance, if yours is the type of merchandise where demographic/socio-economic factors are of less account, e.g. photo/optical retailing, then it may be more appropriate to segment the market according to the types of user, and ascribe to each type of user the characteristics and shopping attitudes that mark them out. The photo/optical retail market might be segmented better as follows:

(i)   *The event recorders* – buy on price, low skills, low brand awareness, broad age-group, etc. Tend to buy cheap automatics, and want memories rather than art.

(ii) *The interested recorders* – less price sensitivity, rising skill level, higher brand awareness. Will likely buy the more expensive automatics and take the trouble to master the extra facilities to get better quality results.

(iii) *The active participants* – demonstrate skill level and technical understanding, high brand awareness, technical quality and features more important than price. Will tend to eschew automatics in favour of SLR cameras with interchangeable lenses and separate flash gun, and take pride in the results.

(iv) *The camera buff* – highly skilled, sees photography as an art form, is heavily into creating special effects, and probably owns, or has access to, developing and printing equipment. Will be technically demanding in his requirements, but at the same time aware of value for money, since he can do a lot of comparison shopping via the specialist photography magazines.

(c) Conversely, if your target segment is age-specific, e.g. young fashion clothing, then it will be prudent to break it down into its component attitude groups – in this case by attitude to fashion – and to understanding the behavioural characteristics of each.

Step 3
For each relevant section identified from the previous steps, define the key success factors for any competitor in the market. As we discussed earlier, the demands of customers on the range, brands, pricing, quality standards, store layout, and customer service provided, will differ for each segment.

Step 4
Evaluate your company against key competitors on these critical success factors on as structured a basis as possible, to establish your real and perceived strengths and weaknesses.

Step 5
Set objectives, strategies, and action plans, showing agreed time scales, responsibilities, and expected results.

Steps 3, 4 and 5 will be covered in more detail in later chapters.

Summing up

The objectives of market segmentation are:

- To help determine marketing direction through the analysis and understanding of trends and customer behaviour.
- To help ensure that the company targets those areas of the market where it has the greatest relative distinctive competence and opportunity of profitable success.
- To help determine realistic and obtainable marketing and sales objectives.
- To help improve decision-making by forcing managers to consider the options ahead in depth.

Completing the marketing audit: 2 The product audit

Summary

Chapter 5 defines what a product is, product life analysis and its impact on purchasing strategy, the product portfolio, and the Boston matrix. It outlines certain weaknesses in the Boston matrix approach, and goes on to discuss in detail the use of the directional policy matrix as a tool of analysis for retail operations.

What is a product?

The central role that the product plays in retail marketing management makes it such an important subject that mismanagement in this area is unlikely to be compensated for by good management in other areas.

The vital aspects of product management we shall discuss in this chapter are concerned with the nature of products, product life cycles, how products make profits, the concept of the product portfolio, and new product development. The purpose of this discussion is to help us to carry out a product audit in order that we can set meaningful marketing objectives. But before we can begin a proper discussion about product management, it is necessary first to understand what a product is, since this is the root of whatever misunderstanding there is about product management.

At the outset it is necessary to state that, in retailing, the product or service on sale cannot be divorced from the actual store context itself. Indeed for many customers, especially where similar categories of goods are on sale in many stores, the most important determinant of success is often the store itself, what its image is, the nature of the total shopping

Figure 5.1

experience and so on. This is becoming increasingly important in grocery retailing, where the leading players attempt to offer a unique shopping experience.

We have already looked at customers; now we begin to look at what we sell to them. Let us begin by explaining that a product is a problem-solver, in the sense that it is an answer to the customer's problem (see Figure 5.1), and is also the means by which the company achieves its objectives. And since it is what actually changes hands, it is clearly a subject of great importance.

The important point about this is that a company which fails to think of its business in terms of customer benefits rather than in terms of physical products is in danger of losing its competitive position in the market. This is why so much attention is paid to bringing the customers in.

We can now see that when customers buy a product, they are buying a particular bundle of benefits that they perceive as satisfying their own particular needs and wants. We can also begin to appreciate the danger of leaving all product decisions to those who do not fully understand this important point and assume that the only issue in product management is the actual technical performance, or the functional features of the product itself. These ideas about the 'extended' product are incorporated in Figure 5.2.

The importance of the brand

It will be clear here that we are talking not just about a physical product, but a relationship with the customer, a relationship that is personified either by the company's name (the store's name), or the brand names on the products it carries. With a number of UK retailers the two are synonymous. For example, Body Shop is the name over the door and the only brand name used on the product. Similarly, while Marks & Spencer's is the company's name, the only brand name carried is St Michael, and the two are indistinguishable.

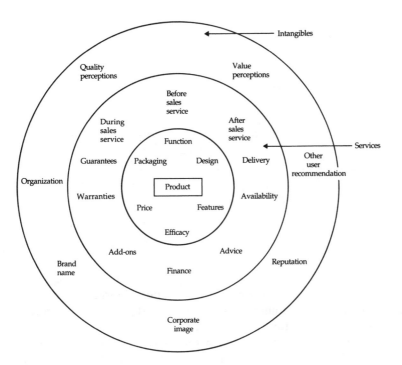

Figure 5.2

However, many retailers carry a portfolio of well known brands in addition to their own-label products. Tesco and Sainsbury's stock ranges from Kelloggs, Heinz, Cadbury-Schweppes, Nestlé and Coca Cola. Dixons has Panasonic, Sony, Hitachi, Philips, Amstrad, IBM, etc. Similarly, Currys will carry ranges from companies like Bosch, Hotpoint, Hoover, Zanussi and Kenwood.

They do this because they recognize the commercial value of the 'product surround' of the brands. Allied to their own company name over the door, these brands add credibility to their merchandise range, and help to bind their customers to them. Most people will be aware of the Coca Cola/Pepsi Cola blind taste tests, in which little difference was perceived when the colas were drunk 'blind'. On revealing the labels, however, 65 per cent of customers claimed to prefer Coca Cola. They were reacting to the 'product surround', or the 'added values' of the brand – the additional attributes, or intangibles, that the consumer perceives as being embodied in the product, and which distinguish the brand from being merely a commodity. Nescafé has a similar status in

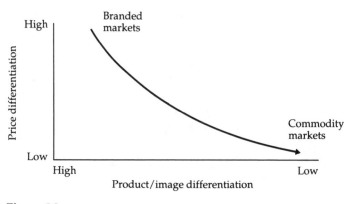

Figure 5.3

the coffee market. In the same way, among retailers, Marks & Spencer's communicates an aura of quality and reliability that enables it to protect its advantage over competing store groups.

A strong, well-maintained brand, whether it is the store name or an individual brand, gives the retailer the ability to command a premium price. That ability will recede very quickly if there is any neglect in maintaining, and protecting, the distinctive values of the brand. What would happen is that it would become increasingly difficult to differentiate the physical characteristics of the product from its competitors, and it would be easy to emulate it, until one would find that purchasing decisions were being made on the basis of price and availability. At this stage, the brand has become a commodity, having completed the 'commodity slide' depicted in Figure 5.3.

Brand loyalty and store loyalty

Many products build themselves such a strong consumer franchise that if they were to go out of stock, the consumer would be unwilling to accept a substitute. Usually a number of alternative solutions are available. Generally it has been observed that the consumer:

1 Switches the purchase to another size, but remains with the brand.
2 Purchases an alternative or substitute brand, i.e. switches brand.
3, Delays the purchase until the next visit to the store.
4 Looks for the product at another store, i.e. switches store.

5   Purchases a product from another (but not totally different) product group.

The implication for store loyalty and brand loyalty would seem to be quite clear: a balanced product range is one which (among other criteria) considers the need to contain the customers' selection processes within the store, but one which at the same time minimizes the retailers' investment in inventory. Thus, we see here the need for a balanced width within the product range, i.e. the number of product groups carried, and within product groups, comprising the product range, the number of items per product group, and the depth. This can and does vary by product group.

The compatibility of assortments refers to how well the various product lines complement each other in terms of the store's total effort to match its market offering to the perceived market opportunity. Finally, there is the compatibility of the product offering with the store image. If the store is majoring on low prices for a range of staple products, then a relatively narrow product range, together with tightly controlled service levels, would seem a logical product range policy, e.g. MFI furniture stores. Conversely, an image for customer service based on choice and availability clearly needs support with high inventory investment.

Customer service

Much of what has preceded has relevance for customer service. Clearly, depth, width and compatibility have a direct impact on customer service. The impact on costs has been commented on, but the revenue (and therefore earning capacity in terms of profitability) should be considered. Very simply, this means that often customer service and sales can be profitably increased by increasing one or both of product range, depth and width, and by giving some thought to product range compatibility.

Space return

Clearly the margin return on inventory investment is an important, useful and flexible measure of profitability. Equally important is the value return per square foot/metre or linear foot/metre of selling space, which in turn implies some optimal space allocation decision rule. This matter will be discussed in more detail later in the book along with the profit contribution mix.

Developing the product range

We have already identified the four variables over which the retailer has control. One of the most important variables open to us is the product range and we must consider this variable before we can go on to think about pricing. We need to assess the wants of our customers and the strengths and weaknesses of our range compared to our competitors' in order to decide what needs to be done in order to build sales and achieve profits. The whole process can be described as a product audit, which seeks to answer such questions as:

- What benefits do customers seek from this type of product?
- Does our product provide more benefits than those of our competitors?
- What competitive product advantages are causing us to lose market share?
- Does our product range still provide sufficient benefits to customers in relation to our costs and selling prices?
- Does each of our products still earn sufficient sales revenue and profit?

The answers to these questions will help to provide a basis for a successful product strategy.

Strategy implies a chosen route to a defined goal, and an element of long-term planning is needed to help follow that route. The product strategy of a company sets out the goals, and the routes to those goals for each subdivision in the range. The purpose of such a strategy is to help the company grow in terms of sales and profits or, in especially adverse conditions, to minimize the reductions in sales and profits.

Four strategies, described in a concept called the 'Ansoff Matrix' help us to view the possibilities for each product line and the groups of customers to whom we might sell those profits. This matrix is illustrated in Figure 5.4.

Market penetration either consists of increasing sales to existing customers or of finding more of the same type of customer for one product line. For example, '10p off a packet of soap powder until the end of April' and other such offers are examples of sales promotional techniques aimed at achieving market penetration. Their objective is to increase sales of a specific soap powder to people who already buy that brand, to attract people who buy another brand of washing powder, or to attract people to our particular store because of the price advantage.

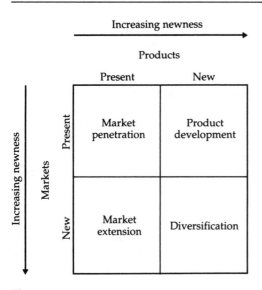

Figure 5.4

Product development comprises the modification of a product in some way, such as quality, style, performance, variety and so on. One example would be adding a new version of pizza with a new topping to appeal to existing pizza eaters, or to improve the quality of a range of suits so that a premium price can be charged.

Market extension means either finding new uses for a product, thereby attracting new customers, or taking the product into entirely new markets. The opening of stores in new parts of the country or in Europe are obvious examples of market extension.

Diversification covers both product development and market extension, i.e. the company selling a new product in a new market. An example of diversification was Marks & Spencer's introduction of a home furnishing range. Here, a whole new product range was introduced, with the express purpose of attracting a whole new raft of customers, as well as aiming to increase sales to M&S's traditional food and clothing clientele.

Choosing the right strategy

In retail operations we are aiming to increase the revenue from sales as much as possible, while keeping costs as low as possible. By that means we maximize profits. If one strategy will earn more income from sales than another, and if it will also do so more cheaply, then that is the option most likely to be chosen. Often it appears to be easiest to work with existing products and with existing customers, since in both cases you are dealing with things that you already understand. For this reason market penetration strategies are often the first choice. Sometimes, however, these strategies may not be the easiest, because they are based on trying to take market share from a competitor, and he may put up a fight!

Strategies of product development and market extension will seem more risky, since in each case you will be working with something new – either products or customers. Each will have a quantity of the unknown. However, whether they are in reality more risky than market penetration will depend upon your strengths as opposed to the strengths of your competitors, and upon the opportunities present in the situation.

You will be faced with the most unknowns when you go for diversification. You will then be taking a new product into an unfamiliar market, and this strategy is likely to be full of challenges. Diversification may sometimes, however, be the most appropriate strategy, probably the only one available for products that are developed 'ahead of their time' as a result of technological innovation. We are all familiar with the time taken to build a mass market for inventions such as television, washing machines, and personal computers – each bearing testimony not just to the difficulty but also to the rewards possible in pursuing strategies of diversification.

Managing the product range – the product life cycle

Any product that is launched on to the market will go through a number of stages related to the passage of time and the generation of sales. This concept is called the product life cycle. Whenever a new product is introduced, it is a substitute for something. Plastics, for example, substituted for wood and metal, electronic calculators substituted for mechanical calculators and slide rules. For all sorts of reasons customers often resist substitution: they may not believe that the new product will live up to its promises; they may have to write off investment in an old product; the new product is in competition with the old one, which probably still fulfils the need for which it was developed. Additionally, the new product may not compete very well on elements such as cost or performance. When electronic calculators were first launched, they were bulky, expensive and liable to failure. They did not succeed immediately in competition with the slide rule.

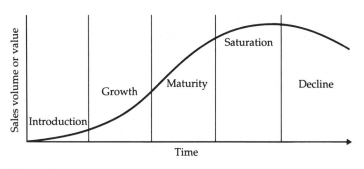

Figure 5.5

The product life cycle postulates that if a new product is successful at the introductory stage (and many fail at this point), then gradually repeat purchase grows and spreads and the rate of sales growth increases. At this stage competitors often enter the market and their additional promotional expenditures further expand the market. But no market is infinitely expandable, and eventually the rate of growth slows as the product moves into its maturity stage. Eventually a point is reached where most households have the product and there is too much product on the retail market, price wars break out, and some firms drop out of the market, until finally the market itself eventually falls into decline. Figure 5.5 illustrates these apparently universal phenomena.

Even if a product succeeds at the introductory stage, demand is likely to grow only slowly. The one exception is where a product is a 'fad' or 'fashion', with little consumer resistance to change in price or, in fact, anything. The sales just take off and the retailer may have a problem in meeting demand. The product's sales peak quickly and may decline equally quickly. The life cycle is almost over before it can be plotted, and is like an inverted V rather than the normal shape of the life cycle.

During the growth stage things are different. The product benefits have become accepted. More people want it, and it can be produced more cheaply – partly due to production difficulties having been overcome, partly due to increased sales leading to larger quantities being produced. At this stage more and more competitors enter the market and the money that is spent on promotion increases the awareness of the product and the interest in buying it.

Sales grow very rapidly in the growth stage, but no market is infinitely expandable. The product is said to have reached maturity when, for example, nearly every student has a pocket calculator, or 90 per cent of households have a refrigerator.

Eventually there are too many competitors in a market that is no longer growing. Saturation has occurred and price wars break out as each firm tries to sell more of its product. At this point some retailers stop stocking the product. Other substitute products begin to appear and the established product goes into decline.

At some stage a retailer will decide that a product has come to the end of its profitable life cycle and should be allowed to die. It may be decided that the opportunity costs of stocking the product are too high, and it is more profitable to invest in other product lines. There are plenty of examples of products that have reached this stage – personal cine cameras, black and white television sets, and, to a great extent, long playing records.

The product life cycle is useful to us therefore because it focuses our attention on the sales pattern that is likely if no corrective action is taken. Several strategies are available to sustain profitable sales over a product's life cycle, and, in effect, extend the growth phase.

We can use the life cycle to monitor the sales of a range of products, such as footwear, or to look at individual lines, such as ladies' casual shoes. However, we must also consider that the range is composed of not just one type of product but is the sum total of the lines of all of the buying groups. This of course has obvious advantages. When one product group is doing badly, another may be doing well, making profits and helping to keep the company prosperous. If we have a succession of products at different stages of their life cycle, we can ensure that there is always something to take the place of ageing products. This mix of products is called a product portfolio. Figure 5.6 shows an example of a product portfolio for a company with three products. One product (A) is in severe decline, product (B) is at saturation stage, while (C) is in the introductory stage.

Additionally, we must consider the effects of seasonality. Although a product life cycle may show growth from one year to another, this may mask considerable fluctuations in sales within the year. Sales of swimwear, which are concentrated in 6 months of the year, may balance sales of winter coats, and accessories such as gloves and scarves, in the other six months. The mix of life cycles in the portfolio needs to take this seasonality into consideration, and of course has a significant effect on the cash generation and usage throughout the seasons, as well as throughout the lives of the products.

From a management point of view the product life cycle concept is useful in that it focuses our attention on the likely future sales' pattern if we take no corrective action. There are several courses of action open to us in our attempts to maintain the profitable sales of a product over its life cycle. Figure 5.7 illustrates the actual courses taken by a British

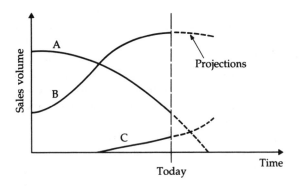

Figure 5.6

company in the management of one of its leading products. As sales growth began to slow down, the company initiated a programme of product range extensions and market development that successfully took the brand into additional stages of growth. At the same time the company was aggressively seeking new products and even considering potential areas for diversification.

Even more important are the implications of the product life cycle concept on every element of the marketing mix. Figure 5.7 gives some guide as to how the product has to change over its life cycle. In

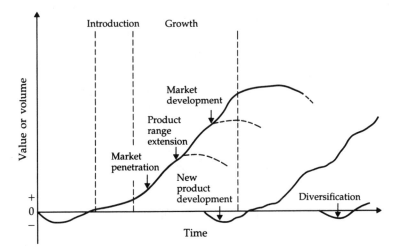

Figure 5.7

addition to this, however, every other element also has to change. For example, if a company rigidly adhered to a premium pricing policy at the mature stage of the product life cycle, when markets are often overcrowded and price wars begin, it could well lose market share. It could be regretted later on when the market has settled down, for it is often at this stage that products provide extremely profitable revenue for the company. It will become clearer later in this chapter why market share is important.

The same applies to promotion. During the early phase of product introduction the task for advertising is often one of creating awareness, whereas during the growth phase the task may need to change to one of creating a favourable attitude towards the product. Figures 5.8, 5.9 and 5.10 illustrate the life cycle of a total retail company and two of its many store types ('products').

Drawing a product life cycle, however, can be extremely difficult, even given the availability of some form of time series analysis. This is connected with the complex question of market share measurement.

Firstly, let us remind ourselves that a firm needs to be concerned with its share (or its proportion of volume or value) of an actual market rather than with a potential market. For the purpose of helping us to draw life cycles, it is worth repeating the definitions given in Chapter 3:

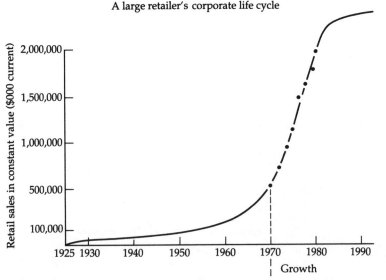

A large retailer's corporate life cycle

Figure 5.8

Supermarket stores – divisional life cycle

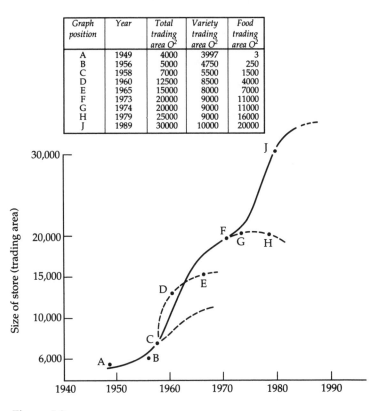

Graph position	Year	Total trading area O²	Variety trading area O²	Food trading area O²
A	1949	4000	3997	3
B	1956	5000	4750	250
C	1958	7000	5500	1500
D	1960	12500	8500	4000
E	1965	15000	8000	7000
F	1973	20000	9000	11000
G	1974	20000	9000	11000
H	1979	25000	9000	16000
J	1989	30000	10000	20000

Figure 5.9

- Product class e.g. men's socks.
- Product sub-class e.g. sports.
- Product brand e.g. Adidas.

The product brand, for the purpose of measuring market share, is concerned only with the aggregate of all other brands that satisfy the same group of customer wants. Nevertheless the retailer also needs to be aware of the sales trends of other kinds of men's socks in the market, as well as of sales overall.

One of the most frequent mistakes made by companies that do not understand what market share really means is to assume that their company has only a small share of some market. However, if the company is commercially successful, it probably has a much larger share of a smaller market segment.

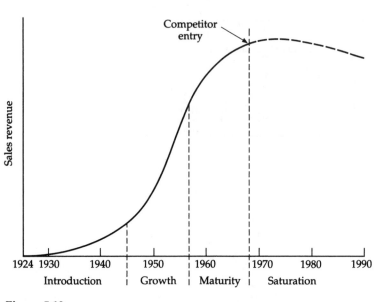

Variety stores – divisional life cycle

Figure 5.10

Table 5.1   Guide to market maturity

Maturity stage factor	Embryonic	Growth	Mature	Declining
1 *Growth rate*	Normally much greater than GNP (on small base).	Sustained growth above GNP. New customers. New suppliers. Rate decelerates toward end of stage.	Approximately equals GNP.	Declining demand. Market shrinks as users' needs change.
2 *Predictability of growth potential*	Hard to define accurately. Small portion of demand being satisfied. Market forecasts differ widely.	Greater percentage of demand is met and upper limits of demand becoming clearer. Discontinuities, such as price reductions based on economies of scale, may occur.	Potential well-defined. Competition specialized to satisfy needs of specific segments.	Known and limited.

3 *Product line proliferation*	Specialized lines to meet needs of early customers.	Rapid expansion.	Proliferation slows or ceases.	Lines narrow as unprofitable products dropped.
4 *Number of competitors*	Unpredictable.	Reaches maximum. New entrants attracted by growth and high margins. Some consolidation begins toward end of stage.	Entrenched positions established. Further shakeout of marginal competitors.	New entrants unlikely. Competitors continue to decline.
5 *Market share distribution*	Unstable. Shares react unpredictably to entrepreneurial insights and timing.	Increasing stability. Typically, a few competitors emerging as strong.	Stable with a few companies often controlling much of the total sales.	Highly concentrated or fragmented as customer segments and/or localized.
6 *Customer stability*	Trial usage with little customer loyalty.	Some loyalty. Repeat usage with many seeking alternative suppliers.	Well-developed buying patterns with customer loyalty. Competitors understand purchase dynamics and it is difficult for a supplier to win over accounts.	Extremely stable. Suppliers dwindle and customers less motivated to seek alterntives.
7 *Ease of entry*	Normally easy. No one dominates. Customers' expectations uncertain. If barriers exist, they are usually technology, capital or fear of the unknown.	More difficult. Market franchises and/or economies of scale may exist, yet new business is still available without directly confronting competition.	Difficult. Market leaders established. New business must be 'won' from others.	Little or no incentive to enter.
8 *Technology*	Plays an important role in matching product characteristics to market needs. Frequent product changes. Aimed at improving the technical specification.	Product technology settles down into one or two successful applications.	Technology stabilizes. Product stocking requirements well-known and relatively undemanding. May be a thrust to renew the industry via the new technology.	Technological content is well-known, stable and accessible.

The important point to remember at this stage is that the concept of the product life cycle is not an academic figment of the imagination, but a hard reality that is ignored at great risk. It is interesting to see how many commercial failures can be traced back to a naive assumption on the part of managements that what was successful as a policy at one time will continue to be successful in the future.

Table 5.1 shows a checklist used by one major company to help it determine where its markets are on the life cycle.

Diffusion of innovation

An interesting and useful extension of the product life cycle is what is known as the 'diffusion of innovation'. This will be referred to again in Chapter 6.

Diffusion is:

1   The adoption
2   of new products or services
3   over time
4   by consumers
5   within social systems
6   as encouraged by marketing

Diffusion refers to the cumulative percentage of potential adopters of a new product or service over time. Everett Rogers examined some of the social forces that explain the product life cycle. The body of knowledge often referred to as 'reference theory' (which incorporates work on group norms, group pressures etc.) helps explain the snowball effect of diffusion. Rogers found that the actual rate of diffusion is a function of a product's:

1   Relative advantage (over existing products).
2   Compatibility (with life styles, values, etc.).
3   Communicability (Is it easy to communicate?).
4   Complexity (Is it complicated?).
5   Divisibility (Can it be tried out on a small scale before commitment?).

Diffusion is also a function of the newness of a product itself, which can be classified broadly under three headings:

• Continuous innovation, e.g. the new miracle ingredient.

- Dynamically continuous innovation, e.g. disposable lighter.
- Discontinuous, e.g. microwave oven.

However, Rogers found that not everyone adopts new products at the same time, and that a universal pattern emerges, as shown in Figure 5.11.

From the real life cycle analysis shown in the Figure 5.12 it can be seen that this retailer was never particularly innovative in buying in new products. In fact, it shows that he tended to buy in the product at the maturity stage, so giving the market another 'kick'. His policy was then to stock it in depth, price it low, and put a lot of promotional advertising effort behind it. A quick glance at Figure 5.13, however, reveals that, *by mistake*, this retailer occasionally bought into a range of merchandise somewhat earlier in its life cycle. The trouble was that he still stocked in depth, priced low and promoted heavily, thus giving away margin unnecessarily.

In general the innovators think for themselves and try new things (where relevant); the early adopters, who have status in society, are opinion leaders and they adopt successful products, making them acceptable and respectable; the early majority, who are more conservative and who have slightly above average status, are more deliberate and only adopt products that have social approbation; the late majority, who are below average status and sceptical, adopt products much later; and the laggards, with low status, income, etc., view life through the rear mirror and are the last to adopt products.

This particular piece of research can be very useful, particularly for advertising and personal selling. For example, if we develop a typology for innovative customers, we can target our early advertising and sales

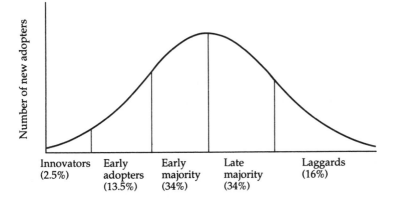

Figure 5.11

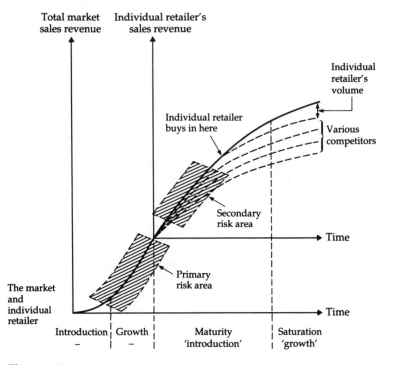

Product life cycle at total market and an individual retailer's level

Figure 5.12

effort specifically at them. Once the first 3 per cent of innovators have adopted our product, there is a good chance that the early adopters will try it, and once the 10-12 per cent point is reached, the champagne can be opened, because there is a good chance that the rest will adopt the product.

We know, for example, that the general characteristics of opinion leaders show that they are venturesome, socially integrated, cosmopolitan, socially mobile, and privileged. So we need to ask ourselves what the specific characteristics of these customers are in our particular market. We can then tailor our advertising and selling message specifically for them.

Retailers need to understand this phenomenon because it relates specifically to the types of customer that frequent their stores and to the category of products in question and where they are on the diffusion of innovation curve. A store not frequented by innovators and early adopters is hardly likely to do particularly well with products that are relatively new to the market.

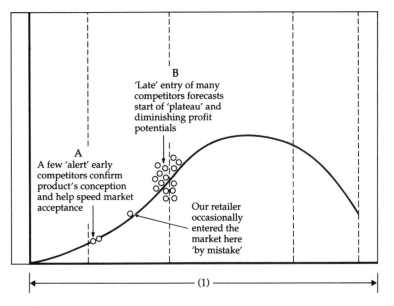

B
'Late' entry of many
competitors forecasts
start of 'plateau' and
diminishing profit
potentials

A
A few 'alert' early
competitors confirm
product's conception
and help speed market
acceptance

Our retailer
occasionally
entered the
market here
'by mistake'

(1)

Figure 5.13

The product life cycle and buying

Before we leave the idea of the product life cycle, it will be useful to examine its relation with the retailer's buying strategy. A PLC-based buying model can be of great assistance because:

- It suggests guideline strategies and priorities.
- The advanced knowledge the PLC provides increases the number of options open to the buyer.
- It helps buyers to coordinate their activities with other functions, such as advertising and promotions.
- It permits the buyer to make decisions with greater accuracy, relevance and foresight.

The introduction or trial phase

The characteristics of this stage of the product life cycle are:

1　Low sales.
2　The uncertainty of how long this phase will last.

3   Losses or low profits, due to high initial advertising and promotion costs.
4   Inexperienced retail personnel.
5   Inexperienced customers.
6   The vulnerability of the product.
7   Relatively few distributors (wholesale or retail).
8   The product is often produced and marketed on a trial or pilot basis.

The buyer has to help the infant product through this initial phase, while not committing too many resources. This is a perfectly reasonable stance to take, because history shows that many new products do not survive the trial phase.

The buyer's actions will focus on:

1   Maintaining low inventories of the product.
2   Seeking knowledge suppliers who can provide good technical back-up services.
3   Obtaining suppliers with the potential to grow with the product, who are patient enough to supply small quantities at the outset, and who are flexible enough to vary their products and services as rapidly-changing needs dictate.
4   Setting up good lines of communication with suppliers.
5   Paying careful attention to quality control (especially important when customers have not yet had the opportunity to form an opinion of the product's quality).

Growth phase

The growth phase is characterized by:

1   Rapid rise of sales in a relatively short time.
2   Much less vulnerability than at the former phase.
3   Possibility of substantial profits.
4   Many other suppliers becoming available.
5   The product now being in full-scale production.

At this phase the retail buyer has to do everything possible to obtain the right level of intake from the suppliers. It will be necessary to:

1   Look out for new sources of supply.
2   Ensure that quality control is maintained as the manufacturing tempo increases.

3   Build bigger inventories or schedule more frequent and rapid deliveries of the product.

Maturity phase

The product enters its maturity phase when the rate of growth of sales volume stabilizes. Usually at this phase:

1   Sales continue to increase, but at a decreasing rate.
2   Most retail competitors are staking the product.
3   Price competition begins.
4   Profits begin to decline.

The buyer is now faced with optimizing his return on existing stocks of the product, while also beginning to reduce the company's forward commitment. The resulting actions will follow these lines:

1   Obtaining more favourable supply contracts on a flow basis since demand is more predictable.
2   Looking for lower cost prices without sacrificing quality.
3   Critically reviewing weaker suppliers.
4   Watching out for other cut-price retail competitors (they often enter the field towards the end of the maturity phase).
5   Minimizing all peripheral costs associated with the product.

Saturation phase

This phase has many of the characteristics of the maturity phase, but they are now present in extreme forms. In addition:

1   It is no longer possible to increase sales despite strenuous efforts.
2   Profits decline sharply.
3   Competition is extremely severe.

The buyer now has to do many of the same things as in the maturity phase, but with more urgency. The strategy is to reduce the company's commitment still further. To this end the buyer will take action to:

1   Put more emphasis on cost-cutting in all areas, not just cost price of goods.
2   Balance inventory levels carefully, minimizing investment wherever possible.

3   Make the best of the rampant, and sometimes ruthless, price-cutting that will exist.
4   Deal with marketing-orientated suppliers rather than production-orientated suppliers.
5   Expect (but not look for) a gradual erosion of quality in the goods received.
6   Keep looking for low-cost substitute goods and services.

Decline phase

Eventually the saturation phase gives way to the decline phase, in which sales are declining and profits have been virtually eliminated, despite the company's efforts to stem the tide. Moreover, suppliers and retail competitors are giving up the product in favour of newer, more profitable lines.

Faced with this situation, the buyer has to continue to reduce the company's commitment to the product and begin developing a withdrawal plan. In doing this:

1   Activities with any long-run effect should be discontinued.
2   Out-of-pocket expenses should be avoided.
3   Inventory levels should be critically examined and revised.

Abandonment phase

This final stage of the product life cycle is extremely important, since, unless old products are pruned from the range, the company's energies cannot be turned effectively to the newer and more profitable items.

The buyer clearly has to delete the product and eliminate all further company commitment to it. To do this, it will be necessary to:

1   Dispose of surpluses no longer needed via auction or clearance sales.
2   Assume buying responsibilities for new or replacement items that can be recommended as suitable alternatives.
3   Give timely notice to suppliers of impending deletion action, thereby preserving a relationship that could be mutually beneficial at some time in the future.

Product portfolio

As we have seen, at any point in time a review of a company's different products would reveal different stages of growth, maturity and

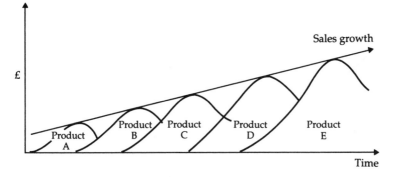

Figure 5.14

decline. If our objective is to grow in profitability over a long period of time, our analysis of our product portfolio should reveal a situation like the one in Figure 5.14, in which new product introductions are timed so as to ensure continuous sales growth.

The ideal of a portfolio is for a company to meet its objectives by balancing sales growth, cash flow, and risk. As individual products progress or decline, and as markets grow or shrink, then the nature of the company's portfolio will change. It is therefore essential that the whole portfolio is reviewed regularly and that an active policy towards new product development and divestment of old products is pursued. In this respect the work of the Boston Consulting Group, begun in the early 1960s, has had a profound effect on the way managements think about this subject and about their product/market strategy.

Unit costs and market share

There are basically two parts to the thinking behind the work of the Boston Consulting Group. One is concerned with market share; the other with market growth.

It is a well-known fact that we become better at doing things the more we do them. This phenomenon is known as the learning curve. It manifests itself especially with items such as labour efficiency, work specialization, and methods improvement.

Such benefits are themselves a part of what we can call the experience effect, which includes such items as process innovations, better productivity from staff and resources, store design improvements, and so on. In addition to the experience effect, and not necessarily mutually exclusive,

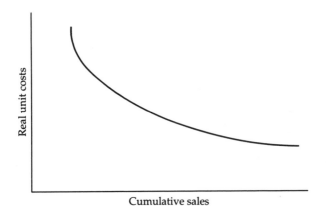

Figure 5.15

are economies of scale that come with growth. For example, capital costs do not increase in direct proportion to capacity, which results in lower depreciation charges per unit of sales, lower operating costs in the form of the number of staff, lower marketing sales, administration, and research and development costs, and lower raw materials and distribution costs. It is generally recognized, however, that cost decline applies more to the value-added elements of cost than to bought-in supplies. In fact the Boston Consulting Group discovered that costs decline by up to 30 per cent for every cumulative doubling of output. This phenomenon is shown in Figure 5.15. While there are many implications from this for marketing strategy, particularly in relation to pricing policy, we will confine ourselves here to a discussion of the product/market implications.

There is an overwhelming body of evidence to show that this real cost reduction actually occurs, in which case it follows that the greater your volume, the lower your unit costs should be. Thus, irrespective of what happens to the price of your product, providing you have the highest market share (hence the biggest volume), you should always be relatively more profitable than your competitors. This is illustrated in Figure 5.16.

As a general rule, therefore, it can be said that market share *per se* is a desirable goal. Indeed research has confirmed that market share and profitability are linearly related. However, as we made clear in Chapter 4, we have to be certain that we have carefully defined our market, or segment. This explains why it is apparently possible for many small firms to be profitable in large markets. The reason is of course that in reality they have a large share of a small, more specialized, market

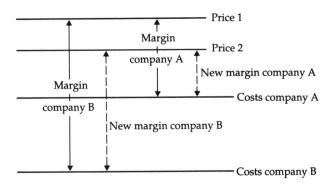

Figure 5.16

segment. This is another reason why understanding market segmentation is the key to successful marketing. It would be unusual if there were not many caveats to the above 'law', and, although what these might be is fairly obvious, it should be noted that the evidence provided by the Boston Consulting Group shows overwhelmingly that in general these 'laws' apply universally, whether for consumer, industrial or service markets.

Turning now to market growth, we observe that in markets that are growing at a very low rate per annum it is extremely difficult and also very costly to increase your market share. This is usually because the market is in the steady state (possibly in the saturation phase of the product life cycle) and is dominated by a few big firms that have probably reached a stage of equilibrium, one very difficult to upset.

In markets that are going through a period of high growth, it is fairly obvious that the most sensible policy to pursue would be to gain market share by taking a bigger proportion of the market growth than your competitors. However, such a policy is very costly in promotional terms, so that many companies prefer to sit tight and enjoy rates of growth lower than the market growth rate. The major problem with this approach is that they are in fact losing market share, which gives cost advantages (hence margin advantages) to competitors.

Since we know from previous experience of product life cycles that the market growth rate will fall when this stage is reached and the market inevitably becomes price sensitive, the product will begin to lose money and we shall probably be forced out of the market. Indeed, seen in this light, it becomes easier to understand the reasons for the demise of many industries in those countries of the world where the Japanese have entered the market. Typical of this is the motor-cycle industry in the UK in which the output of the Japanese increased from thousands of units to millions of units during a period of market growth, while the output of the British remained steady during the same period. When the market growth rate started to decline, the inevitable happened. Even worse, it was virtually impossible for the UK industry to recover from such a situation, and the Japanese, with their advantageous cost position, now dominate practically every market segment, including big bikes.

The Boston matrix

The Boston Consulting Group combined these ideas in the form of a simple matrix, which has profound implications for the firm, especially in respect of cash flow. Profits are not always an appropriate indicator of portfolio performance, as they will often reflect changes in the liquid assets of the company, such as inventories, capital equipment, or receivables, and thus do not indicate the true scope for future development. Cash flow, on the other hand, is a key determinant of a company's ability to develop its product portfolio.

The Boston matrix classified a firm's products according to their cash usage and their cash generation along the two dimensions described above, i.e. relative market share and market growth rate. Market share is used because it is an indicator of the product's ability to generate cash; market growth is used because it is an indicator of the product's cash requirements. The measure of market share used is the product's share relative to the firm's largest competitor. This is important because it reflects the degree of dominance enjoyed by the product in the market. For example, if company A has 20 per cent market share and its biggest competitor also has 20 per cent market share, this position is usually less favourable than if company A had 20 per cent market share and its biggest competitor had only 10 per cent market share. The relative ratios would be 1:1 compared with 2:1. It is this ratio, or measure of market dominance, that the horizontal axis measures. This is summarized in Figure 5.17.

The definition of high relative market share is taken to be a ratio of one or greater than one. The cut-off point for high as opposed to low market growth should be defined according to the prevailing circumstances in the industry, but this is often taken as 10 per cent. There is, however, no reason why the dividing line on the vertical axis cannot be zero, or even a minus figure. It depends entirely on the industry or segment growth or decline. Sometimes, in very general markets, gross domestic product (GDP) can be used.

The somewhat picturesque labels attached to each of the four categories of products give some indication of the prospects for products

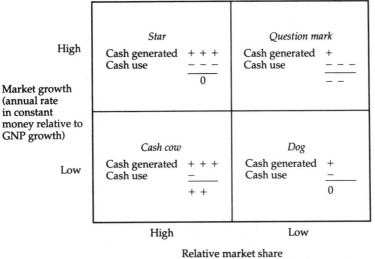

Figure 5.17

in each quadrant. Thus, the 'Question mark' is a product which has not yet achieved a dominant market position and thus a high cash flow, or perhaps it once had such a position but has slipped back. It will be a high user of cash because it is in a growth market. This is also sometimes referred to as a 'Wildcat'.

The 'Star' is probably a newish product that has achieved a high market share and is probably more or less self-financing in cash terms.

The 'Cash cows' are leaders in markets where there is little additional growth but a lot of stability. These are excellent generators of cash and tend to use little because of the state of the market.

'Dogs' often have little future and can be a cash drain on the company. They are probably candidates for divestment, although often such products fall into a category aptly described by Peter Drucker as 'invest-ments in managerial ego'.

The art of product portfolio management now becomes a lot clearer. What we should be seeking to do is to use the surplus cash generated by the 'Cash cows' to invest in our 'Stars' and to invest in a selected number of 'Question marks'. This is indicated in Figure 5.18.

The Boston matrix can be used to forecast the market position of our products in, say, 5 years from now if we continue to pursue our current policies. Figure 5.19 illustrates this process for a retailer with four product lines. The area of each circle is proportional to each product's

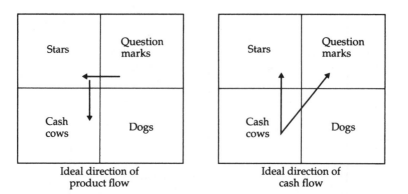

Figure 5.18

contribution to total company sales volume. In the cash of this particular company it can be seen that they are following what could well prove to be disastrous policies in respect of their principal products. Product A, although growing, is losing market share in a high-growth market, as is Product D. Products E and C are gaining market share in declining markets.

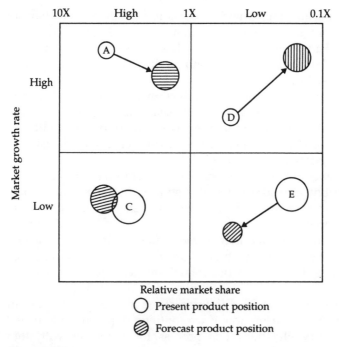

Figure 5.19

Such a framework also easily helps to explain the impracticability of marketing objectives such as 'to achieve a 10 per cent growth and a 20 per cent return on investment'. Such an objective, while fine as a long-term policy, if applied to individual products in the portfolio, clearly becomes a nonsense and totally self-defeating. For example, to accept a 10 per cent growth rate in a market that is growing at, say, 15 per cent per annum, is likely to prove disastrous in the long run. Likewise, to go for a much higher than market growth rate in a low-growth market is certain to lead to unnecessary price wars and market disruption.

This type of framework is particularly useful to demonstrate to senior management the implications of different product/market strategies. It is also useful in formulating policies towards new product development.

Weaknesses in the Boston matrix approach

Unfortunately many companies started using the Boston matrix indiscriminately during the 1970s, and as a result it gradually lost its universal appeal. The reason, however, had more to do with lack of real understanding on the part of management than with any major defects in the methodology.

Nonetheless there are circumstances where great caution is required in its use. Imagine for a moment a company with 80 per cent of its

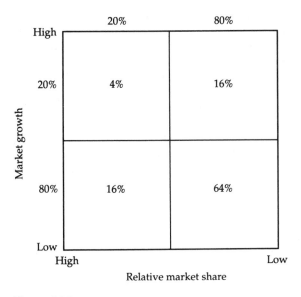

Figure 5.20

products in low growth markets, and only 20 per cent of its products market leaders. The matrix would look as depicted in Figure 5.20. As can be seen, almost 65 per cent of the company's products are 'Dogs'. To divest oneself of these may well be tantamount to throwing the baby out with the bath water!

Consider also those industries in which market share for any single product in the range has little to do with its 'profitability'. Often a product with low market share enjoys the same production, distribution and marketing economies of scale as other products in the portfolio, e.g. in the case of beers and food products. Let us take a product that is manufactured from basically the same components as other large market share products, is manufactured in the same plant as part of a similar process, and is distributed on the same vehicles and via the same outlets. In such a case it is easy to see how this product's low market share can indeed be extremely profitable.

None of this, however, invalidates the work of the Boston Consulting Group, the principles of which can be applied to companies, divisions, subsidiaries, strategic business units, product groups, products, and so on. Providing great care is taken over the 'market share' axis, it is an extremely valuable planning tool.

The next 3 pages have been abstracted from Weymes (Cranfield Research Papers in *Marketing and Logistics*, 22, 1978–9), 'The Application of The Boston Matrix to Retailing'.

The investment required to introduce a product into a retail store is minimal, compared to the launch of a new product into the market by a manufacturing company. A product new to a retail store will represent only a small proportion of store participation but, if the product is to succeed, its growth must be high. To attain high growth, a large amount of prominent shelf space may be allocated to the product, together with in-store and, possibly, promotional campaigns. As sales growth increases, then so does the product's store participation factor. With high growth and participation factors, the product moves from the 'Wildcat' to the 'Star' sector. The product has now become a large generator of revenue, and while sales growth remains high, the product should remain in a prominent position supported by promotional activity. This will ensure that as many households as possible will become familiar with the product. As sales growth declines, the product should maintain market share, moving into the 'Cash cow' sector. The product is now established in the market. Promotional support should be withdrawn and the product moved from the prime display area.

Provided the product is a non-fashion item in a stable market, it should maintain its high level of participation and remain a cash

A successful product A fashion product An unsuccessful product

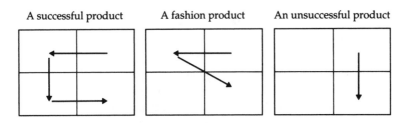

Figure 5.21

generator for the store. Fashion items tend to lose sales as soon as promotional support is withdrawn, especially when a substitute item has been introduced into the market.

Thus, the fashion item may move directly from the 'Star' to the 'Dog' sector. Certain fashion items may not achieve the required sales and will drop from the 'Wildcat' to the 'Dog' sector, while others will become established in the market and move to the 'Cash cow' sector. These product movements are shown in Figure 5.21.

A product in the 'Dog' sector is one experiencing low participation and low growth. It is generating revenue, but only a small amount, while occupying shelf space that could be used more profitably after deletion.

The difference between the manufacturer Boston matrix and the retailer Boston matrix

The main difference between the Boston matrix and the Portfolio matrix lies in the Boston Consulting Group's use of the experience curve. Manufacturing costs are reduced proportionately each time production is doubled. But of course the retailer is not in the manufacturing business. The difference between the two matrices lies in the 'Star' sector. Products in the Boston 'Star' sector may be cash absorbers, as they are being financed in order to gain market share. In the retail 'Star' sector, products are high generators of revenue. The cash generated may not be required for reinvestment but may be used for other purposes such as store expansion or general promotional activities. The cost of the retail 'Star' is the opportunity cost forgone in allocating the product to a prime display site within the store, together with the cost of the associated promotional activity. The 'Dog' of the retail matrix also differs slightly. The 'Dog' from the manufacturing portfolio can be a cash drain – when the reinvestment required is greater than the revenue generated. The retailing 'Dog' may not be a cash drain, but it has an opportunity cost associated with

The portfolio matrix

Star	Wildcat
High cash generators requiring a prime site in the store in order to attract custom. May be unstable especially if a fashion item	Product new to the store requires shelf space and promotion in order to become established. Small cash generator
Cashcow	Dog
A steady cash generator and occupies secondary shelf space. Little or no promotion required	Small cash generator. Possible candidate for deletion but may be supporting a product in the star or cashcow sectors. Occupying valuable shelf space

Abstracted from Cranfield Research Papers – *Marketing and Logistics*, 22, 1978–9.

Figure 5.22   *The portfolio matrix*

it. This is the cost of the shelf space occupied by the 'Dog' which could be used by another product. This opportunity must be weighed against the benefits derived from maintaining the product in the store. All of this is summarized in Figure 5.22.

In the above description of the retail store model, only the product level has been discussed.

The argument for product groups and departments is similar, but a *product group* or *department* in the 'Dog' sector is more serious than a *product* in this sector. Every effort should be made to re-adjust the product mix of the products within these categories so that their performance is improved.

The retailer matrix does not offer the ultimate solution to merchandise management. However, the matrix does act as an indicator to the performance of a product, product group and department; but any final decision must be based on qualitative information. This matrix can be a most useful tool to lawyers and merchandisers as they work together on the balance of the products within the store, and on planning future policies.

A specific example of the application of the Boston matrix to a major retailer

One of the authors took these basic concepts into one of Australia's largest general merchandising retailers, and amended and applied the new analytical tools to help buying managers develop long-range marketing plans for different categories of merchandise, with extremely interesting results. Table 5.2 on page 113 shows the sample calculations from which the portfolios were constructed. They represent actual sales

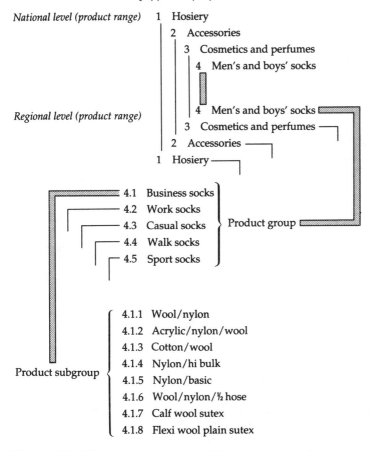

Figure 5.23 *Hierarchy of product portfolios in accessories department*

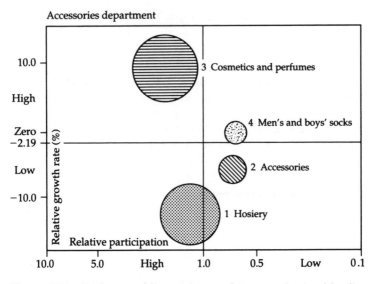

Figure 5.24   *Product portfolio matrix – product range (national level)*

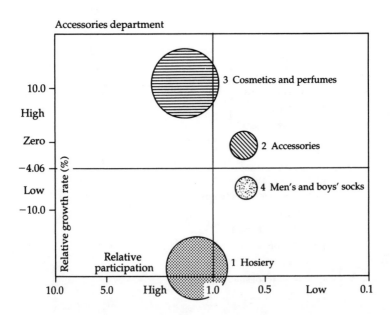

Figure 5.25   *Product portfolio matrix – product range (region l level)*

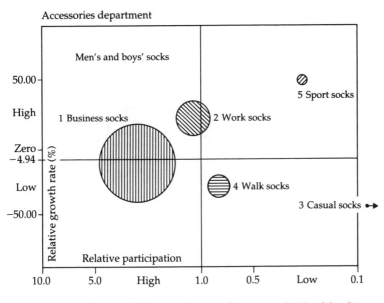

Figure 5.26 *Product portfolio matrix – product group (region 1 level)*

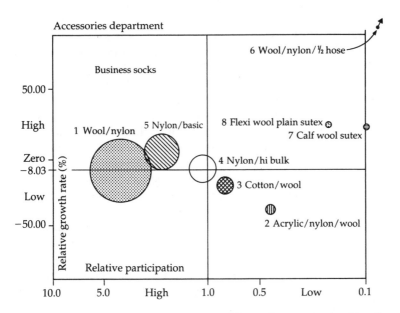

Figure 5.27 *Product portfolio matrix – product sub-group (region 1 level)*

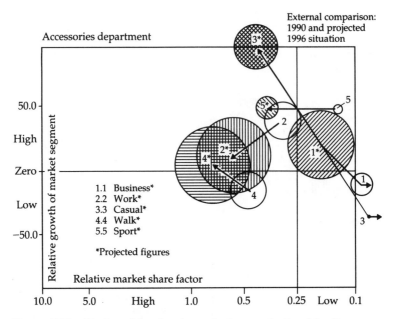

Figure 5.28   *Men's and boys' socks product group (national level)*

figures for different categories of merchandise for the years 1982 and 1983. The notes explain the details of the calculations.

Figure 5.23 shows the categories of merchandise used in the portfolios at their several levels of disaggregation, Figure 5.24 the data in graphical form at the highest level of merchandise aggregation at the national level, and Figure 5.25 the data in graphical form at the highest level of merchandise aggregations, but this time at Region 1 level for comparison purposes. Figure 5.26 shows the data in graphical form at the next level down of merchandise aggregation at the Region 1 level, while Figure 5.27 shows the data in graphical form at the next level down of merchandise aggregation at the Region 1 level, and, finally, Figure 5.28 shows a traditional Boston matrix at the national level.

Thus, Figures 5.23 to 5.27 show the tool applied internally, using a progressively more detailed disaggregation of the data. Figure 5.28 shows the traditional Boston matrix approach.

This kind of application leads to a number of interesting questions, which arise automatically, depending on where the location of the circle is. These include issues relating to positioning of merchandise in the store, pricing, promotion and range content. Of these, the most important relates to the future marketing policy, both for individual items of merchandise and for whole categories. Additionally, the three major considerations are:

Table 5.2 Accessories department – product portfolio matrix – product range (national level)

Product group	Sales ($)[a]		Sample Calculations	1983[b] participation % (D)	Av. expected participation with 4 product groups (%) (C) (E)	Relative[a] participation (D ÷ E) (F)
	Y/E Jan. 1982 (A)	Y/E Jan. 1983 (B)	Av. growth rate (%) ((B−A)÷A)×100 (C)			
Women's hosiery	5,739,316	5,004,395	− 12.81	28.52	25.00	1.14
Accessories	3,121,412	2,938,408	− 5.86	16.74	25.00	0.67
Cosmetics and perfumes	6,314,189	6,854,086	+ 8.55	39.05	25.00	1.56
Men's and boys' socks	2,767,799	2,752,859	− 0.54	15.69	25.00	0.63
	17,942,716	17,549,748	− 2.19	100.00	100.00	

Notes:
(a) The overall average growth of sales is effectively the 'weighted average' or relative growth indicator, i.e. it sets the position of the horizontal axis in the matrix and hence separates 'high' and 'low' relative growth rates.
(b) Participation (or sales share) of each product group within the range is calculated by dividing the sales revenue of each individual product group by the total 1983 sales revenue, and converting it into percentage terms.
(c) Average expected participation depends solely on the number of participating product groups – simply divide this number into 100.
(d) Relative participation is a factor obtained by dividing actual (1983) participation (Column D) by the average expected participation (Column E). The resulting factor (Column F) is effectively a measure of 'dominance' of the relevant product group. The dividing line between 'high' and 'low' relative participation (or dominance) is therefore usually set as 1.00 on a logarithmic scale, i.e. 1.00 is the position for the vertical axis in the matrix.

- What does the customer expect from the store?
- What is happening in the external market?
- What is the profitability (contribution)?

It is clear that such an approach is little more than a visual representation of a retailer's statistics, and that, like all management aids, it does not actually tell us anything we do not already know. Its real value lies in the clarity and the analytical depth and creativity with which it is applied. Certainly the managers who have used it to develop retail marketing plans have found it to be an extremely valuable aid to marketing diagnosis and clarity of strategic thinking.

Nonetheless work in this vital area of retail management is still in its infancy, and there is much research still to be done before any valid claims of efficacy as a management tool can be made with any confidence.

Further developments of the Boston matrix

It is complications such as those outlined earlier that make the Boston matrix less relevant to certain situations. While it is impossible to give absolute rules on what these situations are, suffice it to say that great caution is necessary when dealing with such matters. In any case two principles should be adhered to always. Firstly, a business should define its markets in such a way that it can ensure that its costs for key activities will be competitive; it should define the markets it serves in such a way that it can develop specialized skills in servicing those markets and hence overcome a relative cost disadvantage. Both of course have to be related to a company's distinctive competence.

However, the approach of the Boston Consulting Group is fairly criticized in such circumstances as those described above as relying on two single factors, i.e. relative market share and market growth. To overcome this difficulty, and to provide a more flexible approach, General Electric and McKinsey jointly developed a multi-factor approach, using the same fundamental ideas as the Boston Consulting Group. They used market attractiveness and business strengths as the two main axes and built up these dimensions from a number of variables. By means of these variables, and some scheme for weighting them according to their importance, products (or businesses) are classified into one of nine cells in a 3 × 3 matrix. Thus, the same purpose is served as in the Boston matrix, i.e. comparing investment opportunities among products or businesses, but with the difference that multiple criteria are used. These criteria vary according to circumstances, but generally include those shown in Figure 5.29.

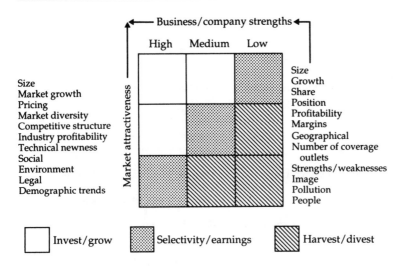

Size
Market growth
Pricing
Market diversity
Competitive structure
Industry profitability
Technical newness
Social
Environment
Legal
Demographic trends

Size
Growth
Share
Position
Profitability
Margins
Geographical
Number of coverage
   outlets
Strengths/weaknesses
Image
Pollution
People

Invest/grow   Selectivity/earnings   Harvest/divest

Figure 5.29

It is not necessary, however, to use a nine-box matrix, and many managers prefer to use a four-box matrix similar to the Boston box. Indeed this is the authors' preferred methodology, as it seems to be more easily understood by, and useful to, practising managers.

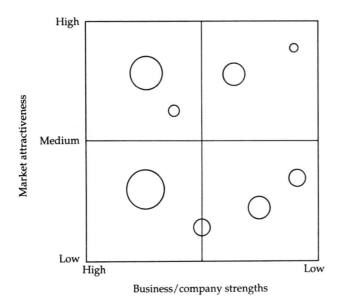

Business/company strengths

Figure 5.30

Table 5.3 Factors contibuting to market attractiveness and business position

Attractiveness of your market	*Status/position of your business*
Market factors	
Size (money units or both)	Your share (in equivalent terms)
Size of key segments	Your share of key segments
Growth rate per year:	Your annual growth rate:
total	total
segments	segments
Diversity of market	Diversity of your participation
Sensitivity to price, service features and external factors	Your influence on the market
Cyclicality	Lags or leads in your sales
Seasonality	
Bargaining power of upstream suppliers	Bargaining power of your suppliers
Bargaining power downstream	Bargaining power of your customers
Competition	Where you fit, how you compare in
Types of competitor	terms of products, marketing capability,
Degree of concentration	Customer service, financial
Changes in type and mix	strength, management strength
Entries and exits	Segments you have entered or left
Changes in share	Your relative share change
Substitution by new	Your vulnerability to new
technology/products	technology/product change
Degrees and types of integration	Your own level of integration
Financial and economic factors	Your margins
Contibution margins	Your scale and experience
Leveraging factors, such as economies	
of scale and experience	Barriers to your entry or exit (both
Barriers to entry or exit (both financial and non-financial)	financial and non-financial)
	Your capacity utilization
Capacity utilization	
Product factors	Your ability to cope with change
Maturity and volatility	Depths of your skills
Complexity	Level of your technical skills/training
Differentiation	of staff
Patents required	
Socio-political factors in your environment	Your company's responsiveness and flexibility
Social attitudes and trends	Your company's ability to cope
Laws and government agency regulations	Your company's aggressiveness
Influence with pressure groups and government representatives	Your company's relationships
Human factors, such as community acceptance	

Table 5.4   Market attractiveness evaluation

Factor	Scoring criteria			Score	Weighting	Banking
	10	5	0			
1 Market size (£m)	≥£250	£51–250	≤£50	5	15	0.75
2 Volume growth (units)	≥10%	5–0%	<	10	25	2.5
3 Competitive intensity	Low	Medium	High	6	10	0.6
4 Market profitability	>15%	10–15%	<10%	8	25	2.0
5 Vulnerability	Low	Medium	High	6	15	0.9
6 Cyclicality	Low	Medium	High	2.5	10	0.25
					Total = 7.0	

This form illustrates a quantitative approach to evaluating market attractiveness. Each factor's score is multiplied by the percentage weighting and totalled for the overall score. In this example, an overall score of 7 out of 10 places this market in the highly attractive category.

The four-box directional roles matrix is show in Figure 5.30. Here the circles represent sales into a market or segment, and, in the same way as in the Boston matrix, each is proportional to that segment's contribution to turnover.

The difference in this case is that rather than using only two variables, the criteria used for each axis are totally relevant and specific to each company using the matrix. It shows:

- Markets categorized on a scale of attractiveness to the firm.
- The firm's relative strengths in each of these markets.
- The relative importance of each market.

The specific criteria to be used should be decided by key executives using the device, but a generalized list is given in Table 5.3. It is advisable to use no more than five or six factors, otherwise the exercise becomes too complex and loses its focus. Read on, however, before selecting these factors, as essential methodological instructions on the construction of a matrix are given later in this chapter and in Chapter 13.

For each factor chosen, select a scoring system relevant to your own circumstances, and weight each factor (out of 100) according to its importance to you. Then put each of your chosen 'markets' through this device, multiplying each score by the weighting factor to indicate its level of attractiveness to you relative to other 'markets'.

A worked example of this quantitative approach to evaluation once the criteria for market attractiveness have been selected is given in Table 5.4.

Some important instructions for using the directional policy matrix in marketing planning

Table 5.5 is a typical calculation made by an organization to estimate its strengths in a market.

From Table 5.5 it will be seen that:

1 This organization is not market leader.
2 All competitors score above 5.0.

The problem with this and many similar calculations is that rarely will this method discriminate sufficiently well to indicate the relative strengths of a number of products in a particular company's product/market portfolio. Some method then, is required to prevent all products appearing on the left of the matrix. This can be achieved by using a ratio, as in the Boston matrix referred to earlier in this chapter. In this case a ratio will indicate a company's position relative to the best in the market, so our organization probably needs to make some improvements when compared with the 'leader'. To reflect this, our weighted score should be expressed as a ratio of Competitor A (the highest weighted score). Thus 6.7 divided by 7.8 = 0.86:1. If we were to plot this on a logarithmic scale on the horizontal axis, this would place our organization to the right of the dividing line, as follows:

3x   1   0.3

Table 5.5

1 *Critical success factors* (What are the few key things that any competitor has to do right to succeed?)	2 *Weighting* (How important is each of these CSFS? Score out of 100.)	3 *Strengths/weaknesses analysis* (Score yourself and each of your main competitors out of ten on each of the CSFS, then multiply the score by the weight.)			
		CSF/ Comp.	You	Comp. A	Comp. B	Comp. C
1 Product	20	1	9=1.8	6=1.2	5=1.0	4=0.8
2 Price	10	2	8=0.8	5=0.5	6=0.6	10=1.0
3 Service	50	3	5=2.5	9=4.5	7=3.5	6=3.0
4 Image	20	4	8=1.6	8=1.6	5=1.0	3=0.6

A scale of 3x to 0.3 has been chosen because such a band is likely to encapsulate most extremes of competitive advantage. If it doesn't, just change it to suit your own industry's circumstances.

Market attractiveness factors

The first time managers try using the directional policy matrix, they frequently find that the circles do not come out where expected. One possible reason for this is a misunderstanding concerning the use of market attractiveness factors. Please remember, you will be most concerned about the potential for growth in volume, growth in profit, and so on for your organization in each of your 'markets'. For example, even if a 'market' is mature (or even in decline), but the potential for your company to grow is there, it would obviously be more attractive than one in which there is little or no potential growth (as would be the case, for example, if you already had a high market share). Likewise, even if a 'market' is currently very profitable for your company but there is little or no potential for increasing the profit, this 'market' might be considered less attractive than one that is currently not so profitable to your company but which offers good potential for increasing your profits.

In considering the position of the circles at some time in the future, you should remember that they can only move vertically if the matrix shows the current level of attractiveness at the present time. This implies carrying out one set of calculations for the present time according to the agreed market attractiveness factors, in order to locate markets on the vertical axis, then carrying out another set of calculations for a future period (say, in 3 years' time), based on your forecasts according to the same market attractiveness factors. In practice it is quicker and easier to carry out only the latter calculation, in which case the circles can only move horizontally.

Once agreed, under no circumstances should market attractiveness factors be changed, otherwise the attractiveness of your markets is not being evaluated against common criteria and the matrix becomes meaningless. But scores will be specific to each market.

Please note, however, that you must list the 'markets' that you intend to apply the criteria to before deciding on the criteria themselves, since the purpose of the vertical axis is to discriminate between more and less attractive 'markets'. This will prevent all your 'markets' appearing in the top half of the matrix, which would clearly make the exercise pointless.

The criteria themselves therefore must be specific to the population of 'markets' under consideration, and, once agreed, must not be changed for different 'markets' in the same population.

A word of warning should also be offered at this point. It should be stressed that markets positioned in the lower half of the matrix should not be treated as unattractive. They should be treated as relatively less attractive than markets positioned in the top half of the matrix.

Another important point about the directional policy matrix is that it can be used not just for markets, but for countries, markets within countries, segments within markets, and outlets within markets. Each time, however, the criteria will obviously be different. It can even be used for franchised retail operations.

Definition of market

Many managers get confused about exactly what to plot on the directional policy matrix, so the following section is intended to clarify this issue. Let us take a hypothetical two-dimensional matrix, Figure 5.31. Each combination (cell) can be considered a segment. Is this organization's market:

1 The actual product/customer cells served?
2 The intersection of product functions A, B, C and customer groups 2, 3, 4?
3 Product functions A, B, C for all customer groups?
4 Customer groups 2, 3, 4 for all product functions?
5 The entire matrix?

Descriptions of 'market' and market segment, while useful, do not really help all that much to solve the conundrum – 'An identifiable group of customers with requirements in common that are, or may become, significant in determining a separate strategy'. The answer, then, is clearly a matter purely of management judgement, and at the beginning of any planning exercise with the directional policy matrix, the most important priority must be to define the unit of analysis correctly.

For example, it is clearly possible to put twenty-five circles (or crosses where there is no turnover) on a portfolio matrix, with markets 1-5 on the vertical axis and each of products A-E on the horizontal axis, i.e. (5) above. But that would almost certainly result in a confusing output.

It would also be possible to put six circles on a matrix, i.e. the actual product/customer cells served (1) above, with markets, 2,3 and 4 on the vertical axis and products A, B and C as appropriate for each of these served markets on the horizontal axis. Alternatively, instead of products

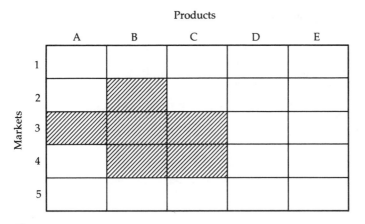

Figure 5.31

A, B and C being individually plotted on the horizontal axis where appropriate, an aggregate value or volume could be printed for all products in any served market. Indeed, any of the combinations (1) to (5) above could be used.

What would not make sense would be to plot products A, B and C on the horizontal axis (in our example, Market 3). This would clearly serve no useful purpose. If any managers wished to do this, they would have to put products A, B and C on the vertical axis and look at their respective sizes and strengths on the horizontal axis. In such a case all we have done is swop the nomenclature, making a 'product' equivalent to a 'market', which is clearly acceptable. The message here is that it is perfectly feasible to use 'product' as 'market', especially in cases where there is only one market and, say, three or four products. In such a case, unless all four products were identical in all respects, each would in practice represent a different market to us. This is certainly the case for a School of Management portfolio completed by one of the authors in 1984. Here, the 'product' (for example the MBA programme) equals 'market'. This is shown in Figure 5.32. (By astute management, some of these circles have since been moved to the left of the matrix.)

There has, then, to be more than one market on the vertical axis. We would suggest at least three, and probably no more than ten, which can be either existing or potential markets. It follows therefore that there will be more than one 'product' on the horizontal axis.

Finally, it may be useful to conclude this section with a definition of a portfolio matrix: 'The use of graphic models to develop a relationship between two or more variables judged by the planner to be of significance in the planning context'.

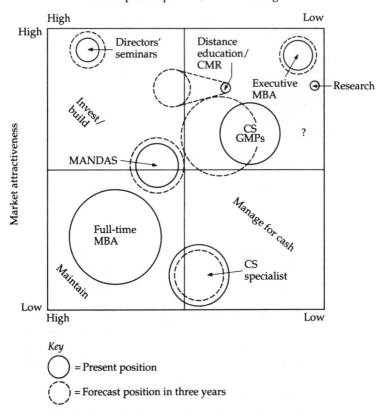

Our competitive position/business strengths

Figure 5.32   *School of management product portfolio*

Whichever approach is used, it can be seen that obvious consideration should be given towards marketing objectives and strategies that are appropriate to the attractiveness of a market (market growth in Boston matrix) and the extent to which such opportunities match our capabilities (market share in Boston matrix). What these objectives should be will be discussed in Chapter 6.

An example of the application of the directional policy matrix to retailing

Put at its simplest, this extension of the Boston Consultating Group matrix allows a retailer to use a graphic approach to planning a portfolio (or range) of products, by applying a set of criteria that are precisely relevant to a specific retailing operation. The vertical axis has as its measurement 'attractiveness (to us) of a specific piece in a range of merchandise'. This ranges from low to high and would probably include variables such as:

- Profitability.
- Competitive intensity.
- Source of supply.
- Market size.
- Market growth.
- Vulnerability.
- Regulatory environment.

It is easy to see how a simple scoring and weighting system can be applied by a retailer to each piece of merchandise under review, so that it can be judged to be either more or less attractive. The horizontal axis will use a similar scoring and weighting system to help assess a retailer's competitiveness with a particular piece/range of merchandise. Thus the horizontal axis can be labelled 'our competitiveness', and can similarly range from high to low. Issues such as the following will be considered:

1   Do we have the right image?
2   Are we big enough?
3   Can we grow?
4   Do we have funds to invest?
5   How large is our market share?
6   Do we have the right products?
7   How well-known are we in this market?

The resulting points on the vertical and horizontal axis will represent that product's position on the matrix as reflected by the application of the chosen criteria. By redrawing the circles to represent that product's contribution to total turnover, we can see the relative importance of each piece of merchandise at a glance.

Even a cursory glance at the hypothetical product configuration in Figure 5.33 will show that the marketing policies pursued for each of the different items will vary according to which box it is located in:

Box 1   has products that are high turnover items in which we are very well placed competitively, but, for reasons known only to us, are not particularly attractive. We should probably maintain our position here, but extend the minimum marketing effort in doing so. There will clearly be consequences for our marketing mix in such a decision.

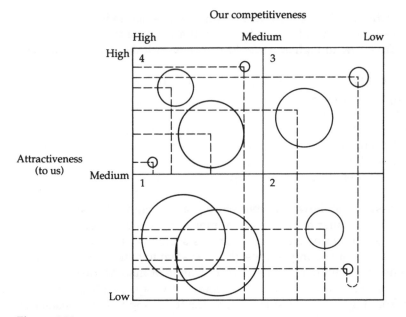

Figure 5.33

Box 2 offers the worst of both worlds. Not only are these items unattractive to us, but we are not very good at them either. Here we should clearly seek either to get out of this market or, if we cannot, at least pursue marketing policies consistent with their position.

Box 3 This is interesting in that we find these products attractive, but we are not very good at them. The choice is either to invest by making ourselves more competitive or to do the minimum consistent with profitability goals.

Box 4 This is the best of all, for these products are both attractive to us, and, at the same time, we are good at them. It does not take a genius to work out that these are the products that we should devote more of our marketing attention to, since it is here that our hope for greater productivity lies.

Ranging, footage, point of sale, promotion, advertising, and pricing policies all fall neatly into place in a more rational and logical manner when such an analysis is done on a range of merchandise within the store. Nonetheless, as already stated, there is also a need for considerably more research here before the efficacy of approaches such as these can be advocated with total confidence. They need to be developed and tested within a number of different retailing environments.

Some further insights and new developments

Finally, let us give some encouragement to those who are looking to the traditional body of marketing knowledge for new insights into retailing strategy. Once a retailer begins to understand the potential power of the matrix approach to diagnosis and strategic decision making, a whole new world begins to open up. Take, for example, the irksome problem of branded products versus own label versus generics. By using a little imagination, we can represent the issues graphically on a two-dimensional matrix.

Figure 5.34 shows three boxes, 1, 2 and 3, which approximately represent generic products (box 1), own label products (box 2) and brand leaders (box 3).

Box 1 This will include products such as sugar, salt and other commodity-type items for which there tends to be little perceived risk on the part of the consumer and for which consumer brand-awareness is comparatively low. (This equates

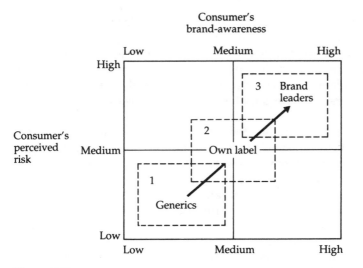

Figure 5.34

to the 'overall cost leadership/undifferentiated marketing' box of the Porter matrix, see page 145). It would probably be fruitless to enter this market on an own-level basis unless exceptional circumstances favoured such a decision.

Box 2   This is the danger box and will be full of products that are not outright brand leaders and for which the consumer's perceived risk in making a purchase is only moderately high. Nonetheless it is here that the retailer's greatest opportunity lies in introducing his own-label brands and competing on price with advertised products. It will be a matter of judgement which products fall into the risk-free area of box 2.

Box 3   This box is peopled by brand leaders and often new products or new concepts. It is here that the true marketing companies sit – like Procter & Gamble, Mars, Heinz and the like. Such companies have consistently invested in product quality and consumer awareness, and it is dangerous nonsense for a retailer to convince himself that he can replace brand leaders with own-label products and cheaper substitutes, for consumers eventually leave the store for another where they can obtain the brand of their choice. It is not the same for all products of course, as research at Cranfield has shown. Nonetheless it behoves the retailer to ascertain what he can and cannot do with many of his brand leaders before reducing their shelf space and believing he can 'get away' with it.

On the other hand, those suppliers who have allowed their products to become 'pimply little me-too products' (by replacing above-the-line advertising with below-the-line promotional activities, thus encouraging the consumer to jump from one special offer to another, leading eventually to price wars and product quality deterioration) have no one but themselves to blame for the consequences. Certainly it is totally unfair to blame retailers for what suppliers see as the misuse of their buying power.

In addition, it is clear that for retailers with the right image it is perfectly feasible to join some of the blue chip producers in the top right-hand corner, given appropriate product quality and share-of-consumer mind strategies. Marks & Spencer's is a perfect example.

Another example of the application of the matrix approach to problem-solving can be seen in Figure 5.35. Surely such a simple two-dimensional model could be used experimentally to judge the optimum space allocation for certain key products?

Finally, could the ever-present price issue be tackled by experimentation with a simple model as represented in Figure 5.36? Here it can be

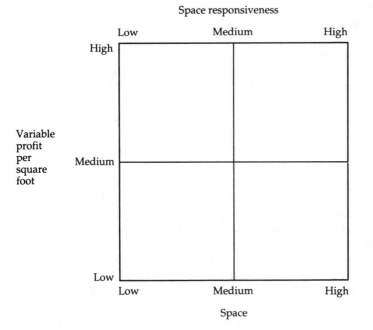

Figure 5.35

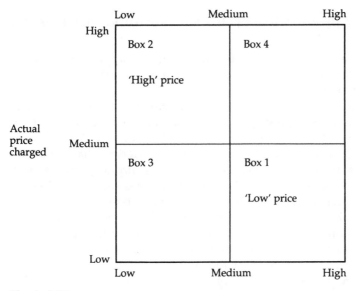

Figure 5.36

seen that there are certain products (often high turnover brand leaders) where the consumer is highly aware of minor differences in price. A leading dog food might be an example of such an item. It would clearly be dangerous not to price keenly in this area.

On the other hand, Box 2 contains many products in which actual consumer price awareness is comparatively low. To charge low prices here (Box 3) could possibly be an unnecessary and unfruitful policy, as indeed would be charging high prices for high price-awareness products (Box 4) unless of course there were special circumstances, such as in the case of convenience stores, speciality stores and so on.

This section of the chapter has briefly addressed the issue of competitive marketing strategy in a retailing context, using a portfolio approach. It has suggested that there is perhaps a lot to learn from experimentation with some of the artefacts of marketing used so successfully by many leading manufacturing organizations around the world, and has concentrated on two such tools – the portfolio matrix of the Boston Consulting Group and the directional policy matrix. It went on to suggest that the underlying concepts can be used in many different ways, and concluded that more research and experimentation is necessary before the efficacy of such approaches can be written about with more confidence and eventually introduced into the ongoing planning fabric of the world's great retailing organizations.

Combining product life cycles and portfolio management

Figure 5.37 illustrates the consequences of failing to appreciate the implications of both the product life cycle concept and the dual combination of market share and market growth.

Companies A and B both start out with 'Question marks' ('Wildcats') in years 5 and 6 in a growing market. Company A invests in building market share and quickly turns into a 'Star'. Company B, meanwhile, manages its product for profit over a 4-year period so that, while still growing, it steadily loses market share, i.e. it remains a 'Question mark' or 'Wildcat'. In year 10, when the market becomes saturated (typically competitive pressures have intensified), Company B with its low market share (hence higher costs and lower margins) cannot compete and quickly drops out of the market. Company A, on the other hand, aggressively defends its market share and goes on to enjoy a period of approximately 10 years with a product that has become a 'Cash cow'. Thus, Company B by pursuing a policy of short-term profit maximization lost at least 10 years' profit potential.

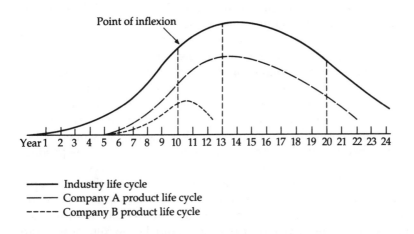

Point of inflexion

Year 1 2 3 4 5 6 7 8 9 10 11 12 13 14 15 16 17 18 19 20 21 22 23 24

—————— Industry life cycle
— — Company A product life cycle
----- Company B product life cycle

Figure 5.37 *Short-term profit maximization versus market share and long-term profit maximization*

Relevance of life-cycle analysis and portfolio management to the marketing audit

It will be recalled that this discussion took place against the background of the need to complete a full and detailed marketing audit before setting marketing objectives. Such analyses as those described in this chapter should be an integral part of the marketing audit.

The audit should contain a product life cycle for each major product, and an attempt should be made (using other audit information) to predict the future shape of the life cycle. It should also contain a product portfolio matrix showing the present position of the products.

The job of collecting information to input into product life cycles is a continuous process based on current sales and past sales. This is greatly facilitated by the use of PCs, which allow a more detailed analysis much faster.

Product management

A surprising number of people or departments can play a part in the process of product management, either directly or indirectly.

Firstly, consider the strategic decisions on the direction of the business and the launching of totally new product ranges. Many of these decisions are taken at board level where a picture of the direction and portfolio of products of all of the buying groups can be viewed.

The day-to-day responsibility for the development and management of product ranges generally lies with the individual buying groups, where decisions on ranges, colours, varieties, etc. for the next season are continually being made. However, although this is a very fast moving and pressured area of the company, there is considerable scope here to put into practice many of the ideas we have discussed, such as product life cycle analysis, the use of the Boston matrix and the directional policy matrix at the level of the product range. You will find that these concepts can be applied at all levels of the business, right down to considering individual items. For example, a product life cycle could be drawn for the total sales of men's underwear. This could be broken down into socks, vests and underpants. Socks could be broken down into work socks, casual socks, sports socks and so on, as was illustrated earlier in this chapter (Figure 5.26).

At various stages in product development other departments also come into the process. In some companies market research is carried out by the marketing information department, while often an advertising department takes responsibility for the process of communicating with the customer. Marketing research is continually being collected in the stores, where there is day-to-day dialogue with customers. Where test marketing is being undertaken, of course the feedback from the stores is crucial. It can be seen therefore that the management of products is a complex area that can be further complicated by the number of people concerned with it. It is also apparent that the management and development of products occurs at many levels within the company. However, at all levels it is possible to apply the ideas provided in this chapter to achieve improved profitability and performance.

Here is a summary of action steps you may find useful:

1   Select a major product and draw a life cycle of:

    (a) The product itself.
    (b) The market (segment) in which it competes.

2   Explain why it is the shape it is.
3   Predict the shape and length of the life cycle in the future.
4   Say why you are making these predictions.
5   Plot your products on a Boston matrix.
6   Explain their relative positions.
7   Forecast where they will be (and why) in, say, 5 years from now.
8   List your main markets or segments.

9 List criteria for attractiveness (to you).
10 List criteria for business strengths (you *vis-à-vis* competitors).
11 Devise a scoring and weighting system for each axis.
12 Put the markets or segments through the criteria.
13 Draw circles around the co-ordinates. The diameter of each circle should be proportional to that segment's contribution to turnover.
14 Are the circles where you want them to be?

Setting marketing objectives and strategies

Summary

Chapter 6 defines what marketing objectives are and how they relate to corporate objectives, and shows how to set them. There is a section on competitive strategies. Where and how to start the process of marketing planning is described, using the process known as 'gap analysis', and new product development is discussed as a growth strategy. Finally, there is an explanation of what marketing strategies are and how to set them. Without doubt, this is the key step in the marketing planning process, for it will by now be clear that following the analysis that takes place as part of the marketing audit, realistic and achievable objectives should be set for the company's major products in each of its major markets. Unless this step is carried out well, everything that follows will lack focus and cohesion. It is really a question of deciding on the right target. After all, it is no good scoring a bull's-eye on the wrong target!

Marketing objectives and their relation to corporate objectives

There are no works on marketing which do not include at least one paragraph on the need for setting objectives – a mandatory step in the planning process. The literature on the subject though, is not very explicit, which is surprising when it is considered how vital the setting of marketing objectives is.

An objective will ensure that a company knows what its strategies are expected to accomplish, and when a particular strategy has accomplished its purpose. In other words, without objectives, strategy decisions and all that follows will take place in a vacuum.

Following the identification of opportunities and the explicit statement of assumptions about conditions affecting the business, the process of setting objectives in theory should be comparatively easy: the actual objectives themselves being a realistic statement of what the company desires to achieve as a result of a market-centred analysis, rather than generalized statements born of top management's desire to 'do better next year'. However, objective setting is more complex than at first it would appear to be.

Most experts agree that the logical approach to the difficult task of setting marketing objectives is to proceed from the broad to the specific. Thus, the starting point would be a statement of the nature of the business, from which would flow the broad company objectives. Next, the broad company objectives would be translated into key result areas, which would be those areas in which success is vital to the firm. Market penetration and growth rate of sales are examples of key result areas. The third step would be creation of the sub-objectives necessary to accomplish the broad objectives, such as sales volume goals, geographical expansion, product range extension, and so on.

The result of this process should be objectives that are consistent with the strategic plan, attainable within budget limitations, and compatible with the strengths, limitations and economics of other functions within the organization.

At the top level, management is concerned with long-run profitability; at the next level in the management hierarchy the concern is for objectives that are defined more specifically and in greater detail, such as increasing sales and market share, introducing products and so on. These objectives are merely a part of the hierarchy of objectives, in that corporate objectives will only be accomplished if these and other objectives are achieved. At the next level management is concerned with objectives that are defined even more tightly, such as to create awareness among a specific target market about a new product, to change a particular customer attitude, and so on. Again, the general marketing objectives will only be accomplished if these and other sub-objectives are achieved. It is clear that sub-objectives *per se*, unless they are an integral part of a broader framework of objectives, are likely to lead to a wasteful misdirection of resources.

For example, a sales increase in itself may be possible, but only at an undue cost, so that such a marketing objective is only appropriate within the framework of corporate objectives. In such a case it may well be that an increase in sales in a particular market segment will entail additional capital expenditure ahead of the time for which it is planned. If this were the case, it may make more sense to allocate available store capacity to more profitable market segments in the short term, allowing sales to decline in another segment. Decisions such as this are likely to be more easily made against a backcloth of explicitly stated broad company objectives relating to all the major disciplines.

Likewise, objectives set for advertising, for example, should be wholly consistent with wider objectives. Objectives set in this way integrate the advertising effort with the other elements in the marketing mix, and this leads to a consistent, logical marketing plan.

So what is a corporate objective and what is a marketing objective? A business starts at some time with resources and wants to use those resources to achieve something. What the business wants to achieve is a corporate objective, which describes a desired destination, or result. How it is to be achieved is a strategy. In a sense this means that the only true objective of a company is, by definition, what is stated in the corporate plan as being the principal purpose of its existence. Most often this is expressed in terms of profit, since profit is the means of satisfying shareholders or owners, and because it is the one universally accepted criterion by which efficiency can be evaluated, which will in turn lead to efficient resource allocation, economic and technological progressiveness and stability.

This means that stated desires, such as to expand market share, to create a new image, to achieve an x per cent increase in sales, and so on, are in fact strategies at the corporate level, since they are the means by which a company will achieve its profit objectives. In practice, however, companies tend to operate by means of functional divisions, each with a separate identity, so that what is a strategy in the corporate plan becomes an objective within each department. For example, marketing strategies within a corporate plan become operating objectives, and strategies at the general level within the marketing department themselves become operating objectives at the next level down, so that an intricate web of interrelated objectives and strategies is built up at all levels within the framework of the company plan. The really important point, however, apart from clarifying the difference between objectives and strategies, is that the further down the hierarchical chain one goes, the less likely it is that a stated objective will make a cost-effective contribution to company profits, unless it derives logically and directly from an objective at a higher level.

Corporate objectives and strategies can be simplified in the following way:

Corporate objective – desired level of profitability.
Corporate strategies – which products and which markets (marketing).
– what kind of facilities (production and distribution systems and stores).

- size and character of the staff/labour force (personnel).
- funding (finance).
- other corporate strategies such as social responsibility, corporate image, stock market image, employee image, etc.

It is now clear that at the next level down in the organization, i.e. functional level, what products are to be sold into what market segments become market objectives, while the means of achieving these objectives, using the marketing mix, are marketing strategies. At the next level down there would be, say, advertising objectives and advertising strategies, with the subsequent programmes and budgets for achieving the objectives. In this way a hierarchy of objectives and strategies can be traced back to the initial corporate objective. Figure 6.1 illustrates this point.

How to set marketing objectives

The Ansoff matrix can be a useful tool for thinking about marketing objectives.

A firm's competitive situation can be simplified to two dimensions only – products and markets. To put it even more simply: Ansoff's framework is about what is sold (the 'product') and what it is sold to (the 'market'). Within this framework Ansoff identifies four possible courses of action for the firm:

- Selling existing products to existing markets.
- Extending existing products to new markets.
- Developing new products for existing markets.
- Developing new products for new markets.

The matrix in Figure 6.2 depicts these concepts.

It is clear that the range of possible marketing objectives is very wide, since there will be degrees of technological newness and degrees of market newness. Nevertheless Ansoff's matrix provides a logical framework in which marketing objectives can be developed under each of the four main headings above. In other words, marketing objectives are about products and markets only. Commonsense will confirm that it is only by selling something to someone that the company's financial goals can be achieved, and that advertising, pricing, service levels, and so on,

Marketing planning in a corporate framework

Corporate mission
Define the business and its boundaries
using considerations such as:
– distinctive competence
– environmental trends
– consumption market trends
– resource market trends
– stakeholder expectations

Corporate objectives
e.g. ROI, ROSHF, image (with stock market, public and employees), social responsibility, etc.

Corporate strategies
e.g. involve corporate resources, and must be within corporate business boundaries

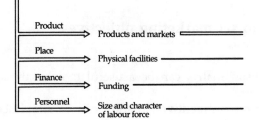

Product → Products and markets

Place → Physical facilities

Finance → Funding

Personnel → Size and character of labour force

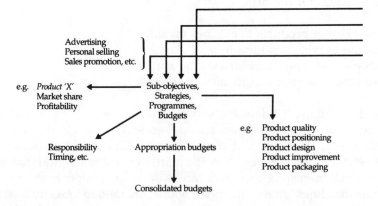

Advertising
Personal selling
Sales promotion, etc.

e.g.   *Product 'X'* ← Sub-objectives,
Market share   Strategies,
Profitability   Programmes,
                      Budgets

e.g.   Product quality
       Product positioning
       Product design
       Product improvement
       Product packaging

Responsibility   Appropriation budgets
Timing, etc.

Consolidated budgets

Figure 6.1

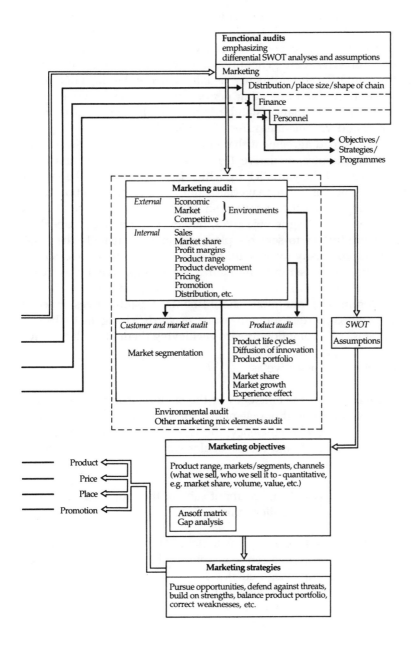

Figure 6.1 continued

are the means (or strategies) by which it might succeed in doing this. Thus, pricing objectives, sales promotion objectives, advertising objectives, and the like should not be confused with marketing objectives.

Marketing objectives are generally accepted as being selected qualitative and quantitative commitments, usually stated either in standards of performance for a given operating period, or conditions to be achieved by given dates. Performance standards are usually stated in terms of sales volume and various measures of profitability.

There is also broad agreement that objectives must be specific enough to enable subordinates to derive from them the general character of action required and the yardstick by which performance is to be judged. Objectives are the core of managerial action, providing direction to the plans. By asking where the operation should be at some future date, we determine objectives. Vague objectives, however emotionally appealing, are counter-productive to sensible planning, and are usually the result of the human propensity for wishful thinking, which often smacks more of cheerleading than serious marketing leadership. What this really means is that while it is arguable whether directional terms such as 'decrease', 'optimize', 'minimize' should be used as objectives, it seems logical that unless there is some measure, or yardstick, against which to measure a sense of locomotion towards achieving them, then they do not serve any useful purpose.

Ansoff defines an objective as:

> '... A measure of the efficiency of the resource-conversion process. An objective contains three elements: the particular attribute that is chosen as a measure of efficiency: the yardstick or scale by which the attribute is measured: and the particular value on the scale which the firm seeks to attain.'

Marketing objectives, then, are about each of the four main categories of the Ansoff matrix. In retailer terms:

1 Existing products to existing customers. These may be many and varied and will certainly need to be set for all existing major products and customer groups (segments).
2 New products to existing customers.
3 Existing products to new customers.
4 New products to new customers

Thus, in the long run, it is only by selling something (a 'product') to someone (customers) that any retailer can succeed in staying in business profitably. Simply defined, product/market strategy means the route

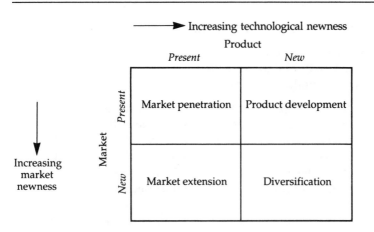

Figure 6.2   *Ansoff matrix*

chosen to achieve company goals through the range of products the company offers to its chosen market segments. The product/market strategy therefore represents a commitment to a future direction for the firm. Marketing objectives, then, are concerned solely with products and market segments/customers.

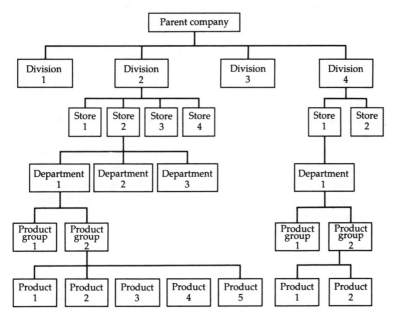

Figure 6.3

At the store level a manager is concerned with:

- Departments within a store.
- Product groups within departments.
- Products within product groups.

His job is to attain a good balance within the product mix.

Figure 6.3 indicates the nature of the manager's task. It is here of course that portfolio management techniques become particularly valuable.

The general marketing directions, which lead to the above objectives, flow of course from the life cycle and portfolio analysis conducted in the audit and revolve around the following logical decisions:

1 *Maintain.* This usually refers to the 'Cash cow' type of product/market and reflects the desire to maintain competitive positions.
2 *Improve.* This usually refers to the 'Star' type of product/market and reflects the desire to improve the competitive position in attractive markets.
3 *Harvest.* This usually refers to the 'Dog' type of product/market and reflects the desire to relinquish competitive position in favour of short-term profit and cash flow.
4 *Exit.* This also usually refers to the 'Dog' type of product/market, also sometimes the 'Question mark', and reflects a desire to divest because of a weak competitive position or because the cost of staying in it is prohibitive and the risk associated with improving its position is too high.
5 *Enter.* This usually refers to a new business area.

As already stated, however, great care should be taken not to follow slavishly any set of 'rules' or guidelines related to the above. In addition, the use of pejorative labels like 'Dog', 'Cash cow', and so on should be avoided if possible.

A preliminary list of guidelines relating to the use of the Boston matrix in a retailing environment was given in Chapter 5. A more complete list of marketing guidelines as a precursor to objective setting is given in Table 6.1. Figure 6.4 sets out a fuller list which includes guidelines for functions other than marketing.

A list that is more specific to retailing is given in Figure 6.5. It will be seen that the boxes of this matrix have been given more appropriate labels, names which non-marketing specialists might more readily understand. One word of warning, however – such general guidelines should not be followed unquestioningly. They are included mainly as checklists of questions that should be asked about each major product in each major market before setting marketing objectives and strategies.

Table 6.1 Strategies by portfolio matrix analysis

| | *Relative market share (or business strengths)* | | |
	High	*Low*	
	Invest for growth Defend leadership, gain if possible. Accept moderate short-term profits and negative cash flow. Consider geographic expansion, product range expansion, product differentiation. Aggressive marketing posture, viz. selling, advertising, pricing, sales promotion service levels, as appropriate.		
High			
Relative market growth (%) 10 for market attractiveness)			
	Maintain market position, manage for earnings Maintain market position in most successful product lines. Prune less successful product lines. Differentiate products to maintain share of key segments. Limit discretionary marketing expenditure. Stabilize prices, except where a temporary aggressive stance	*'Cash dogs'** Acknowledge low growth. Do not view as a 'marketing' problem Identify and exploit growth segments. Emphasize product quality to avoid 'commodity' competition Systematically improve productivity. Assign talented managers.	*Genuine 'dogs'* Prune product line aggressively. Maximize cash flow. Minimize marketing expenditure. Maintain or raise prices at the expense of volume.
Low	is necessary to maintain market share.		
0			
	3.0	1.0	0.3

*'Cash dog' refers to those products or markets which fall on or near the vertical dividing line in either a Boston matrix or a directional policy matrix. Please note, for the purpose of consistency, the same labels used by the Boston Consulting Group have also been used for the directional policy matrix.

Main thrust	Invest for growth	Maintain market position, manage for earnings	Selective	Manage for cash	Opportunistic development
Market share	Maintain or increase dominance	Maintain or slightly milk for earnings	Maintain selectively. Segment	Forgo share for profit	Invest selectively in share
Products	Differentiation, line expansion	Prune less successful, differentiate for key segments	Emphasize product quality. Differentiate	Aggressively prune	Differentiation, line expansion
Price	Lead. Aggressive pricing for share	Stabilize prices/raise	Maintain or raise	Raise	Aggressive, price for share
Promotion	Aggressive marketing	Limit	Maintain selectively	Minimize	Aggressive marketing
Distribution	Broaden distribution	Hold wide distribution pattern	Segment	Gradually withdraw distribution	Limited coverage
Cost control	Tight control. Go for scale economies	Emphasize cost reduction, viz. variable costs	Tight control	Aggressively reduce both fixed and variable	Tight, but not at expense of entrepreneurship
Production	Expand, invest (organic, acquisition, joint venture)	Maximize capacity utilisation	Increase productivity, e.g. specialization/automation	Free up capacity	Invest
R and D	Expand, invest	Focus on specific projects	Invest selectively	None	Invest
Personnel	Upgrade management in key functional areas	Maintain. Reward efficiency, tighten organization	Allocate key managers	Cut back organization	Invest
Investment	Fund growth	Limit fixed organization	Invest selectively	Minimize and divest opportunistically	Fund growth
Working capital	Reduce in process, extend credit	Tighten credit, reduce accounts receivable, increase inventory turn	Reduce	Aggressively reduce	Invest

Figure 6.4

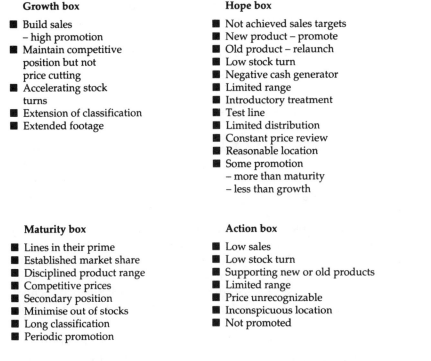

Growth box

- Build sales
  – high promotion
- Maintain competitive
  position but not
  price cutting
- Accelerating stock
  turns
- Extension of classification
- Extended footage

Hope box

- Not achieved sales targets
- New product – promote
- Old product – relaunch
- Low stock turn
- Negative cash generator
- Limited range
- Introductory treatment
- Test line
- Limited distribution
- Constant price review
- Reasonable location
- Some promotion
  – more than maturity
  – less than growth

Maturity box

- Lines in their prime
- Established market share
- Disciplined product range
- Competitive prices
- Secondary position
- Minimise out of stocks
- Long classification
- Periodic promotion

Action box

- Low sales
- Low stock turn
- Supporting new or old products
- Limited range
- Price unrecognizable
- Inconspicuous location
- Not promoted

Above points should be investigated and either delete or push unless it is a
supporting line

Figure 6.5

It is at this stage that the circles in the directional policy matrix can be
moved to show their relative size and position in 3 years' time. You can
do this to show, first, where they will be if the company takes no action,
and, second, where you would ideally prefer them to be. These latter
positions will of course become the marketing objectives. Precisely how
this is done is shown in Chapter 13. It is, however, the key stage in the
marketing planning process.

Competitive strategies

At this stage of the planning process it would be helpful to explain recent
developments in the field of competitive strategies, since an understanding of the subject is an essential prerequisite to setting appropriate
marketing objectives.

One of the principal purposes of marketing strategy is for you to be able to choose the customers, hence the markets, you wish to deal with. In this respect the directional policy matrix discussed in Chapter 5 is particularly useful. The main components of the strategy are:

• The company.
• Customers.
• Competitors.

So far we have said very little about customers, although clearly if we are to succeed, we need to work hard at developing a sustainable competitive advantage. The important word here is 'sustainable', as temporary advantages can be gained in numerous ways, e.g. a price reduction or a clever sales promotion.

Most business people would agree that as markets mature, the only way to grow the business without diversifying is at the expense of competitors, which implies the need to understand in depth the characteristics of the market and of the main competitors in it. The leading thinker in this field is Michael Porter of the Harvard Business School, and any reader wishing to explore this vital subject in more depth should refer to his book *Competitive Strategy*.

Let us look for a moment at the economists' model of supply and demand shown in Figure 6.6. Here we see that when supply is greater than demand, the price will fall, and that when demand exceeds supply, the price will tend to rise. The equilibrium point is when supply matches demand. The only way a retailer can avoid the worst effects of such a situation is by taking one of the following actions:

1 Being the most competitive on price to grow sales
2 Differentiating the product in some way so as to be able to command higher prices, and increase margins

Michael Porter combined these two options into a single matrix, as shown in Figure 6.7. It can be seen that Box 1 represents a sound strategy, particularly in commodity-type markets such as fruit and vegetables, where differentiation is hard to achieve because of the identical nature of the product. In such cases it is wise to recognize the reality and adopt a productive corporate drive towards being the corporate leader. It is here that the experience effect described in Chapter 5 becomes especially important.

However, many companies, such as Body Shop and Holland and Barratt, the health food chain, could not hope to be low-cost operations. Consequently, their whole corporate philosophy is geared to differentiation and

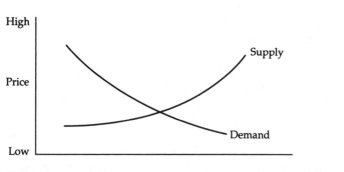

Figure 6.6

what we have called added value (Box 2). Clearly this represents a sensible strategy for any company that cannot hope to be a world cost beater, and indeed many of the world's great companies succeed by means of such a focus. Many of these companies also succeed in pushing themselves into Box 3, the outstanding success box, by occupying what can be called 'retail fortresses'. A good example of this is Marks & Spencer's which dominates the UK's retail clothing markets with its focused quality and customer service approach. Companies like McDonalds also typify Box 3, where low costs, differentiation and world leadership are combined in their corporate strategies.

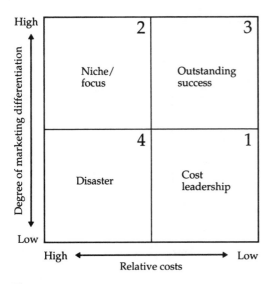

Figure 6.7

Only Box 4 remains. Here we can see that a combination of commodity-type markets and high relative costs will result in disaster sooner or later. A position here is tenable only while demand exceeds supply. When, however, these markets mature, there is little hope for companies who find themselves in this unenviable position.

An important point to remember when thinking about differentiation as a strategy is that you must still be cost-effective. It is a myth to assume that sloppy management and high costs are acceptable as long as the product has a good image and lots of added values. In addition, in thinking about differentiation, please refer back to the section on customer benefits in Chapter 4 (pp. 67–8), for it is here that the route to differentiation will be found. It is also clear that there is not much point in offering benefits that are costly for you to provide but are not highly regarded by customers. So consider using a matrix like the one given in Figure 6.8 to classify your benefits. Clearly you will succeed best by providing as many benefits as possible in the top right-hand box.

Marks & Spencer's is a good example of a company that is proactively changing its global strategy by systematically moving away from standard product ranges in Box 1 (in Figure 6.7) towards speciality products in Box 2 and then going on to occupy a 'global fortress' position in these specialities (Box 3).

The main point here, however, is that when setting marketing objectives, you must have a strong grasp of the position in your markets of yourself

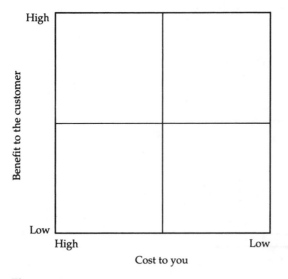

Figure 6.8

and your competitors, and adopt appropriate postures for the several elements of your business, all of which may be different. It may be necessary, for example, to accept that part of your portfolio is in the 'Disaster' box (Box 4). You may well be forced to have some products here, for example, to complete your product range to enable you to offer your more profitable products. The point is that you must adopt an appropriate stance towards these products and set your market line objectives accordingly, using where appropriate the guidelines given in Table 6.1 and Figure 6.4.

Finally, here are some very general guidelines to help you think about competitive strategies.

1 Know the terrain on which you are fighting (the market).
2 Know the resources of your enemies (competitive analysis).
3 Do something that the enemy isn't expecting.

Where to start (gap analysis)

Figure 6.9 illustrates what is commonly referred to as 'gap analysis'. Essentially what it says is that if the corporate sales and financial objectives are greater than the current long-range forecasts, there is a gap which has to be filled.

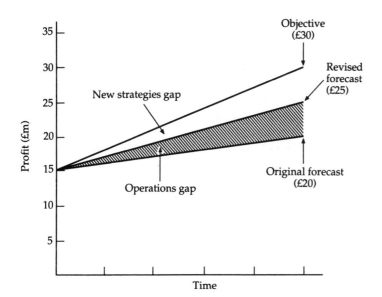

Figure 6.9

The 'operations gap' can be filled in three ways:

1 Promote to increase sales.
2 Reduce operating costs.
3 Increase prices/negotiate lower cost prices to improve margin.

The 'new strategies gap' can also be filled in three ways:

1 Market extension, e.g. find new user groups, enter new segments, expand geographically.
2 Introduction of other products.
3 Diversification, e.g. selling new products to new markets.

Finding a way to increase sales should always be a retailer's first option. It makes sense to attempt to increase profits and cash flow from existing products and customers initially, because this is usually the least costly and the least risky option, and through its present products and markets a company has developed knowledge and skills it can use competitively.

For the same reason it makes sense in many cases to move along the horizontal axis for further growth before attempting to find new markets, since it normally takes many years for a company to get to know its customers and markets and to build up a reputation. That reputation and trust, embodied in either the company's name or its brands, is rarely transferable to new markets, where other companies are already entrenched.

The marketing audit should ensure that the method chosen to fill the gap is consistent with the company's capabilities, and builds on its strengths. For example, it would normally prove far less profitable for a greengrocer to introduce frozen foods than to add another fruit or vegetable product. Likewise, if a product could be sold by the existing sales staff, this is far less risky than introducing a new product requiring new selling skills.

Exactly the same applies to the company's suppliers, distribution, and people. Whatever new products are developed should be as consistent as possible with the company's known strengths and capabilities. Clearly the use of existing store capacity is generally preferable to new investment. Moreover, the type of additional investment is important. Technical personnel are highly trained and specialist, and whether this competence can be transferred to a new field must be considered. A new product may also require new handling and storage techniques, which may prove expensive.

It can now be appreciated why going into new markets with new products (diversification) is the riskiest strategy of all, because new resources and new management skills have to be developed. This is why the history of commerce is replete with examples of companies that went bankrupt through moving into areas where they had little or no distinctive competence, and why many companies that diversified through acquisition during periods of high economic growth have since divested themselves of businesses that were not basically compatible with their own distinctive competence. Perhaps the world's best known example of this was Woolworth's move into high priced merchandise.

The Ansoff matrix of course is not a simple four-box matrix, for it will be obvious that there are degrees of technological newness as well as degrees of market newness. Figure 6.10 illustrates the point. It also demonstrates more easily why any movement should generally aim to keep a company as close as possible to its present position rather than moving it to a totally unrelated position, except in the most unusual circumstances.

Nevertheless, the product life cycle phenomenon will inevitably force companies to move along one or more of the Ansoff matrix axes if they are to continue to increase their sales and profits. A key question to be asked then is how this important decision is to be taken, given the attendant risks.

A full list of the possible methods involved in the process of gap analysis is given in Figure 6.11. From this it will be seen that there is nothing

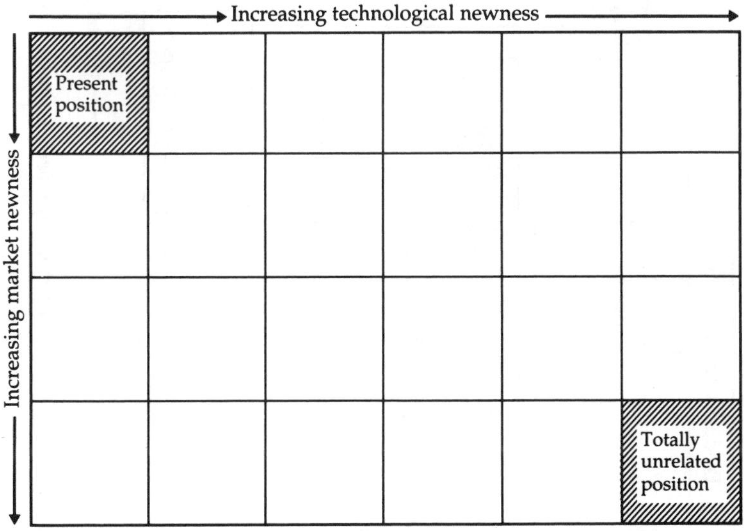

Figure 6.10

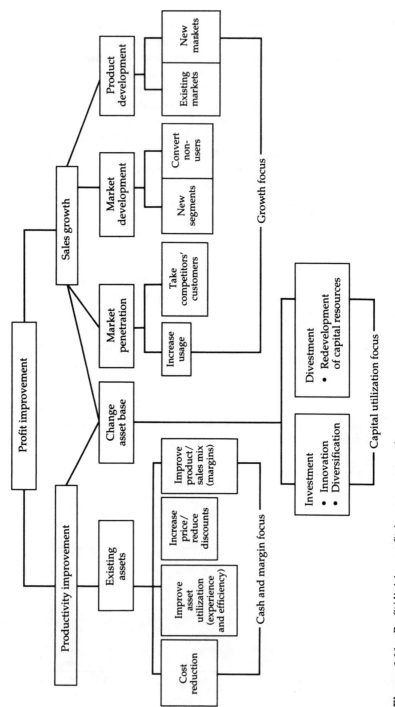

Figure 6.11 *Profit/division profit improvement option*

an executive can do to fill the gap that is not included in the list. The precise methodology to implement this concept is given in the final chapter of this book, which provides a marketing planning system.

At this point it is important to stress that the 'objectives' point in gap analysis should not be an extrapolation, but your own view of what revenue would make this into an excellent business. The word 'excellent' must of course be relative only to comparable businesses. If all the executives in a company responsible for SBUs were to do this, then work out what needed to do done to fill any gaps, it is easy to understand why this would result in an excellent overall business performance.

New product development/market extension/diversification?

The answer to the question in the heading above of course should be comparatively simple if the marketing audit has been completed thoroughly.

It is not the purpose here to explore in detail sub-sets of marketing, such as market research, market selection, new product development, and diversification. What is important, however, in a book on marketing planning is to communicate an understanding of the framework in which these activities should take place.

What we are aiming to do is to maximize synergy, which could be described as the $2 + 2 = 5$ effect. The starting point is the marketing audit, leading to the SWOT (strengths, weaknesses, opportunities and threats) analysis. This is so that development of any kind will be firmly based within a company's basic strengths and weaknesses. External factors are the opportunities and threats facing the company.

Once this important analytical stage is successfully completed, the more technical process of opportunity identification, screening, business analysis, and finally activities such as product development, testing and entry planning can take place, depending on which option is selected. The important point to remember is that no matter how thoroughly these subsequent activities are carried out, unless the objectives of product development/market extension are based firmly on an analysis of the company's capabilities, they are unlikely to be successful in the long term. Figure 6.12 illustrates the process.

The criteria selected will generally be consistent with the criteria used for positioning products or businesses in the nine-cell portfolio matrix described in Chapter 5. The list shown in Table 5.2, however, which is also totally consistent with the marketing audit checklist, can be used to

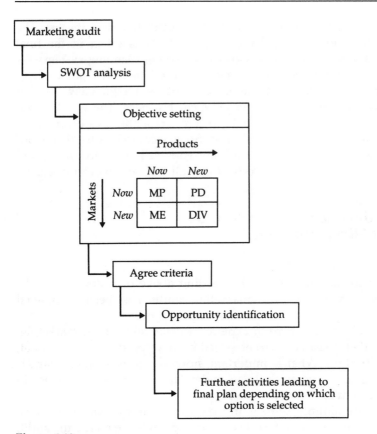

Figure 6.12

select the most important criteria. A rating and weighting system can then be applied to opportunities identified to assess their suitability or not. Those criteria selected and the weighting system used will of course be consistent with the SWOT analysis.

A simple example of a quantitative approach to evaluation once the criteria have been selected is given in Table 5.3.

Although we have said that it is not the purpose of this book to explore in detail any of the sub-sets of marketing, such as market research, it would nonetheless be quite useful to outline the process of new product development and its relation to the gap analysis described above.

After a marketing audit and gap analysis have clarified the place of new product introduction in a broad company context, the organization must examine the micro considerations. These comprise the factors that must be taken into account when a product is assessed in terms of its fit within the product portfolio and its contribution towards objectives.

Figure 6.13 depicts the relation of the new product introduction/development process with the marketing audit and SWOT analysis. New product development can usefully be seen as a process consisting of the following seven steps:

1 *Idea generation* – the search for product ideas to meet company objectives.
2 *Screening* – a quick analysis of the ideas to establish those which are relevant.
3 *Concept testing* – checking with the market that the new product ideas are acceptable.
4 *Business analysis* – the idea is examined in detail in terms of its commercial fit in the business.
5 *Product development* – making the idea into reality.
6 *Testing* – market tests necessary to verify early business assessments.
7 *Commercialization* – full-scale product launch, committing the company's reputation and resources.

Developing new products in the retail environment

Before developing new products, we need to ensure that they fit into the strategies of the company. This question will generally be considered at board level and will concentrate on such factors as the gap between business levels if no further development is undertaken, and the requirements for future profits, the direction of the business, and the fit within the business. Once the need for new product development has been established in the broadest sense, the detailed work of new product development will be passed to the buying departments for action. We need therefore to consider how we might go about this process.

New products will generally be easier to sell if they complement the existing range, because the company will have the required expertise, and the relationship with appropriate suppliers, and customers will expect to find that type of product in our stores. Additionally, new product ideas may help to sell more of existing products. For example, if we introduce a new and successful frozen food to the market, people are likely to buy more of our other products because they like the new one.

The relation between price and quality is also important in new product development, since a move away from the current customer relationship may upset the existing customer images of the company and

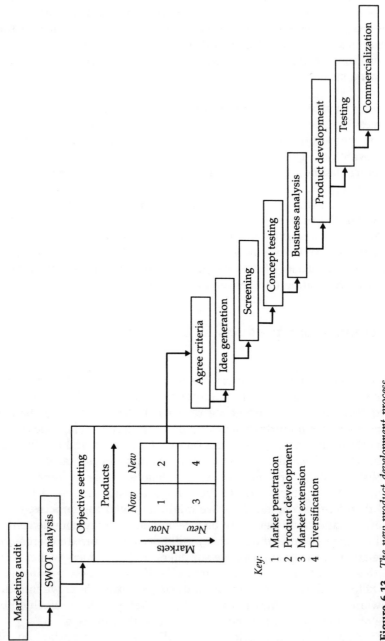

Figure 6.13 *The new product development process.*

Marketing audit

SWOT analysis

Objective setting

Products

Now   New

Markets

Now   1   2

New   3   4

Agree criteria

Idea generation

Screening

Concept testing

Business analysis

Product development

Testing

Commercialization

Key:

1 Market penetration
2 Product development
3 Market extension
4 Diversification

actually inhibit sales. For example, if we were to introduce a new, cheap line of clothing into the range, customers might wonder whether the quality of all products is declining. A wide variety of qualities, sizes or flavours presents a number of problems, including customer confusion and excessive inventory holding.

Considerations that are important generally within new product development may be restricted by the very nature of our business. For example, a profit with an even level of demand throughout the year is preferable to one with seasonal fluctuation, as investment can be recovered more quickly. Often this is just not a possibility. A product that offers some measure of protection from competitive imitation, through patents, large capital outlay, or long development times, is also desirable. However, in most parts of the business, although we can capitalize on supplier links, any further protection is impossible.

In many cases we will be developing products in conjunction with suppliers with whom we have links and the production problems are in part theirs. However, in entering totally new fields, production problems should not be underestimated if both we and the supplier are entering into new technology or new materials. The following factors must be considered.

The question of money

As we have already discovered, cash generation and catalogue development are extremely important. The risk of new product development needs to be set against current products, their development costs and the stream of expected income over time. The new product must meet the company's investment standards in terms of the time taken to pay back and the return on capital employed.

The human factor

The staffing implications of any new product must be considered from the outset. Important questions to be asked are 'How much training will the sales staff require?', 'Are there any special delivery requirements' and 'how will that impact on staff levels?'

Materials

Although in most cases the responsibility for buying raw materials and component parts will be that of the supplier, it is vitally important that we are aware of any potential problems that may arise from the specialized requirements of the product. Any problems in raw material availability may indeed be the suppliers', but ultimately we will be the ones without a product to sell.

Reducing uncertainty in new product development

The ideas for new products come from many sources – customers, competitors, management, other countries, suppliers and trade fairs. Whatever the source, new products are the lifeblood of the company in a dynamic and changing market. The continuing search for profitable new products is a task fraught with risk.

Research has shown that up to 80 per cent of all new product launches fail. Some products, such as groceries and cosmetics, are especially prone to failure. What then can we do to reduce the uncertainty of a new product launch? There is no guaranteed way to avoid problems, but some procedures are useful in helping to quantify the risks in a launch.

The concept test

This can be done at a very early stage in the development of a product, and consists of training interviewers and conducting interviews with existing and potential customers. Any information received at this stage is of course entirely qualitative, but it can give valuable feedback on perhaps the colour ranges, possible uses, or technical requirements of the product idea. Any ideas that appear to be completely unacceptable can be eliminated at this stage or modified to be more acceptable to the target user.

The qualitative screen

The second stage to be considered poses two basic questions:

1 Is this product concept compatible with the company objectives? For instance, does it complement our existing products, or does it project the right image for our company?
2 Is the product compatible with the company resources? For instance, does the company have the right know-how and physical distribution facilities to handle the product?

If the product satisfies the above criteria, it can then progress to the next stage of evaluation.

Economic analysis

At this stage the development of the product can be considered under different assumptions of costs incurred and revenue achieved. Of course the information available may not allow a great deal of detailed analysis, but it will still help to concentrate the thinking on the economic feasibility of the proposal.

The test market

Retailers frequently use a test market to try out a new product. In this case an attempt is made to reproduce the conditions of a launch on a smaller scale, using perhaps six stores representative of different sizes and locations. The sales of the product are then watched and compared if possible with comparable products in the range. An indication of the potential can then be assessed from the performance during the test.

Test markets can never be completely reliable indicators of the ultimate performance. Quite apart from the problems of 'grossing up' small-scale test market results to provide a national picture, there is always the possibility of unusual competitive activity. A rolling launch, extending availability to perhaps twenty stores, can reduce the uncertainty, but this must be set against the time to progress to a full launch and potential competitive gains.

When faced with a new product or indeed when developing existing products, forecasting sales is never easy. This problem is further exacerbated in the retailing industry, owing to the seasonal nature of the business, the need to commit to production with suppliers 6 months ahead of sales, the problems of increasing intake during the sales period and the knock-on effect of any action on future stock levels.

Some retailers still rely on systems that are based solely on the analysis of last year's sales. Past sales are charted, patterns and trends are identified and projections are made from that analysis. However, we have already seen that the product life cycle can have a considerable effect on the development of sales. Extrapolation from the introduction-stage sales figures to the growth phase could result in considerable understocking, while extrapolation from the growth-stage sales figures as a product reaches maturity could result in considerable overstocking. The forecasting of sales figures must attempt to bear in mind many of the concepts that we have discussed in the preceding chapters.

Marketing strategies

What a company wants to accomplish, then, in terms of such things as market share and volume, is a marketing objective. How the company intends to go about achieving its objectives is strategy, which is the route to the achievement of specific objectives and should describe the means by which objectives are to be reached, the time programme and the allocation of resources. It does not delineate the individual courses the resulting activity will follow.

There is a clear distinction between strategy and detailed implentation in tactics. Marketing strategy reflects the company's best opinion as to how it can most profitably apply its skills and resources to the market place. It is inevitably broad in scope. The plan that stems from it will spell out action and timings, and will contain the detailed contribution expected from each department.

There is a similarity between strategy in business and strategic military development. One looks at the enemy, the terrain, the resources under command, and then decides whether to attack the whole front or an area of enemy weakness, to feint in one direction while attacking in another, or to attempt to encircle the enemy's position. The policy and mix, the type of tactics to be used, and the criteria for judging success, all come under the heading of strategy. The action steps are tactics.

Similarly, in marketing, the same commitment, mix and type of resources as well as tactical guidelines and criteria that must be met, all come under the heading of strategy.

For example, the decision to open new stores in the three largest market areas is a strategic decision. The exact location and layout of the stores is a tactical decision.

The following list indicates the general content of strategy statements in the area of marketing that emerge from marketing literature:

1 Policies and procedures relating to the products to be offered, such as numbers, quality, design, branding, packaging and labelling, etc.
2 Pricing levels to be adopted, margins and discount policies.
3 Advertising and sales promotion. The creative approach, the type of media, type of displays, the amount to spend, etc.
4 What emphasis is to be placed on personal selling, the sales approach, sales training, customer service, etc.
5 The type of retail outlet to be used and the relative importance of each.
6 Warehousing, transportation, inventories, service levels, etc. in relation to distribution.

Thus, marketing strategies, the means by which marketing objectives will be achieved, are generally concerned with the four major elements of the marketing mix, as follows:

Product   The general policies for product deletions, modifications, additions, design, packaging, etc.
Price   The general pricing policies to be followed for product groups in market segments.
Place   The general policies for retail outlets and consumer service levels.
Promotion   The general policies for communicating with customers under the relevant headings, such as advertising, sales force, sales promotion, public relations, exhibitions, direct mail, mail order, etc.

The following list of marketing strategies (in summary form), covers the majority of options open under the headings of the four Ps:

1 Product
   (a) Expand the line.
   (b) Change performance, quality or features.
   (c) Deepen the range.
   (d) Consolidate the line.
   (e) Standardize design.
   (f) Positioning.
   (g) Change the mix.
   (h) Branding.

2 Price:
   (a) Change price, terms or conditions.
   (b) Skimming policies.
   (c) Penetration policies.

3 Promotion:
   (a) Change advertising or promotion.
   (b) Change selling methods or point of sale approach.

4 Place:
   (a) Change distribution pattern between stores.
   (b) Change service levels.

Chapter 7 is devoted to a much more detailed consideration of promotion, pricing and distribution. It describes what should appear in advertising, sales, pricing and place plans. This detail is intended for those whose principal concern is the preparation of a detailed 1-year operational or tactical plan. The relation of this chapter to the strategic plan is in the provision of information to enable the planner to delineate broad strategies under the headings outlined above. There is no chapter on product management because all the product options have been covered already, particularly in Chapter 5, in the discussion on the product audit.

There are further steps in the marketing planning process before detailed programmes are put together. These are estimating in broad terms the cost of the strategies, and delineating alternative plans. Both of these steps will be covered in more detail in Chapter 11.

Formulating marketing strategies is one of the most critical and difficult parts of the entire marketing process. It sets the limit of success. Communicated to all the management levels, it indicates what strengths are to be developed, what weaknesses are to be remedied, and in what manner. Marketing strategies enable operating decisions to bring the company into the right relation with the emerging pattern of market opportunities that previous analysis has shown to offer the highest prospect of success.

Before proceeding to describe the next stage of marketing planning, i.e., the construction of actual working plans, we must stress that the vital phase of setting objectives and strategies is a highly complex process which, if done badly, will probably result in considerable misdirection of resources.

This chapter has confirmed the need for setting clear, definitive objectives for all aspects of the marketing programme, and that marketing objectives themselves have to derive logically from corporate objectives. The advantages of this practice are that it allows all concerned with marketing activities to concentrate their particular contribution on achieving the marketing objectives, as well as facilitating meaningful and constructive evaluation of all marketing activity.

For the practical purpose of marketing planning it will be apparent, from the observations above concerning what was referred to as a hierarchy of objectives, that marketing objectives have to be broken down into sub-objectives, which, taken all together, will achieve the company's marketing objectives. By breaking down the company's objectives, the problem of strategy development becomes more manageable, hence easier.

A 2-year study of thirty-five top industrial companies by McKinsey and Company revealed that leader companies agreed that product/market strategy is the key to the task of keeping shareholders' equity rising. Clearly, then, setting objectives and strategies in relation to products and markets is a most important step in the marketing planning process.

Once agreement has been reached on the broad marketing objectives and strategies, those responsible for programmes can proceed to the detailed planning stage, developing the appropriate strategy statements into sub-objectives.

Plans constitute the vehicle for getting to the destination along the chosen route, or the detailed execution of the strategy. The term 'plan' is often used synonymously in marketing literature with the terms 'programme' and 'schedule'. A plan containing detailed lists of tasks to be completed, together with responsibilities, timing and cost, is sometimes referred to as an appropriation budget, which is merely a detailing of the actions to be carried out and of the expected sterling results in carrying them out. More about this in Chapters 7 to 10.

7

The communication plan: 1 Impersonal communications

Summary

Chapter 7 opens by discussing the difference between personal and impersonal communications and provides a method for deciding on the communications mix. It shows how to prepare the advertising plan, and discusses in some detail what advertising objectives are, and how to set them. There is a brief discussion of the role of the diffusion of innovation curve in advertising. The sales promotion plan is then introduced. There is a section on how it can be used, what different types there are, and its strategic role is discussed. A section follows on how to prepare a sales promotion plan. Finally the role of point of sales advertising and public relations is discussed.

Different forms of communication

Now that we have explored the important area of marketing objectives and strategies, let us turn our attention to the question of how we communicate with customers, both current and potential. Companies communicate with their customers in a wide variety of ways, but it is still possible to distinguish the following two main categories:

- Impersonal communications – such as advertising, window and point-of-sale displays, promotions, and public relations.
- Personal communications – the direct person-to-person meeting between the company's staff and the customer. This not only includes selling but also all those other points of communication, such as check-out tills, customer advice desks and so on.

There is an armoury of communication techniques that may be used either singly or in a combination (the communications mix) as the particular situation demands, given the need to achieve maximum impact within finite budgetary constraints. Companies with acknowledged expertise in the area of communicating with customers are continually experimenting with the communications mix they employ in an attempt to become more cost-effective in this important, sometimes expensive, part of their business.

A number of possible means of communicating with customers will now be examined under the two broad headings given above. This chapter will concentrate on the impersonal communications, with the objective of deciding how to go about preparing detailed plans for these important elements of the marketing mix. In Chapter 8 we shall do the same for personal communications.

Communication objectives

Having established that our product range meets customer needs, at the most appropriate price, we must communicate to our customers that the products exist and tell them about the benefits they offer. In this chapter we consider communication about our company in the broadest sense. In doing this we have to consider:

1   What sort of image we are trying to communicate and how that image is communicated in our day-to-day business.
2   Whom do we wish to communicate the image to? We identify many of the groups interested in the company, from employees, to stock market, to banks, and of course the customer.
3   The important factors in selecting a communication method and the types of method available.
4   The ways in which the customer is also influenced indirectly, i.e. methods of communication not under our control, such as newspaper editorials or word-of-mouth customer recommendations.
5   The power of direct communication with the customer at the point of purchase within the stores and its increased importance for high value product lines. (This will be covered in the next chapter.)

Communicating the right image

We have already discussed two of the controllable variables – customers and products – in the preceding chapters. Now we are considering communication, which is broadly concerned with advertising and promotional methods. However, all of the four controllable variables are a part of this communication process, resulting in the 'corporate image' – or individual style and personality of the company. While it is easy to see how the advertising or promotion of a company and its products contribute to its corporate image, it is less easy to see how the other elements can affect it. But consider the following:

- *The product* – the range, the brands, their appearance, function, packaging, and design – all these things can communicate style, quality and reliability.
- *The price* can communicate exclusiveness, quality or prestige, particularly in relation to competing products.
- *The place* – the stores where the products are sold can communicate the quality of exclusiveness of the product. The window displays and internal environment can create an image in the mind of the customer, e.g. as a shop that welcomes the family shopper or one that caters for specialists.
- *The promotion* is solely concerned with communicating the relevant messages and impressions to relevant audiences. It has a direct role to play in reinforcing all the other messages conveyed by the product range, the prices and the stores. Each element must support the communication activities and in turn be supported by them.

Communicating the right message to the right people

If we plan to communicate the right image of our company, we must first decide whom we wish to communicate with. Obviously the customers are a large group and the target of much communication from the company. However, let us consider some of the other interested parties. There are employees, suppliers, the media, banks, analysts, institutional and private shareholders, competitors, to name but a few! Each needs to be informed and influenced by the messages that are addressed to them. Each needs to be given a favourable perception of the corporate image so that they will be more likely to help you than hinder you.

Since some people will fall into more than one group, and different groups have access to your communications with others, the corporate image must always be consistent, even though the individual information needs will vary. Employees will need to know that they are working for a caring company, while a bank will be more interested in the long-term financial future. Customers need different information, although even here it is important that whatever messages we transmit are consistent with other corporate communications.

Each group will also provide valuable feedback on their perception of your corporate image. If the feedback is unfavourable, such as stockbrokers telling you that your company's image is so dated that investors are in danger of losing faith in your ability to compete, then adjustments will be needed very quickly. You must also consider the interaction between the different groups mentioned above. Just producing a glossy, up-to-date annual report will not change the shareholders' view of the company. Shareholders also receive information from the media, and from stockbrokers, who may be influenced by the comments of your competitors and customers.

As you can see, the need for consistency is very important. If all the people with whom you communicate spend time comparing notes on you, then it is vital that you tell the same story to each of them. It would not be a good idea to tell your shareholders that you are innovative, dynamic, adventurous and go-ahead and at the same time reassure your bankers that you are conservative and as unwilling to take risks as you have ever been. Consistency is the message when communicating with people and organizations outside the company.

Choosing a communication method

As was explained earlier, a wide variety of techniques are open to you to communicate with your customers and other influential people. It is important that you are aware of them and how they might be used. Even if you do not use them all yourself, it is probable that your competitors will be using a different combination that may impact on your sales. The majority can be classed under the following groups.

- Advertising.
- Promotion.
- Window and in-store displays.

Let us look at each of these in turn.

Advertising

Advertising can have three main purposes. It can inform, it can persuade, or it can reinforce.

Advertising that offers basic information about the company, and the products or services it offers, is perhaps most important at the early stages of a product's (or company's) life cycle. But this kind of advertising becomes less important as the product becomes established.

Advertising that persuades is often considered to be the main form of advertising. Once an awareness of stores has been created through informative advertising, specific benefits should be emphasized to tell your potential customers why they should use your stores in preference to your competitors'.

Advertising that reinforces existing positive attitudes tells the customer that you are still able to provide the same degree of service and satisfaction as ever. Research has shown that people are more likely to read an advertisement for a store they already use than one about another store. They read the advertisement because they want their existing attitudes reinforced. As a general rule therefore, it is important for any company to remain visible.

Advertising in all forms must be managed as a part of the total retail management effort. Its effectiveness depends not only on how persuasive the message is, but also on the accuracy with which it is targeted, i.e. the accuracy with which you identify the groups of customers to whom you are talking and the benefits they are seeking. All elements of the retail operations mix must be closely linked to the advertising process.

But remember, even the most impressive, elaborate and appealing campaign will fail to convince customers to visit a store twice if that store's products do not meet their needs. Advertising can create awareness and interest in a store, can persuade a customer to try it, and perhaps can lead to purchase.

Prepare the advertising plan

For many years people believed that advertising worked in a delightfully simple way, with the advertiser sending a message and the target receiving it and understanding it. Research, however, has shown that in a society grossly over-supplied with communications, the process is more complex. Figure 7.1 gives some indication of the advertising process.

Advertising, then, is not the straightforward activity that many people believe it to be. It is highly unlikely, for example, that any firm will be able simply to put out an advertisement and expect its sales to increase.

This brings us to perhaps the greatest misconception of all about advertising – that objectives for advertising for the purpose of measuring effectiveness should be set in terms of sales increases. Naturally we hope that

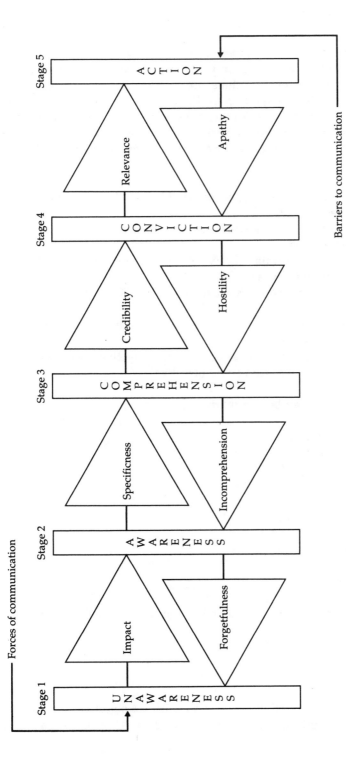

Figure 7.1 *Brand loyalty ladder: the five stages of communication*

advertising will have an important influence on sales levels, but in most circumstances advertising is only one of a whole host of important determinants of these levels (others are product quality, prices, customer service levels, the competence of the store staff, and so on). Generally, then, it is absurd to set sales increases as an objective for advertising.

So what objectives should be set for advertising? Well, we can start by agreeing that we need to set objectives for advertising for the following reasons:

1 We need to set the budget for advertising. Therefore we need some objectives.
2 We need to determine who our target audience is. Therefore we need some objectives.
3 We need to determine the content of advertisements. Therefore we need some objectives.
4 We need to decide on what media to use. Therefore we need some objectives.
5 We need to decide on the frequency of advertising. Therefore we need some objectives.
6 We need to decide how to measure the effectiveness of our advertising. Therefore we need some objectives.

These decisions can be summarized as follows:

1 Why (objectives).
2 Who (target).
3 What (copy platform).
4 Where (media).
5 How (creative platform).
6 When (timing).
7 How much (budget).
8 Schedule.
9 Response.
10 Evaluation.

The whole edifice, however, depends on the first of these.

Advertising objectives

Research has shown that many companies set objectives for advertising that advertising cannot achieve on its own. Apart from increasing sales, the 'annihilation of the enemy' and other such ridiculously unachievable objectives are set. For example, it is unreasonable to set as an objective 'to convince our target market that our store is best' if it is perfectly clear to the whole world that someone else's store is better. You cannot blame your advertising agency if this objective is not achieved!

The first step, then, is to decide on reasonable objectives for advertising. The question that must be asked is: 'Is it possible to achieve the objective through advertising alone?' If the answer is yes, it is an objective for advertising. If the answer is no, it is not an objective for advertising. Advertising through media can do the following:

- Convey information.
- Alter perceptions/attitudes.
- Create desires.
- Establish connections between existing and new product ranges.
- Direct actions.
- Provide reassurance.
- Remind.
- Give reasons for buying.
- .Demonstrate.
- Generate enquiries.

Setting reasonable, achievable objectives, then, is the first and most important step in the advertising plan. All the other steps in the process of putting together the advertising plan flow naturally from this and are summarized briefly below.

Who are the target audience(s)?
1 What do they already know, feel, believe about us and our product/service?
2 What do they know, feel, believe about the competition?
3 What sort of people are they? How do we describe/identify them?

What response do we wish to evoke from the target audience(s)?
1 What are these specific communication objectives?
2 What do we want to 'say', make them 'feel', 'believe', 'understand', 'know' about buying/using our product/service?
3 What are we offering?
4 What do we not want to convey?
5 What are the priorities of importance of our objectives?
6 What are the objectives written down and agreed by the company and advertising agency?

How are our objectives to be embodied in an appealing form?
1   What is our creative strategy/platform?
2   What evidence do we have that this is acceptable and appropriate to our audience(s)?

Where is/are the most cost-effective place(s) to expose our communications (in cost terms *vis-à-vis* our audience)?
1   Where is/are the most beneficial place(s) for our communications (in expected response terms *vis-à-vis* the 'quality' of the channels available).

When are our communications to be displayed/conveyed to our audience?
1   What is the reasoning for our scheduling of advertisements/communications over time?
2   What constraints limit our freedom of choice?
3   Do we have to fit in with other promotional activity on:

(a) Our products/services supplied by our company?
(b) Other products/services supplied by our company?
(c) Competitors' stores?
(d) Seasonal trends?
(e) Special events in the market? (For example, Father's Day).
(f) Store opening/modernization programmes.

Result
1   What results do we expect?
2   How would we measure results?
3   Do we intend to measure results and, if so, do we need to do anything beforehand?

If we cannot say how we would measure precise results, then maybe our objectives are not sufficiently special or are not communications objectives?

Evaluation
1   How are we going to judge the relative success of our communications activities (good-bad-indifferent)?
2   Should we have action standards?

Budget
1   How much money do the intended activities need?
2   How much money is going to be made available?
3   How are we going to control expenditure?

Schedule
1 Who is to do what and when?
2 What is being spent on what, where and when?

The usual assumption is that advertising is deployed in an aggressive role and that all that changes over time is the creative content. But the role of advertising usually changes during the life cycle of a retail concept.

For example, the process of persuasion itself cannot usually start until there is some level of awareness about the store and its products in the market place. Creating awareness is therefore usually one of the most important objectives early on in a life cycle. If awareness has been created, interest in learning more will usually follow.

Attitude development now begins in earnest. This might also mean reinforcing an existing attitude or even changing previously held attitudes in order to clear the way for a new purchase. This role obviously tends to become more important later when competing retailers are each trying to establish their own 'niche' in the market.

Direct mail advertising

In recent years, direct mail has become an increasingly widespread form of advertising. It goes some way towards bridging the gap between personal and impersonal selling by aiming a letter or sales literature at a named prospective purchaser. The key to successful direct mail is the mailing list. Although computers now enable direct-mail techniques to be applied to the consumer markets, success rates are still much lower than in industrial markets and costs are extremely high. This form of advertising is therefore less suitable for low-value items.

The use of direct mail to a retailer's charge–card holders is an example of using direct mail to a highly targeted group of customers, and offers the company certain advantages. Firstly, we have already said that it is easier to sell further products to satisfied customers, as they already hold positive attitudes towards your store. Not only are the charge–card holders likely to hold extremely positive attitudes, but we can also assume that the level of their current purchases is higher than the average customer's, justifying their need for the card. We have also stated that the success of direct mail depends largely on the list of names. Again, this is to our considerable advantage, since we are in constant communication with these customers and we can assume that all the names and addresses on our list are correct, and that they are already interested in the type of products we sell. As you can see, the use of direct mail in this instance brings together many of the ideas that we have already discussed.

Diffusion of innovation

Also relevant to advertising is what is known as the 'diffusion of innovation curve' discussed in Chapter 5 (Figure 5.11). To refresh our memories we will repeat the curve in Figure 7.2.

Research into any product's progress along the diffusion curve can be very useful, particularly for advertising and personal selling. For example, if we can develop a typology for innovative customers, we can target our early advertising and sales effort specifically at them. Once the first 3 per cent of innovators have adopted our new product offering, there is a good chance that the early adopters will try it, and once the 10-12 per cent point is reached, there is cause for celebration, because there is a good chance that the rest will adopt our new product.

We know, for example, that the general characteristics of opinion leaders are that they are venturesome, socially integrated, cosmopolitan, socially mobile, and privileged. So we need to ask ourselves what are the specific characteristics of these customers in our particular business. We can then tailor our advertising message specifically for them.

Finally, we should remind ourselves that advertising is not directed only at consumers. It can be directed at channels, shareholders, media, employees and suppliers, all of whom have an important influence on a firm's commercial success.

The term advertising (often referred to as 'above-the-line expenditure') can be defined as all non-personal communication in measured media. This includes television, cinema, radio, print, and outdoor media.

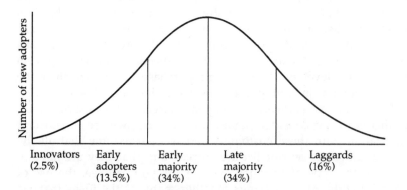

Figure 7.2

Sales promotion

Sales promotion, for which the term 'below-the-line expenditure' is often used as a synonym, is not easily defined. For example, the Americans use the term to describe all forms of communication, including advertising and personal selling. In Britain some use the term to describe any activity concerned with the promotion of sales that is not face to face, some use it to describe any non-media expenditure while others use it specifically to mean in-store merchandising. None of these definitions, however, is an accurate reflection of how sales promotion works, which is why there is so much confusion about many aspects of this important area of marketing activity.

In practice, sales promotion is a specific activity that can be defined as the making of a featured offer to defined customers within a specific time limit. In other words, to qualify as a sales promotion, someone must be offered something that is featured rather than just being an aspect of trade. Furthermore, the offer must include benefits not inherent in the product or service, as opposed to the intangible benefits offered in advertising, such as adding value through appeals to imagery.

Seen this way, every other element of the marketing mix, including advertising, personal selling, point-of-sale material, pricing, after-sales service, and so on, can be used as part of a structured activity in order to achieve specified objectives.

How can we use sales promotion?

Sales promotion is essentially a problem-solving activity designed to get customers to behave more in line with the economic interests of the company than they are doing. Typical tasks for sales promotion are slow stock movement, counteracting competitive activity, encouraging repeat purchase, securing new customers, inducing trial purchase, and so on.

Sales promotion is not necessarily only concerned with volume increases. For example, it can be used to persuade retailers and consumers to bring forward their peak buying from one period to another. To summarize, sales promotion seeks to influence:

Store staff	To sell.
Retail Customers	To buy and sell more, earlier, faster, etc.
Consumers	To buy and use.

Although in recent years sales-promotion activity has increased to such an extent that it can now account for as much expenditure as above-the-line advertising, it is important to realize that on its own sales promotion will not replace selling, change long-term trends, or build you long-term customer loyalty. Nevertheless, while sales promotion is essentially a tactical device, it also has an important strategic role to play, as we shall see later.

What different kinds of sales promotion are there?

The many and varied types of sales promotions are listed in Table 7.1. Each of these different types is appropriate for different circumstances and each has advantages and disadvantages. For example, with a promotion that consists of a free product bonus, it is possible to measure precisely both the cost of the extra products and the additional volume resulting from the offer, it is fast and flexible, it is effective where the customer is bargain-conscious, it can be made to last as long as required, and it is simple to set up, administer and sell. On the other hand, it has no cumulative value to the customer, is unimaginative, and can often be seen as a prelude to a permanent price reduction. Great care is necessary, therefore, in selecting a scheme appropriate to the objective sought.

Strategic role of sales promotion

Because sales promotion is essentially used as a tactical device, it often amounts to little more than a series of spasmodic gimmicks lacking in any coherence. Yet the same management that organizes sales promotion usually believes that advertising should conform to a strategy. Perhaps this is because advertising has always been based on a philosophy of building long-term brand franchise in a consistent manner, whereas the basic rationale of sales promotion is to help the company gain a tactical initiative.

Even so, there is no reason why there should not be a strategy for sales promotion. Then each promotion increases the effectiveness of the next, a bond between seller and buyer is built up, the tactical objectives are linked in with a plan, and there is generally a better application of resources.

Preparing the sales-promotion plan

There is widespread acknowledgement that sales promotion is one of the most mismanaged of all marketing functions. This is mainly because of the confusion about what sales promotion is, which often results in expenditures not being properly recorded. Some companies include it with advertising, others as part of sales expenditure, others as a general

Table 7.1 Types of sales promotion

Target Market	Money		Goods		Services	
	Direct	Indirect	Direct	Indirect	Direct	Indirect
Customers	Price reduction.	Coupons. Vouchers. Money equivalent. Competitions.	Premium offers (e.g. 3 for 2). Free gifts. Trade-in offers.	Stamps. Coupons. Vouchers. Money equivalent. Competitions.	Guarantees. Group participation events. Special exhibitions and displays.	Stamps. Coupons. Vouchers for services. Tickets for events. Competitions.
Store staff	Bonus. Commissions.	Coupons. Vouchers. Points systems. Money equivalent. Competition.	Free gifts.	Coupons. Vouchers. Points systems. Money equivalent.	Free service. Group participation events.	Coupons. Vouchers. Points systems for services. Event admission. Competitions.

Types of promotion

marketing expense, others as a product expense (as in the case of extra product, or special labels, or packaging), while the loss of revenue from special price reductions is often not recorded at all.

Such failures can be extremely damaging because sales promotion is such an important part of marketing strategy. In addition, with increasing global competition, troubled economic conditions, and growing pressures from channels, sales promotion is becoming more widespread and more acceptable. This means that companies can no longer afford not to set objectives, or to evaluate results after the event, nor can they afford to fail to have some company guidelines. For example, a £1 price reduction on a product with a gross margin of £3 has to increase sales by 50 per cent just to maintain the same level of contribution. Failure at least to realize this, or to set alternative objectives for the promotion, can easily result in loss of control and a consequent reduction in profits.

In order to manage a company's sales-promotion expenditure effectively, there is one essential step that must be taken. First, an objective for sales promotion must be established in the same way that an objective is developed for advertising, pricing, or distribution. The objectives for each promotion should be clearly stated, such as trial, repeat purchase, reducing stock levels, a shift in buying peaks, combating competition, and so on. Thereafter the following process should apply:

- Select the appropriate technique.
- Mount the promotion.
- Evaluate in depth.

Spending must be analysed and categorized by type of activity (e.g. special packaging, special point-of-sale material, loss of margin through price reductions, and so on).

One company selling self-assembly kitchens embarked on a heavy programme of sales promotion after a dramatic reduction in consumer demand. While it managed to maintain turnover, it was worried that its sales-promotional activities had been carried out in such a haphazard and piecemeal fashion that it was unable to evaluate the cost-effectiveness of what it had done. It was also very concerned about the promotion's effect on company image and its long-term consumer franchise. So the company made a concentrated study of this area of expenditure, which now represented over half its communication budget. Next time round it had clear objectives, a clear promotional plan properly integrated into the marketing plan, and an established means of assessment.

As for the sales-promotional plan itself, the objectives, strategy and brief details of timing and costs should be included. It is important that too much detail should not appear in the plan; detailed promotional instructions will follow as the marketing plan unfurls. For example, the following checklist outlines the kind of detail that should eventually, be circulated. However, only an outline of this should appear in the marketing plan itself.

1	Objectives	Briefly summarize objectives for new promotion.
2	Background	Market data. Justification for technique. Other relevant matters.
3	Promotional offer	Detail the offer. Be brief, precise and unambiguous.
4	Timing	When is the offer available?
5	Date plan	Assign dates and responsibilities for all aspects of plan before start date.
6	Support	Special advertising, point of sale, window displays, leaflets, etc.
7	Administration	Check branches and depot stocks.
8	Store staff	Targets. Incentives. Store staff briefings
9	Sales reporting	Procedure for collection of required data not otherwise available.
10	Assessment	How will the promotion be evaluated?

Window and in-store displays

Advertising and sales promotions may be described as primary sources of communication. They are under our direct control and we pay for them. Of similar importance in the communication of our marketing message to our customers are our window and in-store displays.

Their importance should never be underestimated, particularly for smaller stores and speciality shops. Indeed window displays are very often the major means of getting the message across for those retailers with limited funds available for advertising. The reason is quite simple. The window displays are there to be seen 24 hours a day, 365 days a year. In certain major shopping locations in London as many as 250,000 people can walk past a shop every day. Those of course are exceptional, but even in quite modest cities and towns passing counts of 10,000 plus are not unusual.

There are several reasons why a retailer should pay careful attention to the design and maintenance of his window displays. As with advertising, existing customers will tend to watch the windows of stores that they use for reassurance that they had previously made the right choice, and that 'their' store was keeping up with expectations. They are not the only ones seeking reassurance. There are many people out in the high streets and shopping centres who lack self-confidence when shopping. They are often reluctant to enter a store on a speculative basis, unless they can see in the window the actual product, or type of product, they are looking for.

For existing and potential customers alike, the windows are a vital vehicle for sales promotions, and for announcing the arrival of new product ranges. If a retailer is trying to adjust his market positioning, or trying to target a new segment of the market, then his windows are an immediate medium for the message.

Therefore, it is important that the displays are carefully designed to be attractive to the chosen target market. Customers seeking exclusivity and high quality will be attracted by the minimalist displays in London's Bond Street and Knightsbridge stores, which in turn will have little appeal to the customer groups seeking wide choice at more affordable prices.

Similarly, once customers have been attracted into the store, it is essential that the marketing message from the windows is carried through into the in-store and point-of-sale displays in a consistent manner. The money spent on ornate and expensive window displays can often be wasted if the same care is not given to the presentation of the merchandise inside the store. Sloppily stocked shelves and fixtures can spoil the perception given by the window displays, and lead to the potential customers feeling they have been cheated or deceived in some way.

Public relations – influencing the customer indirectly

There are also secondary ways of communicating with our customers. These are not under our direct control but will be influenced by the elements discussed above, which we do control. They also have a singular advantage, in that, for the most part, they are either relatively inexpensive or free.

The effective use of press and public relations calls for careful planning and co-ordination. It can lead to an increase in public awareness, understanding, and acceptance of the company's image and policies. Media contacts should be nurtured and utilized to the full.

Well-prepared press releases, and press packs containing the right sort of photographs, are very often the way to generate media interest and articles on your new season's product range, your new shopfit, your new idea for improved customer service, etc. If staff in your company are taking part in community projects, or your company is supporting various charities, then let the media know. They are always on the lookout for human interest stories, and the benefit to you is not only in keeping your company in the public eye, but also in personalizing the relationship between the company and the community, i.e. your customers.

The communication plan: 2 Personal communications/ customer service

Summary

Chapter 8 deals with the nature of customer service and its importance in the marketing mix, and goes on to examine the difference between customer service and personal selling, and their roles in different types of retailing. Quantitative and qualitative ways of measuring customer service are discussed, and we look at the various factors that need to be taken into account by a retailer in preparing staffing plans.

Introduction

We have discussed the process of targeting market segments, selecting the right products and setting up the supply chain, the importance of store design and layout, the need for effective advertising and sales promotion, and the additional benefits to be gained from good public relations. We now turn to the next link in the marketing chain, the critical area of our company's face-to-face contact with its customers.

Customers in the 1990s are better informed than ever before. Most of them are able to choose from the wide variety of shops and stores ranged alongside each other in the high streets and shopping centres. The rapid rate of technical progress and fierce competition has meant that many of the products on offer are of comparable quality, price, and value for money. Why therefore do some firms or organizations succeed while others wallow in mediocrity? The answer lies in the attention they give to the planning and delivery of consistently good levels of customer service.

The Japanese know that the customer is the final arbiter. They already have an enviable reputation for their approach to product development and the quality standards of their manufactured goods. Now they are bringing that same thoroughness and application to bear on the subject of customer service. A survey has shown that as many as 90 per cent of top Japanese companies feel that customer service will be the most important boardroom issue of the mid-1990s.

They are not alone. Many major European and US companies have reached the same conclusion. The airlines are an obvious example. For instance, on the North Atlantic routes they fly the same aircraft and have similar pricing structures. They are locked in battle now trying to convince potential customers that they have better levels of customer service than each other, because they have realized that this is virtually the only area in which they can carve out some differential advantage over the competition in the eyes of those customers. In the process they are spending vast sums of money on training and advertising. Foremost have been British Airways, whose training programmes in the late 1980s have brought about a significant improvement in public perception. The accolade, 'The World's Favourite Airline', has certainly benefited BA's business. Other major concerns sharing the same outlook on the need to invest in a planned approach to customer service, include British Gas, Texaco, and Marks & Spencer's.

What they share is a common belief that their companies have a total commitment to service, from the boardroom right through the organization. It is not something confined to those in direct contact with the customers.

The message for all retailers is that this is an area of growing importance in trying to win the battle of the high streets. Indeed it may turn out to be one of most significant discriminating factors between the winners and the losers.

What is customer service?

Put simply, it is everything we have to do to keep our customers satisfied. It is the outcome of a process whereby, having identified the needs and expectations of customers, we plan and direct the efforts of the entire company to meeting and exceeding those needs and expectations.

For a retailer it is a philosophy that is clearly defined and understood by all employees, not just the store staff. It should be a guiding light to staff at all levels of the organization in all their activities, and particularly when they are in contact with customers.

There has to be genuine understanding that 'The customer is king', and this belief must underlie all customer transactions. A senior director of one retail company had the habit of referring to customers as 'punters' whenever he was in discussions with his staff. As the company concerned was not running betting shops, what he was doing was unwittingly conveying a lack of respect for the customers. As a result, that particular company failed to recognize that these so-called 'punters' were the critical component which could make or break the company.

Some companies labour under the misapprehension that putting all store staff through a cosmetic training course to teach them to smile and say 'Have a nice day' is the answer to providing good customer service. Those who do so are only scratching the surface. It runs far deeper than this. It is a part of the marketing plan that needs just as much care and attention as the product or advertising plans.

The importance of customer service

Research has shown that people who have received poor customer service will, on average, tell ten others about their bad experience, and 10 per cent of those told will tell twenty other people. Unfortunately good news does not travel as fast as bad. Only about half that number will pass on the good news when they have been exceptionally well treated.

It is immediately obvious that there is a significant pay-back to the retailer who gets his customer service right from the start. He minimizes adverse comments about the company, and gains new customers through recommendations from existing clientele.

Apart from isolated rural areas, where a retailer may have 'captive customers' to a certain extent, there are few times when the customer does not have more than one retail outlet from which to choose. Fail to meet their needs and expectations and even the least vociferous will very quickly vote with their feet and shop with the competition.

Customer service and personal selling

Another common fault is to think of customer service only in terms of personal selling. Selling can of course be an important part of customer service, but its relative importance is a function of the type of product under consideration. Sometimes it is of little or no importance and other factors weigh much more heavily. This is best illustrated by looking at a number of examples.

Convenience goods and FMCG (fast-moving consumer goods)

Most days of our lives see us making a number of retail purchases that call for a great deal of customer service. The local CTN (confectionery/tobacco/newsagent) provides service by making sure that it is open on time, the newspapers are easily accessible, that there are enough staff on hand to serve the customers quickly and efficiently so that no one misses their bus or train, that special magazine orders are remembered, etc.

Supermarkets provide service by making sure that there are enough trolleys and baskets at the entrance, that they do not have stockouts on products that the customers expect them to carry, that the shelves and aisles are clearly labelled, that the staff in the store know the layout and location of products for the guidance of customers, and that the check-out points are sufficiently staffed to keep queuing times to a level acceptable to the customers. In the USA, for many years, the level of service has been extended to having staff on hand to pack the goods for the customer at the check-out and load them into their cars, a practice only introduced into the UK by Marks & Spencer's in the late 1980s. The large investments in barcoding and laser-scanning equipment by the majors have not only given them powerful tools for stock control, they have also given them the ability to improve their customer service by speeding up check-out times and providing customers with itemized lists of their purchases.

Similarly, throughout the day, we buy bus or train tickets, petrol, sandwiches and snacks, birthday cards and postage stamps, a pair of tights, a toothbrush, or a battery for the Sony Walkman. In virtually none of these cases does anyone actually 'sell' to us. What they do is to provide a service. For most of these convenience purchases, customers have a variety of retailers to choose from, but being creatures of habit, will tend to be loyal to the one that gives them good consistent customer service.

Speciality goods

Next come a group of goods that we tend to buy less frequently, such as clothing, gardening items, do-it-yourself materials, household articles, video or audio cassettes and so on. Often we might make a special journey at the weekend to purchase these products.

Here, we find a greater degree of personal communication between the store staff and the customers because of the nature of the products concerned. They are in areas where the question of choice is more open, and where customers are often less sure of their exact requirements. There is a high frequency of discussion between customer and store staff before purchase.

For instance, a man who smokes a particular brand of cigarette is highly unlikely to accept an alternative if his brand is out of stock in a shop. He will almost certainly try another shop. However, the same man out shopping for a suit for formal occasions is likely to be far less specific, and may need help from store staff to select the best option for him according to his size, colouring, and pocket, from a bewildering array of greys/navies, single/double breasted, stripes/plains and so on. Equally he will seek help from the staff at the garden centre on the right plants to choose for different parts of the garden, and from the staff at the DIY store on the right tools for different jobs around the home.

In addition to the customer service standards of logical layout, clear labelling, efficient cash and wrap procedures, and courteous staff, as discussed for the convenience and FMCG retailers above, if we are a speciality goods retailer, we must offer a significantly higher level of product knowledge in our dealings with our customers. This type of situation offers a number of advantages to the retailer who has planned this element of the marketing mix properly, and who has trained and motivated his staff.

For a start, the face-to-face contact with the customer makes it possible for the prospective purchaser to ask questions of the salespeople about the product, and for the latter to use their product knowledge to relate to the perceived needs of the customers and help them make the most suitable choice. At the same time this personal contact allows the staff to increase the potential value of the sale by using their selling abilities to suggest additional purchases, i.e. a shirt, tie, and pair of shoes to go with the new suit.

Consumer durables

A new washing machine, television, home computer, video camera, dining-room suite, or set of carpets, are major and infrequent purchases in most households. As such, they are normally carefully considered and researched. Customers will tend to look round competing outlets before making their final decision. The staff in a durable-goods retailer need an even higher degree of product knowledge than previously discussed. They must be able to demonstrate the different products on display, and give an objective assessment of their potential performance and suitability for different uses. They must be aware of delivery times, guarantee periods and conditions, and after-sales service facilities. They must be well-trained in the credit sale options offered by their company, and fully aware of company policy and procedures in the event of a complaint.

However, in these circumstances it is important that the training of the salespeople goes far beyond the basic subjects of specification and availability. They need to understand the whole of the thinking behind the range, how it is positioned in relation to the competition, the segments of the market at which it is targeted, etc. Only when they are fully in the picture, will they be able to give their customers the complete answers to their questions, and convert those questions into sales.

Remember the point made earlier: customers will tend to have done an amount of their own research and will have read brochures. What they need is reassurance that they are making the right decision on this major purchase. The well-trained salesperson will be able to ascertain quickly the needs of the customer, and gain creditability by demonstrating that understanding. Such considerations often weigh more heavily with the customers than armfuls of brochures and technical data when it comes to closing the sale.

To summarize this section, personal selling is only part of customer service, and the amount required is generally a function of the price and complexity of the product, as illustrated in Figure 8.1.

As a rule of thumb, the higher the price to be paid by the customers, the more they will want to confirm they are getting good value for their

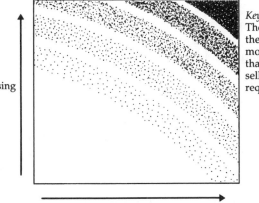

Key:
The darker the shading, the more likelihood that personal selling will be required

Increasing price

Increasingly complex products
(Complexity can be technical/newness/fashionability)

Figure 8.1

money. Equally, with complex or technical products, customers will be seeking substantially more information than can be adequately put across by point-of-sale displays.

Quantitative/qualitative measures of performance

As we discussed earlier, the art of putting together a successful marketing plan lies in making all the components crystal clear and measurable. This is equally applicable to the area of customer service, which might appear at first sight to be a rather abstract concept. However, this is not so. There are a number of ways in which a retailer can get a good fix on progress in this area.

The easy part is of course the measurement of the productivity of store staff, i.e. the personal selling component of customer service. For those retailers where there is little personal selling of product (self-selection stores, supermarkets, etc.), or for those where all staff are interchangeable (taking turns at cash and wrap, shelf-filling, stockroom duties etc), the most frequent measure is 'sales per FTE' (full-time equivalent).

Most retailers operate on a mixture of full-time and part-time staff, so that they are adequately manned for the peak trading periods and save money at off-peak times. By taking the total number of hours worked by a full-time member of staff, we can arrive at the number of 'full-time equivalents'. (For example, in a shop with a turnover of £1,360,000 pa, with six full-timers working 38 hours a week, and five part timers working 19 hours, total hours worked are 323, there are 8.5 FTEs, and sales per FTE are £160,000.) In stores where there are dedicated sales staff, who do nothing else but man the selling area, then it is simple to set individual or team sales targets, as appropriate to the individual situation and the management philosophy of the company.

Stores selling speciality and consumer-durable products are often 'destination stores', i.e. the customer has decided to visit them specifically rather than on impulse. For this type of operation a very useful measure of the degree to which they are meeting their customers' needs is to plan and monitor their 'conversion ratio' – the number of potential purchasers entering the store divided by the number who actually buy on that visit (100 people cross the threshold, 35 buy something, conversion ratio = 35 per cent). As we discussed earlier, these are the types of purchases where the customers look for and need knowledgeable, courteous, and professional customer service. In addition, they have come to the store specially and are prepared to spend money. Assuming the product range is adequate, and this is a factor that needs constant research, then the conversion ratio gives an additional guide to customers' satisfaction with the service they are getting.

An area that can damage a retailer's reputation very quickly is the poor handling of complaints, whether written or verbal. A simple logging of complaints over a control period can establish the present situation and give a basis for targets going forward. Complaints should be separated into those about products and their performance and those on customer service. The latter should be analysed and the appropriate remedial action incorporated into staff-training programmes. Complaints on product will of course go in the first instance to the product team for action, but they also represent an area in which customer service can be measured and improved. Well-trained staff should be in a position to acknowledge obviously faulty merchandise immediately and take the necessary steps through an exchange or refund to satisfy the customer.

If it is necessary to return the goods to the manufacturer, then the retailer should have a control system that monitors the length of time it takes for complaints to be resolved, and work constantly to reduce it. Nothing irritates customers more than waiting for a faulty television, suit, or vacuum cleaner to be returned to them. It is the retailer who incurs their wrath and dissatisfaction, not the manufacturer, so anything he can do to shorten the time taken will be to his advantage. Much of Marks & Spencer's enviable reputation for good customer service comes from a clear policy of no quibble refunds or exchanges on faulty merchandise.

Similarly, if a retailer advertises a service, e.g. 'same day photo processing', or 'suits made to measure in 10 days', then there are immediate performance standards against which customer service can be planned and assessed.

Let us make our final point on written complaints. They should be acknowledged, either in writing or by telephone, on the day of receipt, even if the final resolution may await the return of the goods to the maker. This is a very simple and unambiguous standard to set, and is a clear statement of the retailer's belief in customer service.

The above are all finite ways in which retailers can set quantitative standards in their marketing plans against which to measure improvements in selling and customer service. More qualitative assessments of customers' perceptions can be a by-product of some of the research we discussed in Chapter 4, when looking at ways of comparing our company to its competitors. It is very appropriate to insert a battery of questions on customers' perceptions of our staff, and the service they give, into any image–monitoring exercise.

How many staff do we need?

The facile answer is as many as it takes to ensure complete customer satisfaction! In reality simple economics preclude this, and there are as many answers as there are shops and stores on the high street, because there are so many different factors to take into account. Consider the following:

1 *Size of outlet* – a single floor outlet will need fewer staff than a multi-floor store of the same size per floor.
2 *Type of product* – as discussed above, the higher the price and complexity of the product, the more personal selling is required. More personal selling needs more people.
3 *Opening hours* – the number of trading days, and the hours the outlet is open, may require shift working and flexible working patterns. Changes in holiday entitlements will also affect staff numbers.
4 *Patterns of trade* – bunching of sales into parts of the day, or into certain days of the week, will affect staffing level requirements. For instance, menswear shops do a much higher proportion of their week's business on a Saturday than do womenswear shops, because the higher number of women who do not have full-time employment do more of their clothes shopping during the week. Consequently menswear retailers need a higher staffing level for the weekend.
5 *Sales density* – a shop trading at a sales density of £3,500 per square metre (psm) will need more staff to cope with the customer flow than one on £2,000 psm.
6 *Security* – an unfortunate feature of the modern retail scene is that the rising incidence of theft in many city centre locations means that retailers in those places have to allow for security staff in their staffing plans.

To summarize, customer service is not an ethereal, abstract concept. It is an important part of our communications mix, and calls for the same assiduity in its planning as the other components. As we have discussed, there are ways in which customer service can be measured and performance standards set. It is the time where the retailer comes face to face with the customer, and represents both the greatest opportunity for increased success, and at the same time the greatest threat, if badly handled.

The final point to remember is that, with increasing price competition and homogeneity of product, it is one of the few areas where the retailer can obtain significant differential advantage over competitors.

9

The pricing plan

Summary

Chapter 9 begins by looking at the importance of pricing decisions in retailing, and goes on to discuss the major external and internal factors that need to be considered in preparing a pricing plan, including the dangers of entering price wars and the role of discounting as a strategic tool. Finally, there is an exploration of costs as an input to pricing decision-making, and a caution against cost-plus pricing.

Introduction

As we have discussed, retailing is all about the four P's, Product, Price, Place, and Promotion. Surprisingly therefore, it is rare to find a pricing plan as an explicit part of a retailer's marketing plan.

The reason is not too hard to find. It is relatively easy to manage and measure promotion, in all its various forms, and place (the stores) as discrete subsets of the marketing mix. On the other hand, price is such an integral part of the product and service level offered to the customer that it is rarely separated out and put into a plan of its own. It is more common to find pricing strategies attached to product plans for achieving objectives in relation to certain groups of products or certain market segments, where pricing policies would have a significant part to play in the achievement of those objectives.

However, there are complex issues in regard to pricing that merit separate discussion as a distinct element of the marketing mix. We shall therefore refer throughout to a 'pricing plan', although it will be structured in such a way that the elements of pricing can be integrated into the individual product/segment plans as appropriate.

The same could, of course, be said for each of the other elements of the marketing mix discussed in this book. How they are all integrated into a total plan is discussed in Chapter 12.

The importance of price

Pricing decisions are important for two main reasons. The difference between what the products cost to buy and what we eventually sell them for, the margin, has an immediate effect on the revenue of the company and its profitability.

Secondly, price directly affects the amount sold through its influence on demand – since a higher price can reduce demand, while a lower price can often lead to increased sales. For instance, tour operators retailing holidays will use lower prices to stimulate demand out of the high season, and DIY stockists will often discount home-insulation materials during the summer months.

Naturally the price of products is only one of the controllable variables we have identified – and it must therefore interact and relate to all of the other variables. The price must be consistent with the total 'package' of variables. For example, if a range of products is aimed at the luxury market, then the prices must reflect that decision so that they are perceived as being of that standing by the target customers.

Unless a retailer is in a monopoly position within the market, then all pricing decisions will be influenced by a number of important factors, both from outside and inside the company.

External factors

There are several major factors over which we have no control but which have a significant influence on price:

- The competition.
- Market development.
- Legislation and the financial environment.
- Supply-side structure and activity.

Price and the competition

Most retailers operate in highly competitive markets characterized by a number of well-established companies. In these situations established price brackets occur for specific types of product. For instance, it is unusual to find wide variations in the retail prices of branded cigarettes, confectionery, and soft drinks, despite the miscellany of outlets stocking them.

The question individual retailers need to answer is whether their own position in the market provides them with room to manoeuvre on price.

Where competitive products are very similar, this becomes a real problem – a higher price policy is ruled out because customers will probably switch to a cheaper store. Occasionally a company with a dominant position may try to improve its margins by edging its prices higher in the hope that others will follow suit. This gives the option to the 'price followers' to hold their prices in the hope of gaining extra sales.

However, this scenario is less frequent than the opposite. Dominant retailers tend to have more clout with the suppliers because of the size of their orders, and enjoy better economies of scale on their operating costs. This gives them the option of either enjoying better margins at similar prices, or cutting prices, while still enjoying the same percentage margin as their smaller competitors.

The point here is that all retailers should be aware, as far as possible, of the likely stance that the big players in the market will take in given circumstances, and have planned ahead the appropriate pricing response for their own company.

Price and market development

As well as looking at the individual competitors in a market, it is important to consider the state of development of the whole market in which we operate.

A market in its growth stage offers far greater pricing flexibility to the retailer than a mature one. In the early 1980s the main concern of retailers of video-recorders and blank and pre-recorded tapes was to keep their stock up to date with adequate supplies of the latest technical developments. Price was a secondary consideration. A decade later the market has reached a mature stage, the majority of households (72 per cent of UK households in 1992) have video-recorders, and price competition is rife. In real terms the prices of those products in the 1990s are less than half the price of the early 1980s.

So, if a retailer is considering entering a mature market, the company must be very circumspect in the construction of its pricing plan, as its room for manoeuvre may be limited. The opportunity to charge a premium price will be justified only if there are extra customer benefits that the store can offer.

Price and legislation/the financial environment

Government and local legislation can have very immediate effects on our costs, and therefore the prices we have to charge. The most obvious example of this in the UK is the Value Added Tax. Changes in VAT rates can, and do, happen overnight. A well-prepared retailer will have contingency actions in his pricing plan, so that his company can react swiftly, and without panic, whatever the scenario that unfolds at the Despatch Box.

Being well prepared in these circumstances can give a retailer a range of promotional possibilities. There is the opportunity to advertise that the firm will hold its prices for a given period, and thereby hope for an immediate sales boost. Then it could work quickly with suppliers to reduce the size or weight of products, and maintain the old prices, without damaging the long-term margin. Periodic reviews of pricing plans for such eventualities can be important in sustaining profits in an uncertain environment.

The change to the UBR (Uniform Business Rate) system in the UK in the early 1990s has had a significant effect on the profitability of many regionally based retailers. In some areas the increases were such that price increases, or a sharp drop in profits, were the only alternatives. In others the new system worked to retailers' advantage. For the major operators with a nationwide coverage of stores the swings and round-abouts gave a more neutral effect.

Changes in credit controls and hire-purchase rules can similarly affect a retailer's costs, as can ease of borrowing and interest rates. These changes can be imposed quickly by the dictate of government, and without much warning. Again, although we cannot know exactly what will happen in the future, we can nevertheless periodically consider what pricing actions would be necessary in such eventualities.

Just as governmental actions can affect our cost base as retailers, so clearly they can have a similar effect on our customers' propensity and ability to spend. As was demonstrated in the years 1990-2, high interest rates, allied to rising unemployment and general economic uncertainty, led to a dramatic decline in retail sales. UK retailers during this period were faced with a number of major problems simultaneously. They had to reduce stocks and commitments as the banks and institutions called for a rapid reduction in their borrowing levels. In any case high interest rates were putting pressure on their cost base, which was further exacerbated by the effects of the UBR. Allied to the pressures on customers' disposable incomes, referred to above, the scene was set for a frenzy of price activity, as retailers in virtually all sectors fought to hold market share and maintain a revenue stream to stay in business. We shall return to the subject of price-cutting later in this chapter.

Price and the supply side

The flexibility for individual retailers on pricing can also depend on the structure of the supplier market. For such products as consumer durables in the household electrical and electronic field the capital investment needed for research and development, and then for economic production, means that the suppliers are few in number and large. Often the only movement on cost price available from them would be in response to activity by their own competitors in the supply market, rather than pressure from retailers, with the possible exception of the very large players.

On the other hand, retailers in markets for products such as clothing and furniture are supplied by a wide range of makers of all sizes. The retailer is considerably less constrained, and can shop around and negotiate better cost prices more easily. This, combined with the diversity of product, gives the retailers in these markets greater freedom to make individual pricing decisions. For them the importance of a carefully thought through pricing plan becomes more significant.

Internal factors

Some of the most important influences on price are actually directly under our control, and derive largely from the marketing and business objectives of the company.

The four major factors which are more under our control than anyone else's are:

- The target market.
- The product range.
- Price promotions.
- Costs.

Price and the target market

There must be a clear view of the position in which you wish your store(s) to be held in the perception of your target market, and that view will drive your pricing plan.

If that perception is one of stocking high quality, luxury goods as adjuncts to a gracious life style, then the prices charged will need to be similarly 'gracious', or you will very quickly lose credibility with your target customers. Two dangers exist. The first is to charge too low a price for a recognizably high quality product – buyers tend to distrust a cheap Rolex watch. The second is to stock lower priced merchandise which, as we have discussed earlier, might raise doubts in your target customers' minds as to the exclusivity of your store.

Conversely, if you are stocking commodity products, such as sugar, then charging too high a price will not only lose you sales but also damage your reputation for delivering value for money. That is not to say that you must always seek to match the lowest prices around, even for commodity merchandise. For example, most people will acknowledge that they pay a bit over normal supermarket prices for goods at the local convenience store. However, they accept this because they are willing to pay for the ability to buy these products late at night, on Sundays, and on bank holidays. In other words, the convenience store operator is able to build extra customer benefits into the pricing plan, and charge accordingly. Provided this surcharge is not excessive, then the customers will still perceive that they are getting value for money.

The basic principle holds good for all retailers. In setting prices it is necessary to examine all the bundle of additional benefits that our firm can offer its target customers, and to set our prices according to what we believe our customers will pay for them and still feel that they are getting a fair deal from us.

This last point is one of vital importance to all retailers, no matter where in the price spectrum they may be operating. With the exception of the small proportion of the population who buy solely on price, the vast majority of people view retail prices against their inbuilt perception of value for money. Any retail firm that prejudices its reputation in this area will find it immensely hard to retrieve the situation. Therefore, in putting together the pricing plan, it is always wise to monitor your target customers' perception of your company on this score.

Price and the product range

A retailer carrying a wide variety of product ranges can have an advantage, when it comes to price planning, over a specialist with a narrow portfolio. Trial areas of new products can be introduced at lower prices for a short while to help them get established, with any shortfall on margin being subsidized by the established ranges. A similar approach can be taken with any problem ranges that need to be cleared.

It is easier to combat lower price activity by the competition on a product type if you have others that you can rely on to sell at full margin. In the same way you can lower prices on part of your product range to make it very difficult for a new specialist to get established.

If you stock mostly branded goods, then your pricing will be largely circumscribed by the competition, either locally or nationally, because there are not usually large variations in the cost prices charged by the major brands to any but the retailing giants. Of course there will be a variety of prices in the high street, but they will tend to fall into a reasonably tight band. After all, a pair of Levi's 501 jeans is the same product wherever it is purchased, and it is readily identifiable, so the only comparison a customer needs to make is on the price.

On the other hand, if you are large enough to have products made specially for you, or if your products are mostly unbranded, then careful pricing planning can give additional profit opportunities. Own-label products can usually be bought at lower cost prices than branded goods, since they do not have to carry the latter's selling and promotional costs. Secondly, since they are then unique to the retailer in question, they give the company the chance to price them according to it thinks its customers will pay for them, rather than what the competition is charging. As we discussed earlier, the judgement here is on pricing the merchandise to give good value for money.

Judicious promotional use of unbranded and own-label products at lower prices can be very useful in generating traffic in stores with large amounts of branded merchandise. This is less likely to incur retaliatory price-cutting from the competition than by reducing recognized brands. As mentioned earlier, the converse also applies. If a competitor reduces prices on branded merchandise, then a retailer with a mixed portfolio can respond by taking action on the brands concerned, and using its own-label and unbranded parts of the range to make up the lost margin.

If you are a retailer with a mixture of branded and own-label product, it is worth taking the time to consider, very carefully, the role you wish your own label to carry out. Often the temptation is to use the own-label product as a lead in price level. However, if that name is the same as the one over the store door, then there is a danger of diminishing the credibility of the whole operation. Often it can be better to put effort into developing unique selling features for the own-label products so that they can command a healthy financial margin, and to buy in cheaper brands to use for price-led promotions.

Price promotions

The most obvious examples of using price as a promotion tool are the now traditional post-Christmas and high summer clearance sales. Here the objective is two-fold, – firstly, to stimulate sales turnover during a normally quiet period, and, secondly, to clear remaining stocks of seasonable merchandise and make room for the incoming ranges. In addition, as we discussed above, pricing can be used as a tactical tool to deal with problem products mid-season.

However, there are a wide variety of additional ways in which the planned use of pricing can form part of the promotional strategy of the company. We must emphasize that these activities should be *planned*.

This means that the levels of markdown, or discount, and levels of incremental sales need to be forecast as accurately as possible, and these forecasts built into the pricing and net margin plans. There will of course be occasions when circumstances dictate some immediate, unplanned pricing activity, but these should be the exceptions rather than the rule. Many of the retailing failures of the 1989-92 period were due to companies using indiscriminate price reductions as 'knee jerk' reactions to the prevailing economic conditions, rather than taking a little time to plan their way out of the problem with proper regard for the effect of these actions on their bottom line.

Here are a number of ways in which planned pricing activity can be used as a promotional weapon.

Loss-leaders

Sometimes the dramatic reduction of price on a single product, or small group of products, can be used as a method of generating customer traffic to the store, in the hope that while they are there, they will buy other full margin merchandise. A famous example of this was the Tesco sugar promotion of the 1960s. Arriving at Tesco stores to buy the advertised, amazingly cheap sugar, customers would find it situated right at the back of the store. Small wonder that the majority bought other products along the way.

Quantity discounts

These can be used for two main purposes. The first and most obvious is to stimulate volume sales and increase the size of the individual transaction, e.g. wine merchants offering reductions on a case of twelve bottles. Similarly, prices per unit are generally more attractive for grocery and other items purchased in catering pack sizes. What these retailers are essentially doing is passing back to customers some of the saving in handling and administration costs that they get from selling in bulk, while at the same time increasing their net margin.

Bulk discounts can also be used as a disguised way of giving price reductions to shift problem stock. For instance, 'Buy Two – Get One Free', is in reality a one third-price reduction in a more covert form. This type of promotion can be applied to most types of frequently purchased product, and is often used by clothing retailers to boost sales of such things as shirts, tights, ties, underwear, T-shirts, etc. It is obviously of little use to retailers of washing machines and other such products!

Trade and organizational discounts

These are discounts given against the regular retail prices to bona-fide businesses or organizations. These are very common in builders' merchants and electrical retailers, and are another form of quantity discounts. In the same way many retailers offer discounts to local clubs and societies. Local sports and clothing retailers can often generate substantial incremental turnover by offering a discount to sports clubs, youth groups etc.

Introductory and early season discounts
We referred earlier to the use of pricing as a way of attracting customers to new products, building awareness rapidly during the launch phase. Fashion retailers also use this as a tool to help them identify the likely winning lines in the range, so that they have time to carry out repeat buying for the peak selling period. For this reason you can see winter coat retailers holding short, sharp discount promotions at the end of August/early September, to try and pick the winners to back for the main selling weeks from mid-November onwards.

Voucher discounts
Another way of reducing prices covertly and trying to manipulate the timing of customers' spending is to use discount vouchers. The sort of offer is that for every £X spent, the customer will receive £Y worth of vouchers, which are redeemable against future purchases within a fixed time scale. This approach has several advantages for the retailer. There is a stimulus to the current sales period, and an incentive to the customers to return to the store during a specified future period to make further purchases, using the vouchers. As a result, the retailer has effectively delayed the timing of having to pay for the discount, which will benefit cash flow. Furthermore, because customers usually spend more than the amount on the voucher when they come in to redeem it, there is an added spin-off in that the total percentage discount cost to the retailer can be substantially lower than the initial face value offer to the customer. Finally, there are always a number of customers who lose the vouchers, or forget to use them by the appointed date, in which case the cost to the retailer comes down even further.

Depending on the nature of a retailer's relations with the suppliers, there are sometimes ways in which the latter can be encouraged to join in a cooperative approach to voucher promotions, either by sharing the cost of discount on redeemed vouchers, or by reducing cost prices on additional merchandise bought to support the promotion.

Because of these issues, the use of pricing and discounts should be seen as strategic, as well as tactical, weapons available for use in the achievement of the company's marketing objectives. The degree to which such weapons are effective depends greatly on the price elasticity of demand for the type of products in question, and the behavioural characteristics of the target market segments of the individual retailer.

Caution should be exercised, as it is a well-known fact that many retailers have begun to question the value of price-cuts, especially at a time of falling profitability. They do so because research studies are showing that the average shopper does not have a precise knowledge of the individual prices of all the items in the supermarket trolley or shopping bag, but relies instead on a general understanding of, and feeling towards, the value for money being offered by retailers.

We must stress again the need for careful planning of discount activities. They depend on a trade-off between unit margins and forecast incremental sales. If the additional sales fail to come through at the anticipated level, profitability will fall. Therefore the question of using pricing and discounts as a promotional tool must be considered in the context of the wider implications of marketing strategy and the financial structure of the firm.

Should we enter a price war?

Certain retail sectors are susceptible to price wars. The food sector comes most readily to mind, although the early 1990s have seen fierce price competition in a number of other sectors, most noticeably carpets, clothing, electrical goods, DIY, and fashion jewellery. While some of the thinking necessary in these situations has been covered earlier in this chapter, it is worth considering the possible effects on retailers in such sectors and whether it is really in their interests to enter these price wars.

One of the key considerations is the relative price elasticity of the market for the products in question. What we mean by this is judging whether lowering the market price level will lead to an increase in purchasing by a greater percentage than the percentage reduction in price.

Let us look at two examples. Despite the antics of our offspring at the kitchen table and at the local hamburger joint, the market for tomato ketchup is relatively static and unaffected by price, i.e. it is price-inelastic. Lower the price by 5 per cent and there will be virtually no movement in the total sales level. Therefore there would be little point in either the makers or retailers of tomato ketchup indulging in a price war.

On the other hand, the retail market for television sets has been shown to be relatively price-elastic. As manufacturers and retailers alike competed on price through the 1980s, the market expanded as the new lower prices encouraged the consumers not only to keep pace with changing technology, but also to buy additional sets for their children, bedrooms, etc. Similarly, the carpet price wars expanded the total market by enabling people to carpet areas previously left bare because of cost, or to re-carpet on a more frequent basis.

The attitudes and actions of the suppliers have significance for the retailers in this context. Unless the suppliers are willing to reduce their cost prices to the retail trade during a price war, then all the loss of margin is borne by the retailers. If the demand for the product is price-inelastic, then it will clearly not be in the suppliers' interests to join in and reduce their prices to retailers, as their own profitability will inevitably suffer. Conversely, if demand is deemed to be elastic, then the makers of the product may be able to achieve some economies of scale from additional manufacturing volumes, and pass on some of that saving to the retailers.

Suppliers of strong brands will be very chary about entering price wars unless it becomes clear that volume sales of those brands will suffer long-term damage by retailers substituting cheaper brands for them on their shelves. Nor will they wish to obtain cost price savings by cutting down on their promotional spend, as they have learned by now that this is an encouragement to retailers to buy substitute brands. By keeping their own brand strong, they minimize brand substitution in a price war.

Exactly the same argument applies to the retailer wondering whether to become embroiled in a price war. There is no point in reducing prices if all that results is a long-term drop in profits. There are often other options and factors to consider. If the customers' perception is that the retailer is already price-competitive, then there may be no need to discount further. If customers are using a particular store because of its convenience, cleanliness, service levels, width of range, image and so on, it can sometimes prove detrimental to enter a price war, as some of this image may be tarnished.

To conclude, there are both marketing and financial implications to consider before entering a price war. It is often the case that good retailing skills, allied to skilful promotions, often in conjunction with cooperative suppliers, can ameliorate and overcome the effects of a price war.

However, the business environment is always in transition. The shape of demand curves for products can change through time, and what may be correct today can be questionable tomorrow. There will be times when the retailer feels caught in a 'Catch 22' situation. Sometimes either holding prices steady and losing volume, or reducing them and sacrificing margin, end up in the same forecast shortfall in short-term profit. If this is the case, then the choice must be the course of action that will have the least detrimental effect on long-term profits.

Costs

Undeniably one of the main determinants of the pricing plan is costs. We have left it until now so that it did not overshadow the important other issues we have discussed in this section of the book.

The costs of buying in the products and putting them on sale provide the basis for most retailers' pricing decisions, i.e. a 'cost plus' method. The trouble with such an approach is that it concentrates on what it costs the company to be in business and make a required return on its investment in stock and stores, and makes little attempt to reconcile these costs with what its customers are prepared to pay for the products in question.

To remind ourselves of the relationship between different kinds of cost, Figure 9.1 depicts a simple form of breakeven analysis used in cost-orientated approaches. In this case the company is setting itself a profit target at a certain level of projected sales. Fixed costs are shown as a straight line and all other costs are allocated on a marginal cost basis to produce an ascending curve. At point A revenue covers only the retailer's fixed costs – for rent, rates, heat/light/power, minimum staffing levels, interest and depreciation on capital equipment (shop fixture/fittings and computer hardware), etc. At point B all costs,

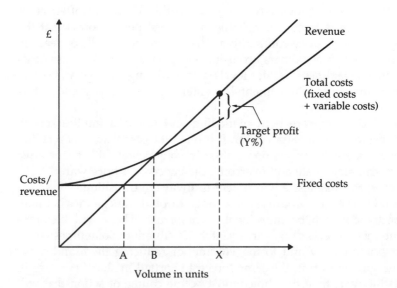

Figure 9.1

including the cost of the stock package, are covered and any additional sales will produce net profit. At point X, Y per cent target profit is being achieved. The assumption is that from point B onwards, any additional sales will incur marginal costs only, such as the cost price from the supplier, additional staff in the stockroom and store, extra shop fixtures, bags and wrapping materials, computer processing and so on. The potential problem with such an approach to pricing, is that it tends to assume that at a given price a given number of products will be sold, whereas in reality the quantity sold is bound to be dependant to a certain extent on the price charged.

Getting the price right is one of the most important tasks facing any retailer, with the possible exception of the CTN (confectionery/tobacco/newsagent) sector, whose prices are largely fixed and marked on the product by the supplier. One of the difficulties retailers face is that of reconciling the views of the accountancy side of the business with those of the marketers.

Many people know the story told on pricing courses of the conversation between the restaurateur who decides to put a peanut rack on the end of his counter and his accountancy expert. Essentially the plan was to sell peanuts for 10p a bag, the cost price being 6p. Unfortunately the accountant insisted that the restaurateur must allocate a proportion of his overheads to the peanut operation, including rent, rates, heat/light/power, salaries, window washing, depreciation, equipment, and so on. These allocated costs, plus a notional rent for the vacant amount of counter space, came to £1,563 a year which, on the basis of a sales level of 50 bags of peanuts a week, amounted to 60p per bag, so demonstrating quite conclusively that at a selling price of 10p per bag the restaurateur would be losing 50p on every bag!

That story is obviously extreme, but it serves to illustrate an important point, namely, that the two sides of the business must work together to try and develop an understanding of other thought processes and problems. It is not easy for accountants to understand the complex decisions that have to be made in an activity that is concerned essentially with human behaviour rather than with things that can be conveniently counted, but try they must. Conversely, marketers have only themselves to blame if they fail to understand the financial consequences of their decisions and the constraints of money on their decision-making.

Working effectively together, however, they can make a formidable team, and have a considerable impact on a retailer's profitability, particularly in the area of costs and their relation to pricing.

Although the peanut example is far-fetched, it does point to one area in which the financial side of the business can help the retailer, and that is by raising the level of awareness of the true costs of stocking various products. Prime retail space is expensive to occupy and run, and high interest rates push up stockholding costs. Therefore it is vital to ensure that every foot of floor space and every item of stock is earning an appropriate return. That is not achieved by applying a simple near-average percentage uplift to the supplier's cost price to cover the fixed costs of the business and a profit margin.

For instance, in a menswear store, a suit will take up twice as much space on a rail as a pair of trousers but may only sell at half the rate. Therefore the 'rent' cost allocated to a suit should be four times that of trousers, and the interest charge for stockholding should be double. Furthermore, since suits require a higher level of personal selling, they should carry a higher proportion of the selling staff costs. There will be similar differences in a department store between the true costs incurred by the furniture department and those in the high stock-turn, self-selection departments.

By supplying analyses of this type, the accountants are able to provide the traders in the product and marketing teams with a true picture of the direct product profitability of all the merchandise ranges stocked. Knowing what the real costs and net margins are across the product portfolio is a signal requirement for a retailer in preparing an effective pricing plan.

The next stage is for the marketers to examine the product portfolio. It may be that there are products producing a low rate of return when measured against the above criteria, but which are necessary to give the required width and credibility to the store's offering. In this case there needs to be a critical assessment of the customer benefits offered by those products and a decision made as to whether they would be able to carry a higher price. If that is not possible, then the other parts of the range need to be examined with the same intent. One assumes of course that, with the help of the accountants and the product team, everything possible has already been done to reduce the operating costs of the business, and to secure a better deal from the product suppliers.

If the products in question are not important to the credibility of the range, and if there is no identifiable route to improving their financial performance, then the next step is to plan their deletion from the portfolio and the introduction of replacement merchandise at a higher net margin. Nor should the process stop when the problem lines have been dealt with. The whole range of merchandise should be examined to ensure that we have taken every potential opportunity for margin enhancement through pricing action.

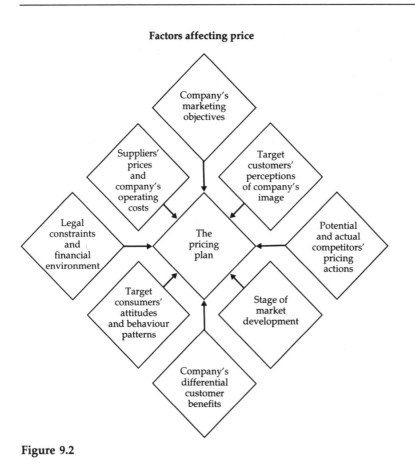

Factors affecting price

Figure 9.2

Conclusion

We must remember that the prices we charge for the products in our stores affect and are affected by the other elements of the marketing mix. Our pricing policy should be determined, and the pricing plan set, only after account has been taken of all the factors that impinge on the pricing decision. Figure 9.2 summarizes the major factors affecting price.

Getting the pricing plan right is not something to be left to chance. If we set our prices too low, we run the risk of either missing our net margin targets if the sales do not come through high enough, or sacrificing potential profit needlessly. Set them too high, and we lose credibility with our discerning customers who will judge us to be uncompetitive and take their custom elsewhere.

While we must pay due heed to our cost structures and monitor pricing by our competition very assiduously, the real key to where we can position our prices, after allowing for differences between different companies' products, depends on our customers' perceptions of the value for money that we offer. To apply the pricing theory discussed in this chapter, and maximize the profit potential of the company, we must do the necessary research to understand our customers' attitudes, consider more carefully what people are prepared to pay for our products, and rely far less on mechanical marking up from the suppliers' prices to us.

10

The place plan

Summary

This chapter looks at the importance of store-location planning and looks at reaching decisions in the first instance on the type of catchment area in which to trade, and thereafter in selecting the individual sites. It then proceeds to address the issues to be considered in designing both the exterior and interior of the store to achieve the desired image, together with some thoughts on controlling the costs of the process. The chapter concludes with a framework for evaluating customer benefits for those companies who seek to supply added customer service, some of which can have implications for their store design.

Introduction

As we have seen, the image built up by a retailer stems from how astutely the marketing mix (the four Ps) is managed. The product, promotion and price elements have already been analysed in some depth. This chapter focuses on the 'place' element.

With the increasing homogeneity of merchandise on the high street, and the speed at which major suppliers react in keeping up with product developments, small wonder that a number of retailers now consider that 'place' is the most crucial element in determining a store's success! They are referring not only to the actual location of the store, but, what is equally important – its image. Bear in mind that the store's image is not the retailer's view of it, it is the view held by the customers. They form their image by filtering and absorbing information that they pick up through the senses, both consciously and subconsciously. Thus, all the sights and sounds, the smell, the 'feel' and the 'taste' of the shopping experience combine in a powerful way, which can work to our advantage or against us.

Whether or not 'place' is actually the single most important factor might be an interesting debating point, but it wouldn't get us any closer to completing our marketing plan. What is patently clear, however, is that opening a store requires a substantial initial investment, and so, from a purely financial standpoint, 'place' plays a significant part in the success of our retailing business, and for this reason must be managed intelligently, with as little as possible left to chance.

This chapter falls into two main sections: factors to be considered in choosing the location of stores, and those issues involved in giving them the right image in the eyes of their target customers. Location decision factors, again, can be split into two sets. The first are to do with the choice of catchment area, i.e. the general geographic locations, the towns, cities or area of cities, in which we should operate, and the second concern the issues to be considered in choosing specific store sites in the selected catchment areas.

General location factors

The sort of customers we are targeting, the type of products we stock, and the scale of our operation, have a significant bearing on the size and location of catchment areas in which we will be able to function profitably. The major food retailers, the chain store groups, and the multiple shop operators, have developed a high degree of sophistication in location decision-making, based on a detailed examination of a wide range of market factors, allied to their own internal modelling techniques. The 'owner-driver' or small retailer does not often need to go to the same level of refinement, but nevertheless can benefit from following the same thought processes. The factors in question are interlocking and are as follows.

Size of population and catchment area of potential location

The population of the catchment area can be considered from a number of different viewpoints. Not all of these will be equally relevant to all retailers.

The first and most obvious requirement for the retailer is to ensure that there are sufficiently large numbers of potential customers in the catchment area of the proposed location. In the case of 'convenience' stores stocking such goods as food, newspapers and magazines, toiletries, confectionery and so on, the catchment area may be just the few streets in the immediate neighbourhood. On the other hand, a large food supermarket may draw customers from several miles around, and a big out-of-town shopping centre, such as Gateshead Metro in NE England, from a distance of over 30 miles away.

Calculating the catchment area for a retail location is no longer a simple matter of taking the population statistics for a town from the local authority, or drawing concentric circles on a map and estimating the number of people within them. Increasingly sophisticated techniques are being used to produce catchment-area maps based on the travelling *times* for customers from all directions rather than simply distance. Thus, a retail location close to a motorway junction will have a much larger geographical catchment area than one in a built-up urban area. The huge Meadowhall shopping centre on the M1 motorway at Sheffield attracts coachloads of shoppers from over 100 miles away, although it is fair to point out that 90 per cent of its customers live within a 20 minutes' drive.

Here are a number of other factors to be looked at when considering straight population figures.

Is the population in the catchment area forecast to grow or decline?

Many city centres have suffered declining populations as people have moved out to commuter towns, and in some places this is forecast to continue. Conversely, some others are making strenuous efforts to reverse this trend, with substantial revitalization programmes for their inner-city areas, and are succeeding in drawing people back to live in the centre again.

Are there seasonal variations?

Holiday areas might have greatly increased populations during the summer months, which shrink back to normal during winter. Areas with universities and colleges will show similar variations in and out of term.

Is there an influx of people during the week?

If the location is a centre for trade and industry, then its weekday population might be much larger than the published population of the area. An extreme example of this is the City of London, where the indigenous population is no more than 15,000 at the weekend, but rises to over 2 million during the working week. Any retail company thinking of opening there must base its business plan on 5-day trading only, as the vast majority cannot justify the cost of opening on Saturdays.

Much of this sort of information is readily available from local authorities and chambers of trade and commerce. Many areas also have regional and local development boards, which are a valuable source of data.

Characteristics of the population

It is not enough for a retail company simply to know the size of the population in a given area. It also needs to know the characteristics of the population and be able to match them up against the characteristics identified for its target customer groups, during the completion of its consumer audit. In this context the following may be relevant.

Age and socio-economic groupings

Knowing the age/SEG breakdown, income levels, and occupations of the population can throw considerable light on their possible life styles and disposable incomes. In the UK, companies such as CACI, Pin Point, Business Blueprints and Chartsearch, are using sophisticated techniques to map the social characteristics of the population in most urban areas. Taking this information, together with the data gathered through national surveys on consumer expenditure, you can derive reasonable estimates of the likely total expenditure on a group of products (food, clothing, electrical, etc.) in such an area.

The possession of such data can be invaluable to retailers in making their top-line decisions on store-siting. For instance, a retailer of young, trendy merchandise would tend to attach a lower priority to locating sites in retirement areas with predominantly older age profiles, sellers of luxury goods will tend to leave deprived inner city locations to discount chains, and retailers of products for babies and young families would be attracted to commuter/dormitory towns and suburbs where young marrieds live.

Ethnic, religious or special consumer groups

Significant ethnic or religious sub-groups in a catchment area may present either a threat or an opportunity to a retail concern thinking of locating there, depending on the type of products it proposes selling. In the same way the particular needs of students in university towns, and of tourists during the season, can present opportunities for certain types of retailer.

As we discussed earlier, the art is to site stores where they will attract the largest number of their target customers. The only exceptions to this 'golden rule' are when a retailer has such a strong image and/or such strong promotion that the customers are prepared to seek it out.

Economic conditions in the catchment area

Some of the issues worth considering under this heading are the following.

Local employment trends
A location dependent on a handful of larger employers can be vulnerable to large-scale unemployment as the economics of different industries change through time. The local chamber of commerce might be a useful source to tap for forecasts on future trends.

Local authority attitudes
Does the local authority work actively with the business community to promote the commercial potential of the area? Some authorities, by their bureaucratic fumbling and short-sightedness, drive away many retailers. The more enlightened set out to help create a retailing environment that acts as a magnet for the surrounding area and brings in extra spending power.

Potential major retail property developments
It is sensible to investigate whether there are any planning applications pending for large-scale redevelopment of current retail space, or for out-of-town developments. If these get the go-ahead, they can have a substantial effect on the existing retail scene. For instance, it is variously estimated that the initial impact of the opening of the Gateshead Metro Centre was to reduce retail turnover in the centre of nearby Newcastle by between 20 and 30 per cent.

Equally, in every town and city centre there is a street, or even stretch of a street, which is recognized as being the best pitch in town. That status can change very quickly if a new covered mall is built even as close as 200 metres away. This was a lesson learnt the hard way by the clothing multiples.

The founders of the Burton, John Collier and Hepworth chains had very astutely built up portfolios of the best, high traffic, corner sites for their tailoring shops. However, the burgeoning of urban shopping centre developments in the 1970s and 1980s meant that, in town after town, they saw the centre of gravity for retailing shift away from them. They were left with the choice of resiting in the new centres and paying high rents, or staying where they were and seeing their relative turnover decline.

Local traffic conditions
What is the public transport infrastructure? With ever-increasing private car usage, is the area sympathetic to the needs of the shopping motorist? Are there any plans for major road schemes that will either enhance or damage the acceptability of the area for the prospective retailer? Are there local restrictions on goods traffic that might make supplying the store difficult?

Local rent and rates
These can vary considerably from area to area, even for locations which, on most of the other criteria, offer similar advantages.

Competition

The presence of competition has its advantages and its drawbacks, depending on the size of the catchment area, the type of product the retailer sells, the size of the retailer, and the number and nature of the competitors.

Large towns and cities usually have a wide spread of competing retailers. While Marks & Spencer's, John Lewis's, Debenhams, etc. have a strong presence in these locations, their individual percentage of the local turnover is relatively low. The advantage for the potential new entrant is that there is less likely to be any retaliatory action to a new opening. The other main advantage is that these locations have an established traffic flow, and there is a good chance of attracting passing shoppers. On the downside, because of the presence of the big players, rents are likely to be higher.

Conversely, in a small town, already catered for by a food supermarket and a number of convenience stores, one would have to be very convinced of one's competitive advantages before opening up in competition.

Certain companies, because of the uniqueness of their offering, in terms of products, price, or service, or a combination of all of them, have become 'destination' stores. In the UK Harrods and Hamleys in London are notable examples, as are Toys R Us and IKEA. Marks & Spencer's exemplifies this on the high street, along with the large food supermarkets and certain department stores. They are the types of operators who can, singlehanded, alter the centre of gravity of retail location. As a result, developers look for such tenants to 'anchor' new precincts and shopping malls. This in turn brings in the national chains, and sets up a high-rent, strongly competitive environment, but, as before, one with a high traffic flow.

However, size is not everything. Unique product ranges can enable retailers to break into the most established shopping locations with a considerable degree of success, and become destination stores in their own right – witness the rise of Body Shop.

The type of product carried has an influence on the attitude to competition. Women shopping for clothing and footwear usually have a repertoire of stores that they will visit before making their final decisions, even if they have a favourite. This is particularly true of the vast medium-priced market and the young fashion customers. For stores stocking these and other products for which there is a high degree of comparison shopping, being close to the competition can be a positive advantage.

It is worth making a final point in this section on general location factors. The major retailers will carry out a thorough analysis of all the significant retail catchment areas on a regular basis, and will constantly update their prioritized list of desired sites according to changes in local conditions. They use national networks of commercial estate agents, specialist market analysis consultancies, and their own in-house property specialists, and also draw on the immense fund of local knowledge possessed by their existing regional and local retail management teams. At the same time they continually review their existing property portfolio to decide whether to invest further through modernizations, extensions, or resiting within the general location. Because the decision-takers cannot have detailed personal knowledge of all locations, they rely on the objective assessment of assembled facts.

There is a message in here for the 'owner-driver' and small operator. Often, and quite understandably, there is a predilection on their part to want to set up in their home town or its immediate environs. Sometimes, in the course of this, they unwittingly, or deliberately, turn a blind eye to some of the facts we have discussed, with an adverse effect on their potential profits. Even if there is no intention of moving home, it is still worth while carrying out one's own analysis of all the potential locations within comfortable and practical travelling distance.

Specific location factors

Having decided on the general location for a store or shop, we now turn to a number of considerations in choosing the individual site.

Type of shopping area

First, we need to be clear on which type(s) of shopping area will best suit the business. Again, much will depend on what type of retailer we are, the type of product and the scale of our business. Here are some of the main types.

Central shopping districts
The prime retailing areas in most cities and large towns are the central shopping districts, which are a mixture of the traditional main high streets and the covered shopping precincts, developed in the last few

decades – modern descendants of Georgian and Victorian shopping arcades. They contain a variety of retail outlets, including department stores, chain and multiple stores, and independent specialists. Served well by public transport, they act as a magnet and attract customers from a wide area. In spite of the inevitably high rents in these locations, the customer flow means that many convenience outlets can live comfortably alongside the major players. This helps to develop a synergistic mix of retailing activities to everyone's mutual advantage.

Secondary high streets and neighbourhood shopping areas

These vary in size. At the larger end are the less busy secondary locations in cities and large towns, which may have a number of national multiple shop operators but will be too small to attract the chain and department stores. Then we go on down the scale until the national multiples no longer find the size of the local market a worthwhile proposition, and the high street is made up of local independent retailers. At the bottom end of the size scale are the neighbourhood shopping parades dedicated to serving the local community, and comprising mostly convenience goods outlets, with an occasional specialist shop thrown in for good measure.

Shopping centres

As distinct from the shopping precincts that arose from the redevelopment of the jumble of shopping streets in the old city centres, the shopping centres we refer to here are the large developments that have arisen away from the middle of the town, and which have been built with the motorist very much in mind. One of the earliest and best known in the UK is the Brent Cross development in North London, but this has been totally eclipsed in size by the huge Gateshead Metro, Sheffield Meadowhall, and Thurrock Lakeside Centres of the late 1980s/early 1990s.

Like the central shopping districts, they contain a mixture of most of the major national retailers, together with a leavening of local specialists. The difference is that the shopping centre has them all under the one roof. With their extensive food courts and, in some cases, entertainment facilities, they are very much 'destination' locations, where families will often spend most of the day.

Because of this, a significant amount of promotional effort is made by the shopping centre landlords to ensure traffic flow to the centre as a whole. This expenditure is usually charged back, in part or entirely, to the tenants on a pro rata basis to their store sizes, via their service charges.

Another version of large-scale retailing in out-of-town locations can come about through cooperation between large companies such as

Marks & Spencer and Tesco, which have opened a large joint development north of London at Brookfield Farm.

However, there is increasing opposition to all these types of development from local community and environmental groups, whose concerns are, firstly, the detrimental effect on the existing high-street shopping areas, which decreases local authority receipts from rates, and, secondly, the effect on the dwindling Green Belt surrounding our towns and cities. Future planning permission is going to be much more difficult to obtain.

Retail parks

Another form of out-of-town development to reach the UK in the 1980s was retail parks, which are groupings or large warehouse-like stores with copious car parking facilities. These stores are generally on one floor only, very simply fitted out, and are occupied for the most part by retailers of lower priced, space-hungry items, for whom the rent levels of the central shopping districts and the covered shopping centres would be prohibitive. The sort of goods most frequently found in the early retail parks were DIY, carpets, furniture, kitchen equipment and so on. These were then followed by a number of discount operations selling clothing and footwear.

The specific site

Having chosen the catchment area and type of shopping area in which we wish to operate, we must next choose the individual site.

There is an increasing preference on the part of consumers for enclosed shopping precincts, either in or out of town. Careful financial planning is needed, as it may be well worthwhile paying the extra rent and service charges to benefit from the higher customer flow.

We must think carefully about the size of store required for a particular location. Some firms have a modular concept, and will look for every store to be, as near as possible, identical in size. This is because they have a standard product range, which they retail to a pattern, and they cater for expansion by looking for additional sites. Others, with a more diverse product range, will open smaller stores in minor markets, stocked with a core range, and add extra merchandise options for their bigger stores in the larger markets.

Retail space is generally too expensive for any of it to be underutilized. Therefore, before we commit to a store of a given size, we must be very sure that we have a product range that is going to fill it, if not from day 1, then certainly in the very near future. Conversely, it is a bad use of money to have to move to a larger site too early in a company's development because inadequate marketing planning has not forecast the space requirements of future product ranges.

If a high-street siting is preferred, we must consider a number of factors. The first is adjacencies, i.e. where are the competing stores positioned and where are the magnet stores that will attract the highest foot traffic. The GOAD organization, subscribed to by all the national retailers, produces schematic maps of all the most important high streets and shopping precincts, showing the occupants and approximate sizes of every site in these locations. From these, it is possible to assess the relative attractiveness of different sides of the road, and of different stretches of what may be, at first sight, all 100 per cent prime pitches. For a specialist retailer, a site between, say, Marks & Spencer's and John Lewis would be a virtual guarantee of customer flow, but one on the opposite side of the street would be considerably less attractive.

We should also consider the size and setting of car parks, and the proximity of bus and rail stations. This information, which is also shown on the GOAD plans, enables the central planners in the major companies to carry out a reasonable amount of desk-top assessment. However, there is no substitute for local knowledge and observation, and this is where the indigenous operator can score. It is important to watch what the traffic flow is like throughout the week, not just on the busiest trading days, and the effect of local market days, etc. Nothing could be more frustrating than having one's shopfront obscured by a market stall on the best trading day of the week, even if King Henry VIII agreed to it in a Royal Charter!

Check with the local authority on its traffic plans. Sympathetic pedestrianization schemes can add considerably to customer flow and shopping comfort. On the other hand, new one-way traffic systems, additional roadside barriers, the resiting of pedestrian crossings and so on, can very quickly lower the prime rating of a site.

If the space requirement for the store is small, then it is worth making enquiries as to the future of the very large older department store sites in the area. They often occupy the best positions, and were built when space costs were less crucial; there is a tendency now for their owners to subdivide them into smaller units, or to lease space within them on a concession basis. This latter route is a way in which a number of companies have built themselves a sizeable retail business without having any independent sites of their own.

If you choose to set up in a multi-floor shopping precinct or mall, then research the traffic-flow patterns of the different floors. It is often the case that the customer flow at ground level is a third greater than that on the first floor, and over double the flow to the second floor or on a basement level. Discrepancies of this size can obviously have a considerable bearing on earning potential. In addition, check out the anticipated opening patterns for the centre going forward, as these could affect the sales and staff cost projections in any viability study.

Store image and design

Having taken pains to pick the optimum site for our store in the chosen catchment area, we must then put the same care and attention into the planning of the store's appearance and the image it will give to our target customers. This image must be consistent with the company's marketing objectives. It must be quite distinctive and distinguish the company from its competitors. Features such as the shopfront, the window and internal displays, and the internal layout all contribute to the customer's perception of the retailer.

Store design and planning require a degree of technical expertise and creativity that the average retailers do not always possess. Often they retain specialist designers and architects to develop the property in a way consistent with their objectives.

It is not the purpose of this book to give a definitive treatise on store design, since the requirements of different types of retailing vary so widely. But we shall point out some common areas that should be considered by any retailer, irrespective of size or product type.

Working with designers

The relation will be much smoother if, right from the outset, the retailer has prepared and discussed with the designer a full and explicit brief. This should contain the following:

- Target customer profile, including ages, sex, SEGs, life styles, and all available market research information on their spending patterns and requirements for the types of products to be stocked.
- Fashion attitude profiles, if appropriate.
- Planned product mix for store, and required stock density for shopfloor, plus any specific stock presentation needs.
- Proposed departmental adjacencies, i.e. what goes next to what.
- Window and internal display policies.
- Stockroom/back office/staffroom requirements.
- Requirements for cash and wrap points/checkouts, together with wiring needs for EPOS, EFTPOS, credit authorization telephones, and security equipment.

- Any other specific needs such as fitting rooms, customer service desks, seating areas, etc.
- The length of time the shopfit is required to last before a remodernization.
- A target price per square foot/metre that the retailer is prepared to pay consistent with the company's business plan.

This last point is extremely important. Designers are very happy to spend as much of a retailer's money as they are allowed to. One of the besetting sins of many retailers in the heady days of the mid/late 1980s was to give their designers too much scope on the costs incurred in shopfitting. The result was high depreciation charges coming through at a time when sales increases slowed dramatically, and was a contributory factor in the high number of retail casualties in the recession of the early 1990s.

Most good design companies are well used to the exigencies of working to a specific budget. What it does is to challenge their creativity on a different plane. If the retailer understands this, and is prepared to work closely with the design team, keeping an open mind on new ideas, on the one hand, and a tight hand on the purse strings, on the other, then the company will go a long way towards achieving the desired result.

The exterior of the store

The external appearance of a store often has to be a compromise between what the company would like and what it is allowed to do. Shopping centre landlords and, to an increasing extent, local authorities are becoming more stringent in the aesthetic protection of their domains.

In older high-street locations there may be the requirement to retain a façade that is subject to a preservation order, or to use specified materials to ensure a blend with surrounding premises. One of the most common restrictions is in the size and design of external signs, especially the projecting type. Occasionally this can work to a retailer's advantage, as in the apocryphal tale of the retailer who, finding his store sandwiched between a Marks & Spencer's and a large Sainsburys, changed the name over his door to 'Entrance', and did a roaring trade!

Irrespective of any restrictions, the external design is one to be considered carefully, as it is the first point of communication with customers. It needs to be distinctive and readily recognizable from a distance. Therefore the materials used, the external lighting, the signage, the size and shape of the windows, and the style and positioning of the door(s), should be in harmony and project the desired image of the store to those target customers.

Window and interior displays

As we discussed earlier, a large number of actual and potential customers pass most high-street stores each day, and the windows are a prime means of speaking to them. Discounters and food retailers tend to use a lot of the glass for promotional posters; fashion clothing and footwear retailers to promote the latest looks; while, at the top end of the spectrum, the luxury goods specialists often go for minimalist window displays that are pure image-builders rather than specific product promoters, confident that their type of customer will come in anyway.

Thought needs to be given to the style of windows that will appeal to our target customers. Should the glass come right to the ground? Should the windows have flat beds or be raised? What sort of equipment and lighting should be used to show our products to best advantage? Very importantly, should our windows have backs on them, or do we want our customers to be able to see right into the store?

Internal displays have a number of potential uses. Furniture, kitchen, and bathroom specialists use them to show what their products could look like *in situ*, as do curtain fabric stores. Fashion retailers use them to suggest 'wardrobe' ideas, to try and engender multiple sales of outfits rather than individual items. Many stores use internal displays at a high level to signpost departments at the back of the store, or close to staircases/escalators to advertise departments on other floors.

Whatever type of window and interior displays are chosen as being most appropriate to appeal to the target customers, care must be taken in the design to ensure that they are economical to maintain and update. Display dressing is a specialist skill, not possessed by the majority of regular shop staff, and is usually provided by full-time display teams in larger operations, or is bought in on a part-time basis by smaller companies. Large displays, using expensive props and materials and complicated to change, can run up substantial costs. Equally, care should be taken in the specification and design of window-lighting systems to ensure that light bulbs can be changed easily by the shop staff, without disturbing the displays or having the expense of calling in an electrician.

The interior of the store

A skilfully designed interior that appeals to customers can have a very positive effect on sales. A colour scheme that they feel comfortable with and is sympathetic to the products, a fixturing system that shows the goods to best advantage without dominating them, a lighting system that shows the merchandise to good effect without being overpowering, and a layout that allows easy access to all parts of the store in a relaxed manner, all contribute to creating a favourable impression. The pulling together of all these elements, and the creation of the right subtlety of interplay between them is the hallmark of a good interior design.

Another feature of good design is the retention of a degree of flexibility for the retailer in the future. Retailing is never static. It changes constantly, sometimes very rapidly. To prosper, the individual retailer must be able to change with it. Therefore it is advisable to keep the fixed architectural elements of the design to a minimum, and to take great care in their planning. In this context the siting and direction of staircases and escalators need to be thought through very carefully, as any mistakes will be hugely expensive to rectify later.

However, it is possible at the design stage to build flexibility into lighting and wiring systems that will avoid major costs as floor layouts are altered, and cash and wrap points moved, etc. Similarly, multi-purpose or free-standing fixturing systems on the walls avoid the need to call in the builders for a product move. Thought should also be given to floor treatments. Different coloured carpets to delineate departments can be very attractive at a store opening, but become a costly nightmare for the retailer 6 months later when the sales-mix changes and departments have to be moved or altered in size.

This flexibility is needed because the key objective of layout planning is to make the most productive use of space. This is normally achieved by apportioning it according to the profitability of various departments or product groups. In most cases the departments or products that produce the highest profit margins are given the best locations in the store.

The most valuable space in a store is near the entrances on the main floor. The products in these areas have the highest level of exposure. They can be seen through the doors and windows by people passing by, and they are seen by customers in effect twice, as they enter and leave the store. Conversely, the least valuable space is on the topmost floor at the greatest distance from the stairs or escalators, or, in a single floor store, the part furthest from the door. Department store operators will often site their coffee shops or restaurants on the top floor for two reasons. Firstly, they generally show a lower return on the space used, but, secondly, because they are destination departments, customers will be exposed to many other products as they make their way there.

As a rule of thumb, convenience, impulse, and other inexpensive items that sell quickly are placed in the high customer traffic areas. More expensive goods, which are purchased less frequently, are placed on the upper floors or in the less prominent parts of the store. Exceptions to this rule of thumb were explored in Chapter 5 in the context of portfolio management.

Layout guidelines

There are some general guidelines to apply when planning a store layout:

1 Aisles need to be wide enough to allow customer traffic to flow without undue crowding. In addition, aisles should enable customers to move from one part of the store to another, and allow for the movement of products into the sales areas for restocking.
2 The layout should give unobstructed views of the selling areas. Not only does this encourage customers to look at the products, it also helps store security by making it easier to keep customers under surveillance.
3 It is beneficial to group related products together in order to encourage purchases of related items.
4 The layout should try to provide a familiar arrangement of departments or products. This enables customers to locate what they are looking for quickly and ensure that each visit to a new store is not a confusing experience. In order to provide a familiar layout, it often becomes a store policy for all its branches to follow set patterns. Equally, it can be based on the layouts of competitors.
5 The layout must enable people to move quickly through or past the areas in which they have no interest.

In general, layout follows one of three patterns, as follows.

Grid pattern
Here traffic is routed in the straight, rectangular pattern favoured by many supermarkets and variety stores. This configuration uses space efficiently, simplifies shopping and is ideal for self-service. On the other hand, it does promote a formal and businesslike atmosphere that does not encourage browsing. Such a layout pattern is unlikely to be suitable for speciality goods, or for those customers who want to make a leisurely choice before purchasing.

Free-flow pattern
Here the objective is to provide a relaxed atmosphere. Products are arranged so that the shopper can have room to browse. This environment can stimulate purchases of an impulse and unplanned nature. The disadvantages of this layout pattern are that space is not used in the most productive way, and although customers stay longer, there are more problems with stock control and shoplifting. Nevertheless this pattern is often desirable in department or speciality stores.

Boutique pattern

This layout provides small speciality 'shops', within the selling floor. For example, there might be a 'knobs, handles and fittings corner'. This pattern combines a free-flow layout and uses it to connect up a range of 'little shops'. Such an arrangement makes it very easy for a customer with a particular interest to see the complete offering in one small area, perhaps with a salesperson who is a specialist in these products in attendance.

Other store services

In an attempt to provide better customer service and perhaps differentiate themselves from competitors, retailers are continually experimenting with issues associated with 'place', which can contribute to their image-building.

Gift-wrapping services, refunds and exchanges, extended store hours, demonstrations, deliveries and so on are all designed to give the customer 'that little bit extra', which may spell success for the company. However, everything has a cost, and so we have to calculate these added benefits in order to check that we are not throwing away potential profit rather than increasing sales.

Figure 10.1 illustrates how additional customer services might be compared and evaluated. The key to interpreting it is as follows:

Services in Quadrant A – Introduce as quickly as possible.
Services in Quadrant B – Proceed with caution, gather data and proceed on the basis of facts.

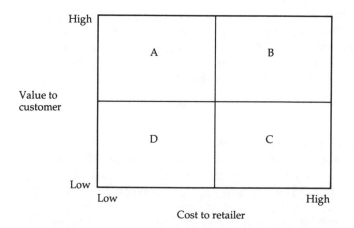

Figure 10.1

Services in Quadrant C –   Drop them as soon as possible.
Services in Quadrant D –   Not really worth bothering with, but no harm
                             is done.

Again the message is loud and clear. The retailer who best understands who the customers are and what they are seeking is in the strongest position to put together the most attractive offer.

Conclusion

From what we have discussed in this chapter, it is possible to see that those who argue for 'Place' being the most important of the four Ps, have a number of strong debating points on their side. There is little doubt that inadequate thought processes and planning on this subject can cost a retailer substantial profit, or even put the company out of business.

Choosing the wrong catchment area in which to trade is a recipe for disaster from the outset, no matter how well the store is designed, as the sales will never come through at the required levels. However, a store in a good location but one that has been poorly designed will never realize its true profit potential, because it has not created the image and appeal sought by its potential customers. If expensively designed, it will also carry a burden of high depreciation and operating costs.

Small wonder therefore that the big retail groups invest substantial time and effort on 'Place', and use the best advice they can find from both inside and outside the company. For the smaller firm with a limited budget for outside help, there is still a considerable amount that can be done from its own resources, using its invaluable local knowledge, to avoid many of the pitfalls we have discussed.

11

Marketing information, forecasting and organizing for marketing planning

Summary

The first part of Chapter 11 deals with the difference between market research and marketing research, how much to spend on marketing research, what the different forms of marketing research are, marketing intelligence systems, and how to organize them. Next, forecasting techniques are briefly covered. Finally, different organizational structures for marketing planning are outlined and discussed, and there is a discussion about the cultural implications of marketing planning.

Introduction

In the next chapter we look at one of the most difficult aspects of marketing planning – actually making it all work by means of a system within the company. This is something that most courses and books somehow seem to overlook. Yet no work on marketing planning can be complete without a fairly detailed consideration or how all the structures and frameworks presented in earlier chapters are to be implemented.

The truth is of course that the actual process of marketing planning is simple in outline. Any book will tell us that it consists of a situation review, assumptions, objectives, strategies, programmes, and measurement and review. What other books do not tell us is that there are a number of contextual issues that have to be considered, and that they make marketing planning one of the most baffling of all marketing problems.

Here are some of those issues:

- When should it be done, how often, by whom, and how?
- Is it different in a large and a small company?
- Is it different in a diversified and an undiversified company?
- Is it different in an international and a domestic company?
- What is the role of the chief executive?
- What is the role of the planning department?
- Should marketing planning be top down or bottom up?
- What is the relation between operational (1-year) and strategic (longer term) planning?

Until issues such as these are understood, the other chapters in this book will remain little more than interesting aspects of marketing planning. So the purpose of the final chapter is to help us to pick up all the pieces of the jigsaw puzzle and put them together to form a picture we can all see and understand.

First, however, we need to set the scene, and in particular to fill in a few gaps concerning marketing information and the organizational side of marketing. Our research has shown very clearly that it is important to recognize at the outset what the realistic constraints on the implementation of a marketing planning system are likely to be. Two such major constraints are marketing information and a company's organizational form, which are considered in this chapter. We shall then go on in the next chapter to demonstrate how marketing planning can be made to work by means of a system, and will include in this a discussion of the role of the chief executive, and the planning department. In Chapter 13 we provide an actual marketing planning system that will enable you to operationalize the concepts, structures and frameworks described in this book. Finally, there will be a glossary of marketing planning terms.

This chapter, then, is in two parts:

1. Marketing information and forecasting
2. Marketing organization.

In the final chapter we consider marketing planning systems design and implementation.

Marketing information and forecasting for marketing planning

It will by now be obvious that without information it is going to be difficult to do many of the things we have been discussing so far. Any plan can only be as good as the information on which it is based, which is why we have been making sure that we know the right questions to ask, such as, 'Who are our customers?', 'What is our market share?' and so on. Throughout this book we have been stressing that the profitable development of a company can only come from a continuous attempt to match the company's capabilities with customer needs. In order that the company can be sure that this matching process is taking place effectively, it is necessary that some type of information flow be instituted between the customer and the firm. This is the role of marketing research.

Difference between market research and marketing research

Put very simply, market research is concerned specifically with research about markets, whereas marketing research is concerned with research into marketing processes. We are concerned here with marketing research, which has been defined by the American Marketing Association as the systematic gathering, recording and analysis of data about problems relating to the marketing of goods and services.

The words in this definition are important. The process has to be systematic because it is necessary to have a structured interaction between people, facilities and procedures designed to generate an orderly flow of pertinent information collected from sources both inside and outside the company, for use as the basis for decision-making in specified responsibility areas of marketing management.

It will be apparent immediately that data by themselves (such as words, figures, pictures, sounds, and so on) are of little use until they are combined with direction and hence become information. But without some purpose in mind, some marketing problem to solve, information is not much use either. Indeed research has shown that one of the biggest problems facing management today is a surplus of data and information, rather than too little. This brings us to our definition of intelligence, which is information consumable and usable by management in converting uncertainty into risk.

Uncertainty of course is when any outcome is considered to be equally possible. When a probability can be assigned to certain outcomes, however, we are talking about risk, which is just quantified uncertainty. Clearly our ability to make successful decisions is enhanced if we are operating under conditions of known risk rather than uncertainty.

Conversion of uncertainty into risk and the minimization of risk are perhaps marketing management's most important tasks. In this process the role of marketing research is of paramount importance.

How much to spend on marketing research

Before looking at the different kinds of research available to the marketing manager, a book written about marketing planning should surely address the issue of the marketing research budget.

Marketing information has to be produced, stored and distributed, but it has a limited life – it is perishable. Like other resources, information has a value in use: the less the manager knows about a marketing problem and the greater the risk attached to a wrong decision, the more valuable the information becomes. This implies the need for a cost/ benefit appraisal of all sources of marketing information, since there is little point in investing more in such information than the return on it would justify. But while costs are easy to identify, the benefits are more difficult to pin down. They can best be expressed in terms of the additional profits that might be achieved through identifying marketing opportunities and through the avoidance of marketing failures that could result without the use of information.

It must be stressed, however, that the decision about how much to spend on marketing information is not an easy one. On the one hand, it would, generally speaking, be foolhardy to proceed without any information at all, while, on the other hand, the cost of perfect information would be prohibitive. One way of estimating how much to spend is based on the theory of probability and expected value. For example, if by launching a retail concept you had to incur development costs of £1 million and you believed there was a 10 per cent chance that the concern would fail, the maximum loss expectation would be £100,000, i.e. £1 million x 0.1.

Obviously, then, it is worth spending up to £100,000 to acquire information that would help prevent such a loss. However, because perfect information is seldom available, it makes sense to budget a small sum for marketing research that effectively discounts the likely inaccuracy of the information. Such an approach can be a valuable means of quantifying the value of marketing research in a managerial context.

Forms of marketing research

Increasing sophistication in the use of the techniques available to the researcher, particularly in the handling and analysis of multivariable data, has made marketing research into a specialized function within the field of marketing management. Nevertheless, any company, irrespective of whether or not it has a marketing department, should be aware of some of the tools that are available and where these may be used.

Marketing research can be classified either as external or internal. The former research activity is conducted within the competitive environment outside the firm, whereas much valuable intelligence can be gained from internal marketing analysis in the form of sales trends, changes in the marketing mix such as price, advertising levels, and so on. External marketing information gathering should always be seen as a complement to such internal information.

Apart from this, there is another basic split: between reactive and non-reactive marketing research. Non-reactive methods are based upon the interpretation of observed phenomena or extant data, whereas reactive research calls for some form of proactive assessment in the market place.

The most widely used method of reactive marketing research comprises the asking of questions by means of a questionnaire survey, which is indeed a ubiquitous and highly flexible instrument. It can be administered by an interviewer, by telephone, or it can be sent by mail, and so on.

All these different methods have their advantages and disadvantages, and all have different cost consequences. For example, the greatest degree of control over the quality of the responses is obtained by getting a researcher to administer each questionnaire personally, but this is very expensive and time-consuming. Telephone interviews are quick and relatively inexpensive, but there is a severe limit to the amount of technical information that can be obtained by these means. The post questionnaire is a much-favoured method, but here great care is necessary to avoid sample bias. For example, is there something special (and possibly therefore unrepresentative of the population) about those who reply to a postal questionnaire?

But without doubt the biggest potential pitfalls with the questionnaire lie in its design. Everyone knows about the 'loaded' question or the dangers of ambiguity, yet these are not always easily detectable. Indeed even the order in which questions are asked can distort the answers. Such pitfalls can be reduced by pilot testing it – in other words, by giving it a trial run on a sub-group of the intended sample to isolate any problems that can arise.

Sometimes it may be more appropriate to gather information not by large surveys but by smaller-scale, more detailed studies intended to provide qualitative insights rather than quantitative conclusions. Depth interviews can provide such insights. These are loosely structured discussions with a group broadly representing the population in which the researcher is interested, in which a group leader attempts to draw from the group their feelings about the subject under discussion. Such in-depth interviews can also take place with individuals, a method that is particularly popular when information is required about narrow market segments.

Experimentation is another type of reactive marketing research that can provide a valuable source of information about the likely market performance of new products or about the likely effects of variations in the marketing mix. Thus, different product formulations, different levels of promotional effort, and so on, can be tested in the market place to gauge their different effects.

Sometimes market experimentation can take place in laboratory conditions, particularly in the case of advertising. Samples of the target audience will be exposed to the advertisement and their reactions obtained. Eye cameras, polygraphs and tachistoscopes are just some of the devices that can be used to record physical reactions to marketing stimuli.

In contrast with such methods are those that are classified as non-reactive, in that they do not rely on data derived directly from the respondent. One of the best known among these is consumer panels, widely used by consumer companies.

The consumer panel is simply a sample group of consumers who record in a diary their purchases and consumption over a period of time. This technique has been used in industrial as well as consumer markets and can provide continuous data on usage patterns as well as much other useful data.

Finally, in many respects the most important of all marketing research methods is the use of existing materials, particularly by means of desk research, which should always be the starting point of any marketing research programme. There is often a wealth of information to be obtained from published information, such as government statistics, OECD, EEC, the United Nations, newspapers, technical journals, trade association publications, published market surveys, and so on. Two or three days spent on desk research nearly always provide pleasant surprises for the company that believes it lacks information about its markets. When combined with internal sales information, this can be the most powerful research method open to a company.

Marketing intelligence systems

Given the importance of information to marketing decision-making, it is clear that time spent on the proper organization of information flows will be a sound investment. Such organization is often referred to as the marketing intelligence system (MIS). Much research has been carried out in this area to show that it is one of the most badly organized areas of management, in spite of the advent of the computer. This poor organization has been shown to be largely due to the failure of management to identify the decisions that have to be taken and the information essential to making these decisions.

Clearly the definition of management information needs is central to the successful construction of an MIS, but it is this vital step that is rarely completed properly, mostly because executives fail to isolate the key determinants of success. For example, they misunderstand the meaning and significance of market share, or they overestimate or underestimate the importance of service levels, and so on. The result is inevitably the kind of 'snow job' that is so evident in many companies, in which data and information are produced on a regular basis in such volumes that it becomes virtually impossible for the recipients to isolate what is or is not important. Consequently the output of such a system is rarely used and management continues to operate largely on the basis of intuition and hunch. The model shown in Figure 11.1 is a helpful guide to the construction of an MIS.

Four steps are essential for the successful construction of an MIS. Firstly, make a detailed list of all current data and information that are produced. Secondly, get each manager to list the decisions he has to make, together with the information essential to the making of these decisions. Thirdly, combine these two in the most logical manner, since there will be many redundancies in information requirements. Taking as an example internally generated sales data, it should be possible to make

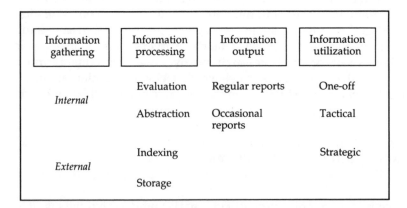

Figure 11.1

a list of all possible combinations of the following: product lines, product group summaries, geographical areas, time scale, comparatives, purchasing patterns, etc.

All of these can be combined, in code form, on a matrix. Now comes the most difficult part of all. Look at every one of the many combinations, write down the purpose for which each of the reports is required. For example, the purpose of a regularly produced product line report would be to provide definitive performance information in simple product lines within defined geographical areas. Thus, the objectives of a weekly/monthly report listing product lines' sales by category might be:

1 To identify the proportionate spread and penetration of individual product lines by category. This is important if the company is seeking to establish products in specific market sectors as a means of market segmentation.
2 To assess increases in sales of new products, in total and by store.
3 To assess loss of sales in stores.
4 To facilitate customer and store targeting.
5 To facilitate evaluation of promotional activity in stores.
6 To facilitate comparison of actual sales to potential, and so on.

Fourthly, there is the difficult task of organizing the system. Having worked out the 'ideal' MIS, you must now evaluate its cost, for clearly while it is tempting to think in terms of building a totally integrated MIS from first principles, experience suggests that it is better to think 'total' but to plan 'piecemeal'.

A building block approach, each block representing a sub-system for meeting a discrete information need, will eventually enable a totally integrated and sophisticated system to be developed in accordance with the needs and experience of the users. However, while the benefits of collecting and storing integrated data are obvious, the problem is that maintaining disaggregated files is expensive, and management must balance this extra cost against the possibility that future market developments may require system modifications that cannot be made because data has been aggregated.

Organizational aspects of MIS

Because the MIS is part of a companywide information system, it could be argued that it should be located within a central corporate information office, so that the integration that is so desirable within the marketing function also takes place on a companywide basis. However, the main issue is not so much where in an organization the information function should be located, as how best, given the constraints of the existing marketing organizational set-up (which will be a function of needs largely dictated by the market place), to facilitate both vertical and horizontal information flows both into and out of the information unit. Thus, while either a central company intelligence unit or one based in a marketing department would suffice, the problem is that of institutionalizing procedures, through systems, to facilitate information flows, and training management in their use. The inputs would come in from all levels of management through systemized procedures, as either items of information or requests for information. The information unit would sift and check the information, analyse it, decide where within the organization it might be useful, and transmit the information to potential users or store it for future use.

Thus, the MIS may be managed by a group within the marketing department, or as part of a companywide system.

Forecasting

Forecasting is one of the most emotive subjects in the whole field of management. Most managers reckon to be experts, or at least are rarely backward in expressing an opinion about the subject, and the marketing man is constantly on the rack, because the one task he inevitably gets wrong is the forecast. While in a book of this kind it is not possible to go into any detail, it would be wrong not to attempt to put this subject into a better perspective than it is currently.

Why is forecasting so difficult?

The size and complexity of the marketing task in all kinds of enterprise has substantially increased in recent years. The growing diversity of customer needs in a rapidly changing environment has resulted in shorter product life cycles, which have therefore become more difficult to manage profitably. Distribution patterns have changed dramatically in most markets, and competitive pressures have intensified with the geographical dispersion of operations and the growing internationalization of the scale of businesses, the management of which has become more competent as a result of the growing professionalism of management educators. The socio-cultural, legal, political environments in which managers have to operate have become more volatile and subject to more rapid change. The volume of data and information available has mushroomed, and processing networks have become more sophisticated, while the availability of quantitative techniques to the management of the marketing function has outpaced the ability to use them effectively. Added to this is the ever-present difficulty of measuring the behavioural aspects, such as the social, cultural and psychological, of marketing.

The result of all this is that it is becoming increasingly more difficult to find and develop profitable markets, and with this comes the difficulty of forecasting with anything like the accuracy that was possible when markets were more stable. Nevertheless it has to be done and it has to be done well, because the consequences of being wrong can be very severe indeed for a company.

While not wanting to go into a detailed description of the many forecasting techniques available to a company, it could be useful to discuss briefly the major boundaries of forecasting as outlined in Figure 11.2.

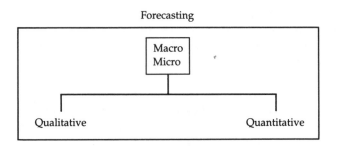

Figure 11.2

From this it will be seen that there are two main types of forecasting, which can be loosely described as macro and micro. Selection of the appropriate technique is dependent on four main factors, the first of which is the degree of accuracy required. It will be obvious that the greater the risk of the decision that depends on the forecast, the greater will be the accuracy required, hence the cost. Second, the method will depend on the availability of data and information. Third, the time horizon is a key determinant of the forecasting method. For example, are we forecasting next period's sales, in which case quantitative extrapolative approaches may be appropriate, or are we forecasting what will happen to our principal market over the next 5 years, in which case qualitative approaches may be appropriate? Lastly, the position of the retail concept in its life cycle will also be a key determinant of the forecasting method. For example, at the introductory stage of a concept's life cycle less data and information will be available than at the maturity stage, when time series can be a useful forecasting method.

From this it will be apparent immediately that we must make an important distinction between macro and micro forecasting. Macro forecasting is essentially concerned with forecasting markets in total, whereas micro forecasting is more concerned with detailed unit forecasts. The discussion in Chapter 2 of the marketing planning process makes it very clear that budgets and plans based on little more than trend extrapolations are unlikely to be successful in the long run, since the really key strategic issues relating to products and markets are rarely given due consideration through such a process. Likewise, it will be recalled that in Chapter 4 in our discussion of market segmentation it was stressed that there are inherent dangers in running sophisticated budgeting systems that are based on little more than crude extrapolations of past sales trends and which leave the marketing strategies implicit. Such systems are the ones that cause serious commercial problems when market structures change.

Thus, some form of macro forecasting has to precede the setting of marketing objectives and strategies. Detailed unit forecasts, or micro forecasts, should come after the company has decided which specific market opportunities it wants to take advantage of and how best this can be done.

Figure 11.2 also shows that there are basically two main techniques for forecasting, which can be described as qualitative and quantitative. It would be unusual if either of these methods was used entirely on its own, mainly because of the inherent dangers in each. What we are really talking about is the need to combine an intuitive approach with the purely mathematical approach.

For example, it is comparatively easy to develop an equation that will extrapolate statistically the world population up to, say, the year 2000. The problem with such an approach, however, is that it does not take account of likely changes in past trends. It would be easy to list a whole series of possible events that could affect world population, and then assign probabilities to the likelihood of those events happening.

The main point we are making is that it is the task of management to take whatever relevant data are available to help predict the future, to use on them whatever quantitative techniques are appropriate, but then to use qualitative methods such as expert opinions, market research, analogy, and so on to predict what will be the likely discontinuities in the time series. Only through the sensible use of the available tools will management begin to understand what has to be done to match its own capabilities with carefully selected market needs.

Without such an understanding, any form of forecasting is likely to be a sterile exercise.

Organizing for marketing planning

The purpose of this brief section is not to delve into the complexities of organizational forms, but to put the difficult process of marketing planning into the context of the relevant environment in which it will be taking place. The point is that you start from where you are, not from where you would like to be, and it is a fact of business that marketing means different things in different circumstances. It is not our intention here to recommend any one particular organizational form. Rather it is to point out some of the more obvious organizational issues and their likely effect on the way marketing planning is carried out.

As a result of the seemingly permanent debate surrounding organizational forms, the authors supervised a research study over a 2-year period between 1987 and 1989, conducted by John W. Leppard, which looked at marketing planning in the context of various organizational settings. One interesting fact to emerge was that most literature on the subject concentrated almost exclusively on the 'medicine' itself and showed relatively little concern for the 'patient' (if indeed the company can be viewed as being ill and in need of attention). That this should happen makes about as much sense as a doctor dispensing the same drug to every patient he sees, irrespective of his or her condition. Certainly the treatment might help a proportion of the clients, but for a vast number it will be at best irrelevant and at worst perhaps even dangerous.

In the case of those promoting the 'marketing planning nostrum' it is particularly ironic to observe how the product has somehow become more important than the customer. Whatever happened to all that good advice about focusing on customers and their situations?

What must be recognized is that there has to be a symbiotic relation between the patient and the cure. It is the two working together that brings success. Similarly the doctor, if the third party adviser might be described as such, must be more prepared to take a holistic approach to the situation. Instead of writing an instant prescription, he should first find out more about his client.

Since the research study referred to above set out to consider how marketing planning might be introduced more effectively into organizations, let us remember that, like the good doctor, we are going to try to understand more about our patients.

Organizational life phases

At first sight every organization appears to be quite different from any other, and of course in many ways it is. Its personnel and facilities can never exist in the same form elsewhere. Its products, services, history and folklore also play their part in creating a unique entity. Yet it is also possible to look at organizations in another way and find that, in addition to uniqueness, there are also similarities.

What then is this commonality all organizations share? As companies grow and mature, it seems that they all experience a number of distinct life phases. Certainly our research experience has convinced us that once the phases of corporate life are explained to managers, they can readily position their own company on its lifeline.

The significance of this is that the senior executives can then understand the nature of their company's growing pains and how these might contribute to current operational problems and even to a particular organizational culture. Moreover, sometimes this culture will be most receptive to marketing planning, at other times less so. Equally, the marketing planning process itself might need to be modified to sit more comfortably within a given corporate culture.

For now, however, let us look at the way companies grow and develop.

Firstly, as firms grow in size so they tend to go through an organizational evolution. Figure 11.3 shows a firm starting off its existence and growing in turnover over a period of time. When such a firm starts off, it is often organized totally around the owner who is generally the creative force behind the enterprise and who tends to know more about his customers and the products stocked than anyone else in the company. This organizational form can be represented as in Figure 11.4, with all decisions and lines of communication revolving around one person. The point here is that formalized marketing planning by means of systems and written procedures will certainly be less relevant than in, say, a diversified multinational. Indeed, for as long as the pivotal person can cope with the situation, the organization can grow and flourish.

However, as this firm grows in size and complexity, as new products and new markets are added, this organizational form begins to break down, the central 'brain' becomes overloaded, and the first crisis appears. This is resolved in one of two ways: either the owner/entrepreneur sells his business and retires or starts up again, or he adopts the more traditional organizational form with which most of us are familiar (Figure 11.5), in which certain functional duties are allocated to individuals to manage by means of their own specialized departments. Some

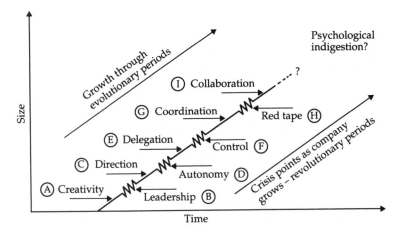

Figure 11.3

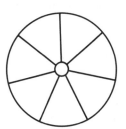

Figure 11.4

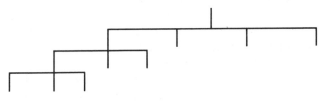

Figure 11.5

aspects of the work will need to be delegated, and systems and procedures will have to be developed to replace the ad-hoc arrangements of the initial phase. Above all, organizational loose ends have to be tidied up and a new sense of purpose and direction instilled in the employees.

Thus, a strong leader is required to bring the company out of the leadership crisis phase and into the next, relatively calm period of directed evolution. Here the leader, who may by now no longer be the founder, directs events from a centralized position. He or she presides over a hierarchical organizational structure that is set up to achieve what the leader prescribes. Again, steady growth can accompany this phase of corporate life until another crisis point is reached. This is the so called autonomy crisis.

Eventually the company will reach a certain size or complexity at which the directive leadership is no longer so appropriate. Individuals working in their particular spheres of activity know more than the central authority. Not only do they resent being told what to do by someone they perceive to be 'out of touch', they actually want to have more personal autonomy to influence company policies and operations. The struggle for power at the autonomy crisis can be accompanied by a tightening of central control, which in turn exacerbates the problem, causing poor morale and even perhaps high staff turnover.

The crisis is eventually resolved by the company providing a much more delegative style of leadership, which does in fact generate more autonomy at lower levels. Again a relatively trouble-free, evolutionary growth period follows from this delegated style.

However, as growth continues, senior management becomes increasingly concerned about the high levels of autonomy lower down the organization. Top managers experience feelings of powerlessness, and sense the need to regain control. This control crisis can be another very destabilizing phase of the company's development. Understandable though the feelings of importance might be for senior management, it seems to be very difficult to turn the clock back to a directive style again. Too much has happened in the intervening years.

The solution to the control crisis seems to be to embark upon a programme for establishing better coordination between the various parts of the organization. This is often achieved by using such mechanisms as formal planning procedures, centralizing some technical functions but leaving daily operating decisions at the local level, setting up special projects for lower-level employees, and so on. Thus another period of relative calm comes with the coordinated evolutionary phase of development.

With continued growth there is a tendency for the coordinating practices to become institutionalized: thus planning procedures become ritualized, special projects become meaningless chores and too many decisions seem to be governed by company rules and regulations. A new crisis point has been reached – the 'bureaucracy' or 'red-tape' crisis. Procedures seem to take precedence over problem-solving.

The only solution seems to be for the company to strive towards a new phase of collaboration in which once again the contributions of individuals and teams are valued as much, if not more, than systems and procedures. There has to be a concerted effort to re-energize and re-personalize operating procedures. More emphasis has to be put on teamwork, spontaneity and creativity.

If a company can win through to the collaborative phase of evolution, then again a period of relatively trouble-free growth can be expected as a reward. However, as we have seen, this pattern of evolutionary growth followed by a crisis appears to be ever-repeating. Each solution to an organizational development problem brings with it the seeds of the next crisis phase. Thus it is that the collaborative evolutionary crisis will probably end when there is a surfeit of integrating mechanisms and perhaps employees begin to lose the ability to function independently.

This last point is purely conjecture, because not many companies seem to have moved far enough along their biographical lifeline for this to be an issue. But from the work we have completed in a number of companies, this idea of company life phases has helped us to understand much more about a client's operating problems and how we might more suitably provide help.

The influence of the culture carriers

The biographical lifeline described above goes some way towards explaining a company situation, but does it go far enough? Is the company culture derived entirely from its past? The answer is negative. Certain individuals, the so-called culture carriers, will influence the situation in ways that promote a particular pattern of behaviours and values within the organization. These will certainly be company-specific in nature and as such could be described as cultural.

Who, then, are the culture carriers and what do they do to be so influential? Much has been written about influencing behaviours, but there is some convincing evidence about the things that leaders do to transmit and embed culture.

Primary mechanisms

Here are the most influential behaviours that signal and reinforce culture:

1   How the leader reacts to crisis or critical events.
2   The criteria he or she establishes for allocating rewards and status.
3   The areas to which the leader pays attention, measures and controls.

4 The criteria he or she establishes for recruitment, selection, promotion, retirement and dismissal.
5 The role model the leader plays to others, by demonstrating certain behaviour, or even by coaching or teaching subordinates.

Secondary mechanisms

1 Organizational systems and procedures.
2 Organizational design and structure.
3 Design of physical space, facilities and building.
4 Formal statements about organizational philosophy, creeds and charters.
5 Stories, legends, myths and parables about important people and events.

One of the main results of the actions of the culture carriers is that they can determine the level at which marketing planning is treated in the organization. Why they do this seems to depend upon the extent to which they use their positions of power and influence for personal aggrandizement or for the good of the company.

Accordingly we have identified four levels of acceptance of marketing planning:

- *Level 1* – marketing planning is deliberately ignored.
- *Level 2* – marketing planning is treated unthinkingly as a formula and the company merely pays lip service to the end result.
- *Level 3* – marketing planning is taken moderately seriously and it is recognized that resources have to be allocated to the process if results are to be achieved.
- *Level 4* – marketing planning is taken very seriously, and it is recognized that not only do resources have to be allocated, but also that the plan could fundamentally change the direction and nature of the business (and with it the existing power structure in the company!).

Thus it can be seen that marketing planning has to be perceived as not just an economic process designed to use resources more effectively, but also as a change mechanism with 'political' undertones. Clearly the level at which marketing planning is accepted by the company is related to the level of risk or readiness to change acceptable to the culture carriers. Figure 11.6 perhaps helps to illustrate these points. How marketing planning impacts on the company can similarly be illustrated, as shown in Figure 11.7. Level 1 is omitted for obvious reasons.

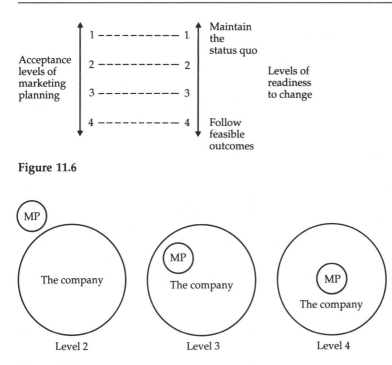

Figure 11.6

Figure 11.7

The more seriously marketing planning is taken, the more central it becomes in the company's operational life. While it could be argued that the level of acceptance of marketing planning is purely a cognitive problem and that the levels reflect understanding, this does not square with our experience. The acceptance of marketing planning seems to be more an attitudinal problem, and being prepared to subscribe to the values inherent in a complete planning process.

Equally, when we talk about marketing planning, we are describing a process that requires an acceptance level of 3 or 4 on our scale. Any lower level will, in our opinion, be a complete waste of time for all concerned, be they educationalists or company personnel.

The marketing planning process and corporate culture

Assuming that marketing planning is acceptable at something deeper than a cosmetic level, it becomes possible to see how the process aligns with different phases of the company's lifeline.

Creative evolution phase

In our research we did not find a single marketing planner at this stage of development. Most of the companies were still really formulating their business ideas, and the senior executive (the culture carrier) was in close touch with his customers and his own staff. The organization had a high level of flexibility to respond to changes in customer needs. In our research many of these companies were showing high growth, and to introduce marketing planning did not appear to offer any additional benefits.

It has to be recognized that some retail companies do not have a sufficiently good concept or service to develop very far along their life path. The infant mortality rate for businesses is very high. However, if the company successfully negotiates this initial phase, eventually it reaches the leadership crisis. As we have seen, a strong leader is required, one who will provide the drive and direction that will lead to the next evolutionary phase.

Directed evolution

Companies at this stage of development fell into two camps. Naturally enough, the underlying style behind the marketing planning process was directive in each case, but the impact and effectiveness were significantly different for each type.

The first type we have referred to as 'Directed Marketing Planning Type 1'. Here, the senior executive took responsibility, or delegated the task of producing a marketing plan. This person would then spend time analysing data, performing a situational review and so on until he or she finished up with a document. Generally an approving mechanism was built into the process, e.g. the board of directors would have to vet the marketing plan before it could be issued, but by and large thereafter the plan acts as a directive for the organization.

The second type – 'Directed Marketing Planning Type 2', called for appropriate members of staff to be told what information to provide about their areas of work, the form in which the information should be provided, and so on. Thus, rather than the plan being directed, the process is spelt out carefully. The resulting information is assembled at a senior level and the resulting planning document is issued as before.

Although in both cases all the creative thinking and control takes place at the top level of the organization, the second method holds a prospect of generating more useful data without sacrificing the directive, power-based culture.

Delegated evolution

As a solution to the autonomy crisis that can develop when directive leadership becomes inappropriate, more delegation becomes an operational feature of organizations.

What seemed to be a problem for marketing planning in these companies was that people in the 'front line' or operating units of large companies were expected to produce marketing plans, but without very much guidance. For example, one company had to send its marketing plans to head office, where they were rigorously examined and then given the corporate thumbs up or down. Only through a process of acceptance or dismissal were the criteria for 'good' plans eventually pieced together.

Our conclusion was that a delegated form of marketing planning can lead to some very high quality inputs and certainly to high levels of commitment on behalf of those involved. Yet ultimately the solely bottom-up planning procedures seem to be difficult to integrate and can be demotivating to those concerned. Somehow the sum of the parts is less in stature than it ought to be.

Coordinated evolution

At this stage the lessons of the directed and delegated phases seem to have been learned. There is much more emphasis on a plan for planning and a means to incorporate top-down direction and bottom-up quality. Equally, a coordinated approach enables the company to make best use of its specialized resources and to generate commitment from the staff.

In many ways the marketing planning processes which are the stuff of textbooks and so on appear to be most suited for a company at this stage of its development. However, as we have seen, it is possible for the planning process to degenerate from essentially a problem-solving process into a fairly meaningless, bureaucratic ritual. It is at this stage that the planning process will become counter-productive.

Collaborative evolution

Here the bureaucracy has to make way for genuine problem-solving again. At present we do not have very much evidence about what this means in practice. But it is possible to speculate that as business environments change at an ever-increasing pace, so new marketing planning procedures might need to be developed. Creativity and expediency would appear to be the passwords to this new phase of development.

Diagnostic tools

We have found it necessary to develop diagnostic tools or instruments to help identify where the company might be on its lifeline and also how the management style reflects the current culture of the organization. Although these are in a relatively early stage of development, both we and client organizations are finding that the information they uncover helps to make more sense of the company situation *vis-à-vis* marketing planning.

Centralization versus decentralization

As we can see from the above, the case for and against centralization could be argued in the context of the organization's stage of development. However, as we have also seen, action can be stimulated by the organizational culture carriers, with the reaction that change might be introduced largely for 'political' reasons. Whatever the underlying reasons, it is important to understand some of the basic strengths and weaknesses of centralization versus decentralization.

Looking firstly at decentralization, it is possible to represent this diagrammatically, as in Figure 11.8. The shaded area of the triangle represents the top level strategic management of the firm. It can be seen that the central services, such as market research and public relations are repeated at the subsidiary company level. It can also be seen that there is a strategic level of management at the subsidiary level, the acid test being whether subsidiary company/unit top management can target new market segments without reference to headquarters.

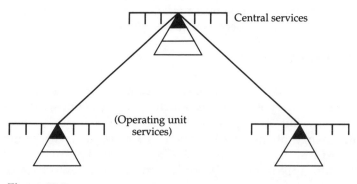

Figure 11.8

The point about this kind of decentralized organizational structure is that it leads inevitably to duplication of effort and differentiation of strategies, with all the consequent problems, unless a major effort is made to get some synergy out of the several systems by means of a companywide planning system. One very large retailer with four different types of retail outlet allowed the subsidiary management to behave independently. When it came to buying, not only did the company miss out on potential buying economies of scale, but the same merchandise appeared in different stores at widely differing prices. The confusion was further confounded because this particular company insisted on using the company's logo on all its stores, irrespective of the different target markets of each store type.

The same problems apply to marketing research, advertising, pricing, distribution, and other business areas. When someone takes the trouble to find out, it is often very salutary to see the reaction of senior managers at headquarters when they are told, for example, that the very same market problem is being researched in many different companies around the group, all at enormous expense.

It is this kind of organization structure which, above all others, requires strong central coordination by means of some kind of planning system, otherwise everyone wastes enormous amounts of corporate resources striving to maximize their own small part of the business. If, however, some system of gaining synergy from all the energy expended can be found, then the rewards are great indeed. The point is, that marketing in this kind of system means something different from marketing in other kinds of system, and it is as well to recognize this from the outset.

A centrally controlled company tends to look as depicted in Figure 11.9. Here it will be seen that there is no strategic level of management in the subsidiary units, particularly in respect of new product introductions. This

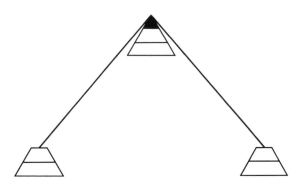

Figure 11.9

kind of organizational form tends to lead to standardized strategies, particularly in respect of product management. For example, when a new product is introduced, it tends to be designed at the outset with as many markets as possible in mind, while the benefits from market research in one area are passed to other areas, and so on. The problem here of course is that unless great care is exercised, subsidiary units can easily become less sensitive to the needs of individual markets, and hence lose flexibility in reacting to competitive moves. The point here again is that marketing in this kind of system means something different from marketing in the kind of system described above.

There is a difference between financial manipulation and business management in respect of the headquarters role. There is a difference between a corporation and its individual components, and often there is confusion about what kind of planning should be done by managers at varying levels in the organization, because the chief executive has not made it clear what kind of business he is managing.

We have looked briefly at two principal organizational forms, both of which consist essentially of a central office and various decentralized divisions, each with its own unique products, processes and markets that complement the others in the group. In enterprises of this type planning within the divisions applies to the exploration of markets and improved efficiency within the boundaries laid down by headquarters. The problems and opportunities that this method throws up tend to make the headquarters role one of classifying the boundaries for the enterprise as a whole, in relation to new products and markets that do not appear to fall within the scope of one of the divisions.

In this type of organization the managers of affiliated companies are normally required to produce the level of profit set by headquarters management within the constraints imposed on them, and such companies need to institutionalize this process by providing a formal structure of ideas and systems so that operating management knows what it is expected to do and whether it is doing the essential things. The point about these kinds of organization seems to be that some method has to be found of planning and controlling the growth of the business in order to utilize effectively the evolving skills and growing reputation of the firm, and so avoid an uncontrolled dissipation of energy. It is probably easier to do this in a centrally organized firm, but, as we have pointed out, both organizational forms have their disadvantages.

Finally, the financial trust type of organization needs to be mentioned briefly, one in which the primary concern of central management is the investment of shareholders' capital in various businesses. The buying and selling of interests in various firms is done for appreciation of capital rather than for building an enterprise with any logic of its own. Planning in this type of operation requires different knowledge and skills, and addresses itself to kinds of problem that are different from those in the two organizational forms described above.

What is certain is that one of the major determinants of the effectiveness of any marketing planning that is attempted within a company will be the way that it organizes for marketing. The purpose of this section has been to point out some of the more obvious facts and pitfalls before attempting to outline a marketing planning system, to which we can turn in the next chapter.

Conclusions

In this chapter we have shown how the acceptance of marketing planning is largely conditioned by the stage of development of the organization and the behaviour of the corporate culture carriers. Thus it is that different modes of marketing planning become more appropriate at different phases of the company's life.

While the marketing planning process itself remains more or less consistent throughout, how that process is managed must be congruent with the current organizational culture. The alternative to this would be to take steps to change the company culture and make it more amenable to a particular planning process.

Since culture tends to act to maintain the existing power structure and the status quo, marketing planning interventions in companies must be recognized as having a 'political' dimension and are not purely educational. Not least among the political issues is the question of whether or not a company's management style can adapt sufficiently to enable the marketing planning process to deliver the rewards it promises.

Can managers who have led a company down a particular path suddenly change track? In other words, is it possible for frogs to change into princes? The iconoclastic books would claim that they can, because this is a much more optimistic message with which to sell copies. However, those who have carried out academic research or are experienced consultants would have some reservations.

We remain open-minded about this issue, believing that if the business pressures on a company are sufficient, intelligent behaviour will win the day. We might be proved wrong, but in the meantime this chapter provides some useful messages for both marketing advisers and senior executives of companies. While we see our research as being an important step along the road to effective marketing planning, we are also realistic enough to recognize that there is still far to travel.

12

Implementation issues in marketing planning

Summary

Chapter 12 opens by discussing the implications of size and diversity of operations on marketing planning. This is followed by a summary of the main elements of the marketing planning process. There is a discussion of the role of the chief executive, and the planning department, followed by some thoughts on the marketing planning cycle and planning horizons. Finally, some insights are provided into how the marketing planning process works.

Introduction

In Chapter 3 we explained some of the many myths that surround marketing planning, and spelt out the conditions that must be satisfied if any company is to have an effective marketing planning system. These are:

1   Any closed-loop marketing planning system, but especially one that is essentially a forecasting and budgeting system, will lead to the stifling of marketing and creativity. Therefore there has to be some mechanism for preventing inertia from setting in through the over-bureaucratization of the system.
2   Marketing planning undertaken at the functional level of marketing, in the absence of a means of integration with other functional areas of the business at general management level, will be largely ineffective.
3   The separation of responsibility for operational and strategic marketing planning will lead to a divergence of the short-term thrust of a business at the operational level from the long-term objectives of the

enterprise as a whole. This will encourage a preoccupation with short-term results at operational level, which normally makes the firm less effective in the long term.

4 Unless the chief executive understands and takes an active role in marketing planning, it will never be an effective system.

5 A period of up to 3 years is necessary (especially in large firms) for the successful introduction of an effective marketing planning system.

Some indication of the potential complexity of marketing planning can be seen in Figure 12.1. Even in a generalized model such as this, it can be seen that in a large diversified group operating in many foreign markets, a complex combination of product, market and functional plans is possible. For example, what is required at regional level will be different from what is required at headquarters level, while it is clear that the total corporate plan has to be built from the individual building blocks. Furthermore, the function of marketing itself may be further

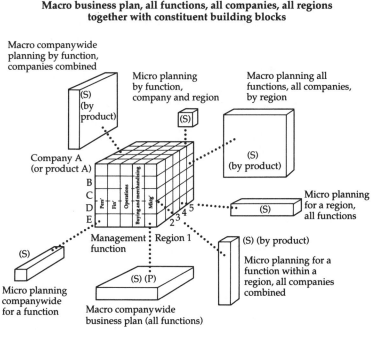

Macro business plan, all functions, all companies, all regions together with constituent building blocks

Key:
P=parent company
S=subsidiary company

Figure 12.1

functionalized for the purpose of planning, e.g. into marketing research, advertising, selling, buying promotion, and so forth, while different customer groups may need to have separate plans drawn up.

Let us be dogmatic about requisite planning levels. First, in a large diversified group, irrespective of such organizational issues, anything other than a systematic approach approximating to a formalized marketing planning system is unlikely to enable the necessary control to be exercised over the corporate identity. Second, unnecessary planning, or over-planning, could easily result from an inadequate or indiscriminate consideration of the real planning needs at the different levels in the hierarchial chain. Third, as size and diversity grow, so the degree of formalization of the marketing planning process must also increase.

The degree of formalization must increase with the evolving size and diversity of operations. However, while the degree of formalization will change, the need for a complete marketing planning system does not. The problems that companies suffer, then, are a function of either the degree to which they have a requisite marketing planning system or the degree to which the formalization of their system grows with the situational complexities attendant upon the size and diversity of operations.

It has already been stressed that central to the success of any enterprise is the objective-setting process. Connected with this is the question of the design of the planning system, and, in particular, the question of who should do what, and how. For example, who should carry out the situation review, state the assumptions, set marketing objectives, and strategies, and carry out the scheduling and costing-out programme, and at what level?

These complex issues revolve essentially around three dimensions – the size, the stage of development of the company and the degree of business diversity. Of these dimensions, the size and the stage of development of the organization are without doubt the biggest determinants of the type of marketing planning system used.

Size/stage of development of organization

As we saw in the previous chapter, all companies move along a biographical 'lifeline' as they develop and overcome the various archetypal organizational crises that beset them as they grow, learn and progress.

At the early stages of the development 'spectrum' are generally small, entrepreneurially run organizations, high on energy, creativity and flexibility, but low on formalised planning. The characteristics of organizations further down the development track are that they tend to be larger and run on 'scientific principles'. Thus planning is an integral part of their culture, there are many functional specialists, an organizational chart to show where they all fit in, and rules and procedures to ensure that the organization operates as smoothly as a Rolls-Royce engine. Invariably the impetus for planning is 'top-down', but unfortunately many of the mechanisms to ensure smooth running only serve to encumber the organization with bureaucratic trappings.

Those organizations furthest along the development spectrum are sometimes larger still, but not necessarily so. What characterizes them is that they have either worked though the 'red-tape crisis' of planning, or have been smart enough to avoid it. They will seek the advantages of coordinating all their resources for the common purpose that planning can bring, but also try to find ways to integrate the vibrancy and élan often associated with smaller organizations. Such organizations are sufficiently experienced and mature to experiment with new and individual approaches to planning and organizational life in general.

In general, the bigger the company, the greater is the incidence of standardized, formalized procedures for the several steps in the marketing planning process. On the other hand, many small companies that have a poor understanding of the marketing concept, with the top manager leaving his strategy implicit, suffer many serious operational problems.

These operational problems become progressively worse as the size of the company increases. As the number and levels of management grow, it becomes progressively more difficult for top management to enjoy an in-depth knowledge of business conditions by informal, face-to-face means. In the absence of written procedures and a structured framework, the different levels of operating management become increasingly less able to react in a rational way to day-to-day pressures. Systems of tight budgeting control without the procedures outlined in this book are in the main only successful in situations of buoyant trading conditions, are often the cause of high levels of management frustration, and are seen to be a major contributory factor in those cases where eventual decline sets in.

Diversity of operations

From the point of view of management control, the least complex environment in which to work is a single store selling a limited product range to a homogeneous customer group. An example is a small family baker who bakes and sells a small range of products to shoppers in the immediately locality.

For the purposes of this discussion, such a retail operation is termed 'undiversified'. Should that baker embark on a programme of expansion and open up many more retail outlets, while at the same time extending the erstwhile simple product range into many new areas, then clearly the control problems will increase proportionately as he diversifies.

In such cases the need for institutionalized marketing planning systems increases with the size of the operation, and there is a strong relation between size and the complexity of the management task, irrespective of any apparent diversity. For example, a retail group might operate in many diverse markets around the country through many different kinds of marketing systems, and with varying levels of market growth and market share. In most respects therefore the control function for headquarters management is just as difficult and complex as that in any large, diversified conglomerate. Success is due to the level of in-depth knowledge top management has about the key determinants of success and failure underlying the product or market nationwide, and because of the underlying homogeneity of retailing.

Because of this homogeneity, it is usually possible for headquarters to impose nationwide policies on operating units in respect of things such as certain aspects of advertising, public relations, packaging, pricing, trademarks, product development, and so on. But in the headquarters of a diversified conglomerate policies of this kind tend to be impracticable and meaningless.

It is often said that common planning in companies comprising many heterogeneous units is unhelpful, and confuses rather than improves understanding between operating units and headquarters. However, the truth is that conglomerates can consist of several smaller multinationals, some diversified and some not, and that the actual risk of marketing rests on the lowest level in an organization in which there is general management profit responsibility. Forecasting and budgeting systems by themselves rarely encourage anything but a short-term, parochial view of the business at these levels, and in the absence of the kind of marketing planning procedures described in this book, higher levels of management do not have a sufficiently rational basis on which to set long-term marketing objectives.

Exactly the same principles apply at the several levels of control in a diversified multinational conglomerate, in that at the highest level of control there has to be some rational basis on which to make decisions about the portfolio of investments; in our research the most successful companies were those with standardized marketing planning procedures to aid this process. In such companies there is a hierarchy of audits, SWOT analyses, assumptions, strategies and programmes, with increasingly more detail required in the procedures at the lowest levels in the organization. The precise details of each step vary according to circumstances, but the eventual output of the process is in a universally consistent form.

The basis on which the whole system rests is the informational input requirements at the highest level of command. Marketing objectives and strategies are frequently synthesized into a multi-discliplinary corporate plan at the next general management profit-responsible level, until at the highest level of command the corporate plan consists largely of financial information and summaries of the main operational activities. This is an important point, for there is rarely a consolidated operational marketing plan at conglomerate headquarters. This often exists only at the lowest level of general management profit responsibility, and even here it is sometimes incorporated into the corporate plan, particularly in capital goods companies, where engineering, manufacturing and technical services are major factors in commercial success.

Here it is necessary to distinquish between short-term operational plans and long-term strategic plans, both products of the same process. Conglomerate headquarters are particularly interested in the progress of, and prospects for, the main areas of operational activities, and while obviously concerned to ensure a satisfactory current level of profitability, are less interested in the detailed short-term scheduling and costing-out of the activities necessary to achieve these objectives. This, however, is a major concern at the lowest level of general management profit responsibility.

To summarize, the smaller the company and the less developed it is, the more informal and personal the procedures for marketing planning are. As company size and diversity increase, so the need for institutionalized procedures increases. This is illustrated in Figure 12.2.

The really important issue in any system is the degree to which it enables control to be exercised over the key determinants of success and failure. To a large extent the issue, much debated in the literature, of where in an international organization responsibility for setting marketing objectives and strategies should lie, is something of a red herring. Of course in a diversified multinational conglomerate detailed marketing objectives and strategies for some remote country cannot be set by someone in London. It is precisely the issue, i.e. finding the right balance between the flexibility of operating units to react to changes in local market conditions and centralized control, that a formally designed system seeks to tackle. Those companies that conform to the framework outlined here have systems which, through a hierarchy of bottom up/top down negotiating procedures, reach a nice balance between the

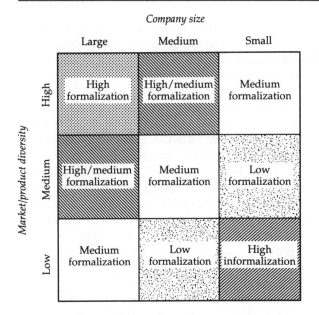

Figure 12.2

need for detailed control at the lowest level of operations and central-ized control. The main role of headquarters is to harness the company's strengths on a global basis, and to ensure that lower level decisions do not cause problems in other areas and lead to wasteful duplication.

Figure 12.3 explores four key outcomes that marketing planning can evoke. It can be seen that in the systems where the individual is totally subordinate to a formalized system (I), where individuals are allowed to do what they want without any system (III), or where there is neither system nor creativity (IV), are less successful than System II, in which an individual is allowed to be entrepreneurial within a total system. System II, then, will be an effective marketing planning system, but one in which the degree of formalization will be a function of company size and diversity.

Creativity cannot flourish in a closed-loop formalized system. There would be little disagreement that in today's abrasive, turbulent, and highly competitive environment it is those firms that succeed in extract-ing entrepreneurial ideas and creative marketing programmes from systems that are necessarily yet acceptably formalized that will succeed in the long run. Much innovative flair can so easily be stifled by systems.

There is ample evidence of international companies with highly formalized systems that produce stale and repetitive plans, with little

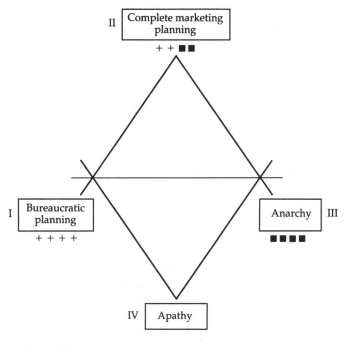

II | Complete marketing planning
+ + ■■

I | Bureaucratic planning
+ + + +

Anarchy | III
■ ■ ■ ■

IV | Apathy

+ Degree of formalization
■ Degree of openness

Figure 12.3

changed from year to year, and plans that fail to point up the really key strategic issues as a result. The scandalous waste this implies is largely due to a lack of personal intervention by key managers during the early stages of the planning cycle.

There is clearly a need therefore to find a way of perpetually renewing the planning life cycle each time around. Inertia must never set in. Without some such valve or means of opening up the loop, inertia quickly produces decay.

Such a valve has to be inserted early in the planning cycle, during the audit or situation review stage. In companies with effective marketing planning systems, whether such systems are formalized or informal, the critical intervention of senior managers, from the chief executive down through the hierarchial chain, comes at the audit stage. Essentially what takes place is a personalized presentation of audit findings, together with proposed marketing objectives and strategies and outline budgets for the strategic planning period. These are discussed, amended where necessary, and agreed in various synthesized formats at the hierarchial levels in the organization before any detailed operational planning takes place. It is at such meetings that managers are called upon to justify their views, which tends to force them to be more bold and creative than they would have been had they been allowed merely to send in their proposals.

Obviously, however, even here much depends on the degree to which managers take a critical stance, which is much greater when the chief executive himself takes an active part in the process. Every hour of time devoted at this stage by the chief executive has a multiplier effect throughout the remainder of the process. And let it be remembered we are not, repeat not, talking about budgets at this juncture in anything other than outline form.

Until recently it was believed that there may well be fundamental differences in marketing planning approaches, depending on factors such as the type of goods and markets subject to planning, company size, the degree of dependence on importance, etc. In particular, the much debated role of headquarters management in the marketing planning process is frequently put forward as being a potential cause of great difficulty.

One of the most encouraging findings to emerge from our research is that the theory of marketing planning is universally applicable, and that such issues are largely irrelevant. While the planning task is less complicated in small undiversified companies, and there is less need for formalized procedures than in large diversified companies, the fact is that exactly the same framework should be used in all circumstances, and that this approach brings similar benefits to all.

In a multinational conglomerate headquarters management is able to assess major trends in products and markets around the world, and is thus able to develop strategies for investment, expansion, diversification and divestment on a global basis. For its part, subsidiary management can develop appropriate strategies with a sense of locomotion towards the achievement of coherent goals.

This development is achieved by means of synthesized information flows from the bottom upwards, which facilitate useful comparison of performance around the world, and the diffusion of valuable information, skills, experiences and systems from the top downwards. The particular benefits which accrue to companies using such systems can be classified under the main headings of the marketing mix elements as follows:

- *Marketing information* – there is a transfer of knowledge, a sharing of expertise and an optimization of effort.

- *Product* – control is exercised over the product range. Maximum effectiveness is gained by concentrating on certain market segments, based on experience.
- *Price* – pricing policies are sufficiently flexible to enable local management to trade effectively.
- *Place* – substantial gains are made by rationalization of the logistics function.
- *Promotion* – duplication of effort is reduced, as is a multitude of different platforms/company images.

The procedures that facilitate the provision of such information and knowledge transfers also encourage operational management to think strategically about its own areas of responsibility, instead of managing only for the short term.

It is abundantly clear that it is through a marketing planning system and planning skills that such benefits are achieved, and that discussions such as those about the standardization process are largely irrelevant. Any standardization that may be possible will become clear only if a company can successfully develop a system for identifying the needs of each market and each segment in which it operates, and for organizing resources to satisfy those needs in such a way that best resource utilization results world-wide.

A summary of the marketing planning process

The purpose of this section is to summarize the earlier chapters, and to ensure that the many threads developed are seen in their correct context, within the marketing planning process.

There are many checklists of things you have to do to go through the motions of marketing planning. But pages of figures and marketing prose, well typed, elegantly bound, and retrievably filed, do not make much difference. They make some, because the requirements of writing a plan demand deep thought. However, it is vital that companies must always search for the requisite level of marketing planning in just the same way they seek to find the requisite level of variety in product range offered in their stores.

It is well to remember, above all else, what the purpose of marketing planning is. The following sub-sections are intended to identify the main barriers to marketing planning and summarize the main points of a requisite marketing planning system, and to provide the basis for the design of a system suitable for any business.

The process itself

'How well should we be doing in present trading conditions?' The answer to this question requires considerable analysis inside and outside the company. Simply looking at the bottom line and saying 'budget achieved' is not enough. It is quite possible to achieve budget and still lose market share – if the budget is not developed from a proper qualitative assessment of the market in the first place.

The real question we should be asking is 'What sales/gross profits should we be achieving in the current trading conditions?' To answer the above questions, it is necessary to have a well-argued 'common format' available in the organization, i.e. a marketing plan.

Undertaking marketing planning is like 'trying to nail a jelly to the wall'; it is a messy process that evolves over time. In effect you are attempting to 'control' the future by deciding what to do about the possible different trading environments. In undertaking marketing planning you join the ranks of those who 'make things happen' in the company. The alternative is to be tossed around like a cork in the sea of competition.

The marketing planning process comprises the bringing together of minds within the company/group/department, and a 'trading off' between the difficult issues raised. By definition, the marketing planning process starts from a 'zero base' each year; the 10 per cent syndrome must be avoided at all times.

The marketing planning process facilitates, and indeed depends on, interactive communication up and down the organization. If this does not happen, all that results are forecasts projected from history rather than the development of genuine objectives based on what is actually happening inside and outside the company.

Remember, the planning process is first and foremost to help you help yourself. It is not something you take part in simply to appease your superiors.

It is sometimes difficult for higher echelons in the organization to synthesize and aggregate the SWOTs from lower levels. However, the task is made easier if, for instance, departments are grouped to reflect the structure of the external market.

Once the marketing planning process has developed through to the agreement of a detailed 1-year operational plan, and once the plan's budget is agreed, then commitment must be total. If, however, during the ensuing fiscal year performance begins to fall behind the budget, it is quite legitimate to manipulate any and all elements of the marketing plan in order to correct the deficit. There is flexibility in the way the elements of a plan can be altered and manipulated, but the budget remains fixed.

Marketing audit

The marketing planning process starts with an audit of the company's operating performance and environment. The marketing audit is essentially a data base of all market-related issues with which the company is concerned. The subsequent SWOT analysis lends structure to the audit in order to facilitate planning activities.

The company must provide a list of detailed questions each manager is required to consider for his area of responsibility. Each manager carrying out his audit will use sales data and if the company has a marketing research manager, it is helpful at this stage if he can issue to all managers a market overview covering major market and product trends, etc.

It will probably be necessary to customize the audit checklist contents according to the level in the organization to which they are addressed. In this way each particular checklist is made meaningful and relevant to each level. Some brief explanatory definitions may also be necessary.

The audit will inevitably require more data preparation than is finally reproduced in the marketing plan. Therefore managers should attempt to start a 'product/market bible' during the year, which can also be used as a reference source at verbal presentations of proposals, etc. What this means is that the marketing audit should be conducted on a continuing (dynamic) basis rather than at a particular point in time. In this way it becomes a useful information source to draw on for decision-making throughout the year.

Do not try to hide behind vague items in the audit, such as 'poor economic condition'. Even in static or declining markets there will be 'growth' points present. Seek these out and decide whether or not to focus/concentrate your efforts on them.

Incorporate product life cycles and portfolio matrices as an integral part of the audit. The diagrams and the corresponding words should match.

It is suggested that the manager draws a product life cycle for each of his important products, and uses the audit information to attempt to predict the future shape of the life cycle. It is also suggested that the manager plots his products on a portfolio matrix and that he uses the audit information to show the future desired position of his products, e.g. for 5 years ahead, if this is the planning horizon. The matrix may therefore have to include some new products not currently in the range.

The audit can be a useful 'transfer' device for when one manager moves job and another takes over. For example, the incoming manager can quickly pick up an understanding of that department's business.

SWOT analysis

It is important to remember that it is only the SWOT analysis, not the audit, that actually appears in the marketing plan. This summary of the audit should, if possible, contain not more than four or five pages of commentary, focusing on key factors only. It should list internal differential strengths and weaknesses *vis-à-vis* competitors and key external opportunities and threats. A SWOT should be completed for each segment or product considered to be crucial to the firm's future.

The SWOT analysis should be interesting to read, contain concise statements, include only the relevant and important data, and give emphasis to creative analysis. To be true markets we must differentiate ourselves from our competitors. The SWOT analysis is a device which assists us to do that.

A SWOT analysis, well done, helps to identify and pin down the real issues that should be addressed in the future as a matter of priority. Too often, however, the SWOT summary is just a smörgåsbord of apparently unrelated points (in which case any underlying theme is difficult to discern).

Having listened to someone presenting a SWOT summary, you should end up with a clear understanding of the main thrust of the business. If a SWOT is well done, someone else should be able to draft the objectives that logically flow from it. The SWOT statement should contain clear indicators   as   to   the   key   determinants   of   success   in   the company/group/department; we can then build on these.

The SWOT statement should in effect encapsulate our perception of the market place, summarize what we are trying to do, and point to required future actions. If pursued aggressively, this approach will make competitors followers.

The SWOT is by definition a summary of the key issues emanating out of the marketing audit. The SWOT is generated from internal debate; it is not just one person's opinion. The SWOT should provide answers to such questions as:

- What do customers need?
- How do they buy?
- What are our competitors doing?

Generally the SWOT should be differential or at least the S and W (internal) part should be. The O and T (external) part of the SWOT is generally non-differential, e.g. the threat of a new sales tax. We have to assess the impact of such a threat (should it happen) earlier than our competitors, and make the appropriate preparations earlier in order to give us the edge.

In writing down each issue in our SWOT summary we should continally follow with the implied question, 'Which means that ...?' In this way we are forced to think about the implications of the issue itself.

Finally, agreed budgets (which come at the end of the process) must reflect internal consistency with the issues raised in the original SWOT analysis. Often this internal consistency is not evident because budgets are done first rather than last, and the qualitative content is done last rather than first (in which case it is just rhetoric).

It is difficult to work to a SWOT prepared by another person, unless of course you took part in the original debate. The quality of a SWOT analysis can suffer if:

1 Each item/issue is over-abbreviated.
2 If the writer concentrates on micro rather than macro issues.

Remember, it is a great self-disclipline to complete a good, tight but comprehensive SWOT.

Assumptions

These also should appear in the marketing plan. List the main assumptions on which the plan is based. If the plan can be implemented irrespective of any assumption made, then the assumption is unnecessary. They should be few but important.

Marketing objectives

These should also appear in the marketing plan. Marketing objectives are about products and markets only (not about advertising, etc.). The words used should reflect what appears in the product life cycle and in the portfolio matrix. Any figures used (such as volume, value, etc.) should also reflect this. There is a detailed explanation of how this should be done in Chapter 13.

Note that if there is, say, a 3-year planning horizon, the 3-year marketing plan should contain marketing objectives with broad revenue and cost projections for the full 3-year period. This plan will be required for the long-range corporate plan. The 1-year marketing plan should contain the same general marketing objectives plus the specific objectives for the first year of the planning cycle. Thereafter the detailed 1-year marketing plan should be about the next fiscal year only. Ideally the 1-year and 5-year plans should be separate, but it is not absolutely necessary.

At an early stage in the planning process it is likely that store managers, for example, will have to discuss their major objectives with their superiors before coming to a final agreement, since those superiors will probably have a better understanding of the broader company objective.

It is necessary to set objectives in order to lay down what we are in fact committing ourselves to, and to force us to think about the corresponding resource implications.

Marketing objectives flow from the SWOT analysis and should be fully compatible with the key issues identified in the SWOT. Marketing objectives should be quantifiable and measurable for performance-monitoring purposes; avoid directional terms such as 'improve', 'increase', 'expand', etc. There will be a hierarchy of marketing objectives down through the organization. Try to set priorities for your chosen marketing objectives.

Many so-called marketing objectives are in fact really marketing strategies. Do not mix the two up. Marketing objectives are what we want to achieve; marketing strategies are how we intend to achieve them.

In some cases, marketing strategies and detailed marketing actions are confused. Actions are the short-term list of activities carried out to a schedule that in aggregate amount to a particular strategy.

Marketing strategies

These must also appear in the marketing plan. As we have said, strategies are how the objectives are to be achieved:

- Product policies, to include mix, functions, design, size, packaging, and so on.
- Pricing policies, to be followed for product groups in market segments.
- Place policies for stores and customer service levels.
- Promotion policies for communicating with customers under the relevant headings, such as advertising, personal selling, sales promotion, etc.

Programmes

Detailed programmes (sometimes referred to as 'appropriation budgets') should appear only in the detailed 1-year operational marketing plan. In the 3-year strategic marketing plan all that are required are the financial implications (budget) of the agreed strategies. A detailed 1-year marketing plan requires specific sub-objectives for products and segments, supported by more detailed strategy and actions statements, e.g. what, where, when, costs, etc. Include budgets and forecasts in this plan, and of course a consolidated budget.

The preparation of budgets and sales forecasts must reflect the marketing objectives, and the objectives, strategies and programmes must reflect the agreed budgets and sales forecasts. Forecasts (in lieu of objectives) are obtained by simply extrapolating past experience. Instead, we should be taking a 'zero-based' view of the current and possible future environments in order to arrive at an achievable set of objectives. Unit forecasts then follow.

The above noted zero-based review (in the form of a marketing audit and corresponding SWOT) is necessary in order to identify possible 'discontinuities' in our future trading environment. Simple extrapolation of historial data ignores the possibility that discontinuities can (and do) occur.

Forecasts (and corresponding budgets based on such forecasts) can be self-fulfilling prophecies, e.g. salesmen sell the products they like to customers they enjoy selling to. If we project the resulting numbers by way of a forecast, we are not reflecting the real market situation.

A somewhat deeper perception of the market place is needed in order to review and reveal realistic marketing objectives and strategies, ones consistent with the company's distinctive competence. Individual budget items must clearly be retraceable to issues identified in the original SWOT. When measuring performance, at all times seek to relate to the outside market as well as your internal budget.

Marketing plans

A written marketing plan (or plans) is the outcome of the marketing planning process. It is effectively a business proposition containing proposed courses of action, which in turn have resource implications.

Written marketing plans verbalize (and formalize) our intuitive model of the market environment within which we operate. Written marketing plans help to make things happen.

The acid test of any marketing plan presentation is to ask yourself 'Would I put my own life's savings into the plan as presented?' If the answer is 'No', then further work is needed to refine your ideas.

A good disclipline in preparing 'internally consistent' marketing plans is to use the following summary format:

SWOT issues ⟶ *Objective* ⟶ *Strategy* ⟶ *Specific actions and timing*

Role of the chief executive

Our research showed that few chief executives had a clear perception of:

- Purposes and methods of planning.
- Proper assignments of planning responsibilities throughout the organization.
- Proper structures and staffing of the planning department.
- Talent and skills required in an effective planning department.

The role of the chief executive is generally agreed as being:

1 To define the organizational framework.
2 To ensure the strategic analysis covers critical factors.
3 To maintain the balance between short- and long-term results.
4 To display commitment to planning.
5 To provide the entrepreneurial dynamic to overcome bureaucracy.
6 To build this dynamic into the planning operation (motivation).

In respect of planning, the chief executive's principal role is to open up the planning loop by means of his personal intervention. The main purpose of this is to act as a catalyst for the entrepreneurial dynamic within his organization, which can so easily decay through bureaucratization. This is not sufficiently recognized in the literature.

When considering the CE's role in the context of the reasons for failure of marketing planning systems, it is clear that, for any system to be effective, the chief executive requires to be conversant with planning techniques and approaches, and to be committed to and take part in the marketing planning process.

Role of the planning department

This department's role is:

1 To provide the planning structure and systems.
2 To secure rapid data transmission in the form of inteligence.
3 To act as a catalyst in obtaining inputs from operating divisions or areas.
4 To forge planning links across organizational divisions, e.g. buying/ store operations, marketing, finance and personnel.
5 To evaluate plans against the chief executive's formulated strategy.
6 To monitor the agreed plans.

The planner is a coordinator who sees that the planning is done – not a formulator of goals and strategies. The planner's responsibility has three basic dimensions: they are directive, supportive and administrative.

Directive role

In his directive role the planning executive acts on behalf of top management to supervise the planning procedure to promote orderly and disciplined implementation of the planning process. This function can be performed well only when managers have both the ability and willingness to make it happen. The planning executive is likely to be more effective by acting in a supportive than in a directive role.

Supportive role

A supportive role brings the planning executive into service as an internal consultant and advisory resource. In this role he:

1   Advises line management on the application of planning principles.
2   Assembles background information to provide insight into the economy, industries, markets, investment alternatives, etc., which are relevant to each retail area he serves.
3   Directs or supports forecasting of the economy supplier industries and end-user markets.
4   Renders assistance in installing progress-monitoring systems and interpreting their output.
5   Renders assistance to line executives in applying advanced methods and procedures.
6   Provides other internal and consulting assistance to line managers in preparing their plans and monitoring their progress.

Administrative role

In their administrative role planners ensure that planning procedures are implemented on schedule and that communications are accurate and rapid. In this role it is suggested that they have limitations. They can provide coordinating and communicating services, but they cannot enforce them. If line management does not participate willingly, someone else with the appropriate authority must take corrective or disciplinary action.

Again, when this is taken in the context of the failures of marketing planning systems, it is clear that an understanding of the proper role of the planning department is an important determinant of planning success.

Marketing planning cycle

The schedule should call for work on the plan for the next year to begin early enough in the current year to permit adequate time for market research and analysis of key data and market trends. In addition, the plan should provide for the early development of a strategic plan that can be approved or altered in principle.

A key factor in determining the planning cycle is bound to be the degree to which it is practicable to extrapolate from sales and market data, but generally speaking successful planning companies start the planning cycle formally somewhere between 9 and 6 months from the beginning of the next fiscal year. It is not necessary, however, to be constrained to work within the company's fiscal year; it is quite possible to have a separate marketing planning schedule if that is appropriate, and simply organize the aggregation of results at the time required by the corporate financial controller.

Planning horizons

It is clear that 1- and 5-year planning periods have been far the most common, although 3 years has become the most common period for the strategic plan, largely because of the dramatically increasing rate of environmental change. Lead time for the initiation of important new retail format or modernization programmes, the length of time necessary to recover capital investment costs, and the size and usefulness of existing stores and office buildings, are the most frequently mentioned reasons for having a 5-year planning horizon. Increasingly, however, these 5-year plans are taking the form more of 'scenarios' than the detailed strategic plans outlined in this book.

Many companies, however, do not give sufficient thought to what represents a sensible planning horizon for their particular circumstances. A 5-year time span is clearly too long for some companies, particularly those operating in volatile fashion-conscious markets. The effect of this is to rob strategic plans of reality. A 5-year horizon is often chosen largely because of its universality.

Some small subsidiaries in large conglomerates are often asked to forecast for 7, 10 and sometimes 15 years ahead, with the result that the forecasts tend to become meaningless exercises. While it obviously makes sense for, say, a glass manufacturer to produce 12-year plans (or scenarios) because of the very long lead time taken in laying down a new furnace, it does not make sense to impose the same planning time-scale on small subsidiaries operating in totally different markets, even though they are in the same group. Such time scales place unnecessary burdens on operating management, and tend to rob the whole strategic planning process of credibility.

The conclusion to be reached is that there is a natural point of focus into the future beyond which it is pointless to look. This point of focus is a function of the relative size of a company. Small companies, because of their size and the way they are managed, tend to be comparatively flexible in the way in which they can react to environmental turbulence in the short term. Large companies, on the other hand, need a much longer lead time in which to make changes in direction. Consequently they tend to need to look further into the future and use formalized systems for this purpose so that managers throughout the organization have a common means of communication.

How the marketing planning process works

There is one other major aspect to be considered. It concerns the requisite location of the marketing planning activity in a company. The answer is simple to give. Marketing planning should take place as near to the market place as possible in the first instance, but the plans should then be reviewed at high levels within an organization to see what issues have been overlooked.

It has been suggested that each manager in the organization should complete an audit and SWOT analysis on his own area of responsibility. The only way that this can work in practice is by means of hierarchy of audits. The principle is simply demonstrated in Figure 12.4.

This figure illustrates the principle of auditing at different levels within an organization. The marketing audit format will be universally applicable, it is only the detail that varies from level to level and from company to company within the same group. For example, any one single company can specify without too much difficulty the precise headings under which information is being sought. In the case of one particular retailing company, under an assessment of the market environment, information and commentary were required on local demographic changes, competition, sales trends and sales per unit store area, and all clearly were provided for this purpose.

At each operating level this kind of information can be gathered in by means of the hierarchy of audits illustrated in Figure 12.4, with each area regional manager completing an audit for his area of accountability. Without such an information-collecting vehicle, it is difficult to formulate any strategic view.

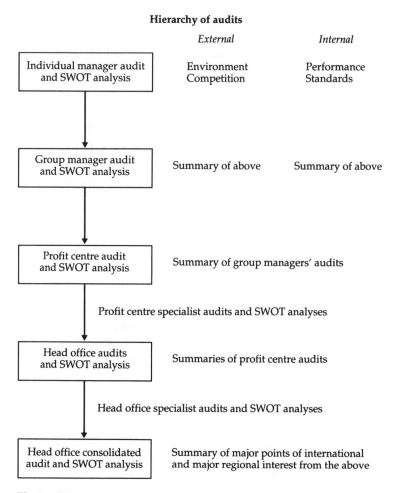

Figure 12.4

It has to be recognized that information and data are not always readily available, but given training, resources and understanding between headquarters and units, it is surprising how quickly information links that are of inestimable value to both sides can be forged.

Since in anything but the smallest of undiversified companies it is not possible for top management to set detailed objectives for operating units, it is suggested that at this stage in the planning process strategic guidelines should be issued. One way of doing this is in the form of a strategic planning letter. Another is by means of a personal briefing by the chief executive at 'kick-off' meetings. As in the case of the audit, these guidelines should proceed from the broad to the specific, and

Table 12.1 Chief executive's strategic planning letter (possible areas for which objective and strategies or strategic guidelines will be set)

Financial	*Retail operators*
Remittances	– Stores
– Dividends	– Modernizations
– Royalties	– Sales densities
Gross margin %	– Cost ratios
Operating profit	– Customer service levels
Return on capital employed	
Debtors	*Buying and merchandising*
Creditors	– Product mix development
Bank borrowing	– Gross/net margin
Investments	– Stock levels/stock turn
Capital expenditure	– Supplies policy
Cash flow controls	– Warehousing
	– Distribution
	– Quality control
Manpower and organization	*Marketing*
Management	Target markets
Training	Market segments
Industrial relations	Branding policies
Organization	Market shares
Remuneration and pensions	Pricing policies
	Image
Systems	Promotion
Computing	Market research
Networks, communications	Customer service requirements

should become more detailed as they progress through the company towards operating units. Table 12.1 contains a list of the headings under which strategic guidelines could be set.

Under marketing, for example, at the highest level in a large group, top management may ask for particular attention to be paid to issues such as the impact of leadership and innovation strategies, vulnerability to attack from competing stores or products, and so on. At operating company level it is possible to be more explicit about target markets, product development, and the like.

It is important to remember that it is top management's responsibility to determine the strategic direction of company, and to decide such issues as when businesses are to be milked, where to invest heavily in product development or market extension for a longer-term gain, and so on. If this is left to operating managers to decide for themselves, they will tend to opt for actions concerned principally with today's products and markets, because that is what they are judged on principally. There

Strategic and operational planning

Top-down and bottom-up

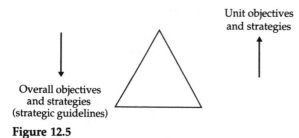

Unit objectives
and strategies

Overall objectives
and strategies
(strategic guidelines)

Figure 12.5

Strategic and operational planning

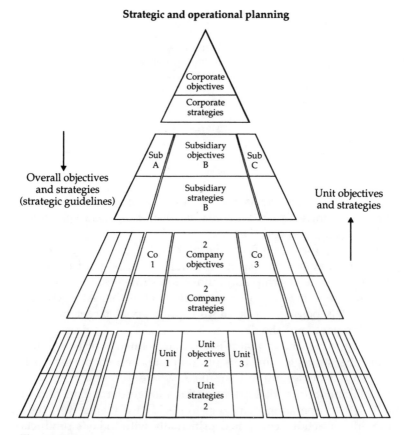

Overall objectives
and strategies
(strategic guidelines)

Unit objectives
and strategies

Figure 12.6

is also the problem of their inability to appreciate the larger, company-wide position.

Nevertheless the process just described demonstrates very clearly that there is total interdependence between top management and the lowest level of operating management in the objective- and strategy-setting process. In a very large company without any procedures for managing this process it is not difficult to see how control can be weakened and how vulnerability to rapid changes in the business environment can be increased. This interdependence between the top-down/bottom-up process is illustrated in Figures 12.5 and 12.6, which show a similar hierarchy in respect of objective- and strategy-setting to that illustrated in respect of audits.

Having explained the point about requisite marketing planning, we can also use these figures to illustrate the principles by which the marketing planning process should be implemented in any company, irrespective of whether it is a small local company or a major multinational. In essence these exhibits show a hierarchy of audits, SWOT analyses, objectives, strategies and programmes.

Figure 12.7 is another way of illustrating the total corporate strategic and planning process. This time, however, a time element is added, and

Strategic and operational planning

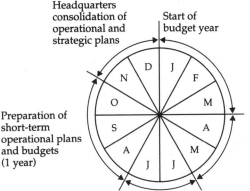

Headquarters consolidation of operational and strategic plans

Start of budget year

Issue of strategic planning letters or chief executive's 'kick-off' meetings
(open loop point 1)
Management audits
Marketing audits
SWOT analyses
Objectives, strategies
Budgets (proposed) long term (i.e. draft strategic marketing plans are prepared)

Preparation of short-term operational plans and budgets (1 year)

'Headquarters' review
Revise and agree long-term objectives, strategies, budgets (open loop point 2) (i.e. strategic marketing plans are finalized)

Figure 12.7

the relation between strategic planning letters, long-term corporate plans and short-term operational plans is clarified. It is important to note that there are two 'open loop' points on Figure 12.7. These are the key times in the planning process when a subordinate's views and findings should be subjected to the closest examination by his superior. It is by taking these opportunities that marketing planning can be transformed into the critical and creative process it is supposed to be rather than the dull, repetitive ritual it so often turns out to be. Figures 12.5, 12.6 and 12.7 should be seen as one group of illustrations showing how the marketing planning process fits into the wider context of corporate planning.

Conclusions

We must stress that there can be no such thing as an off-the-peg marketing planning system. Nonetheless both our research and our experience have indicated that marketing planning remains one of the last bastions of management ignorance, largely because of the complexity of the process and its organizational, political and cultural implications. It is for these reasons, and because so many of the readers of the first edition of this book asked for one, that we have added a final chapter that contains both a very brief summary of the main points described in the book and a simple, step-by-step system that can become the basis of your own planning procedures. The system provided has been used successfully in businesses ranging from big international industrial companies to small domestic service organizations.

In the end marketing planning success comes from an endless willingness to learn and to adapt the system to our people and our own circumstances. It also comes from a deep understanding about the nature of marketing planning, which is something that in the final analysis cannot be taught.

Success comes from experience. Experience comes from making mistakes. We can minimize these if we combine commonsense and sweet reasonableness with the models provided in this book. But be sure of one thing, above all else – by themselves the models will not work. However, if you read this book carefully and use the models sensibly, marketing planning becomes one of the most powerful tools available to a business today.

13

A step-by-step marketing planning system

Summary

This chapter is in two parts. The first part is a summary of the main points relating to marketing planning. The second part is an actual marketing planning system, which operationalizes all the concepts, structures and frameworks outlined in this book in the form of a step-by-step approach to the preparation first of a strategic and second an operational marketing plan. Finally, there is a suggested format for senior headquarters personnel who may have the task of summarizing many SBU strategic marketing plans into one consolidated document.

Part 1: Marketing planning summary

The purpose of marketing planning

The purpose of marketing planning and its principal focus is the identification and creation of sustainable competitive advantage.

What is marketing planning?

Marketing planning is simply a logical sequence and a series of activities leading to the setting of marketing objectives and the formulation of plans for achieving them.

Why is marketing planning necessary?

- Increasing turbulence, complexity, competitiveness of retail markets.
- Speed of technological change.

- For you:

    1   To help identify sources of competitive advantage.
    2   To force an organized approach.
    3   To develop specificity.
    4   To ensure consistent relations.

- For superiors

    1   to inform.

- For non-marketing functions:

    1   To get support.
    2   To get resources.

- For subordinates:

    1   To gain commitment.
    2   To set objectives and strategies.

Ten barriers to marketing planning

This book has described a number of barriers to effective marketing planning. The ten principal barriers are:

1   Confusion between marketing tactics and strategy.
2   Isolating the marketing function from operations.
3   Confusion between the marketing function and the marketing concept.
4   Organizational barriers – the tribal mentality, e.g. the failure to define strategic business units (SBUs) correctly.
5   Lack of in-depth analysis.
6   Confusion between process and output.
7   Lack of knowledge and skills.
8   Lack of a systematic approach to marketing planning.
9   Failure to prioritize objectives.
10   Hostile corporate cultures.

The 'Ten S' approach to overcoming these barriers

Figure 13.1 summarizes the 'Ten S' approach developed by Malcolm McDonald to overcome each of these barriers. The sections which follow elaborate briefly on each of the 'Ten Ss'. Ten fundamental principles of marketing planning are provided.

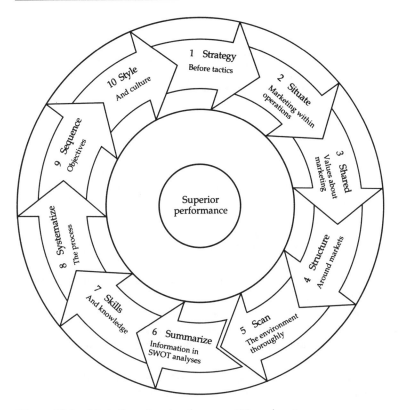

Figure 13.1 *Marketing planning for competitive advantage*

Marketing planning – Principle 1

Develop the strategic marketing plan first. This entails greater emphasis on scanning the external environment, early identification of forces emanating from it, and developing appropriate strategic responses, from all levels of management in the process.

A strategic plan should cover a period of between 3 and 5 years, and only when this plan has been developed and agreed should the 1-year operational marketing plan be developed. Never write the one-year plan first and extrapolate from it.

Marketing planning – Principle 2

For the purpose of marketing planning, put marketing as close as possible to store operations and therefore to the customer. Where practicable, have both marketing and retail operations report to the same person, who may not necessarily be the chief executive officer.

Marketing planning – Principle 3

Marketing is a management process whereby the resources of the whole organization are utilized to satisfy the needs of selected customer groups in order to achieve the objectives of both parties. Marketing, then, is first and foremost an attitude of mind rather than a series of functional activities.

Marketing planning – Principle 4

Organize company activities round target market segments if possible rather than round functional activities, and get marketing planning done in these strategic business units. Without excellent marketing planning in SBUs, corporate marketing planning will be of limited value.

Marketing planning – Principle 5

For an effective marketing audit to take place:

1 Checklists of questions customized according to level in the organization should be agreed.
2 These should form the basis of the organization's MIS.
3 The marketing audit should be a required activity.
4 Managers should not be allowed to hide behind vague terms such as 'poor economic conditions'.
5 Managers should be encouraged to incorporate the tools of marketing in their audits, e.g. product life cycles, portfolios and so on.

Marketing planning – Principle 6(1)

A SWOT should:

1 Be focused on each specific segment of crucial importance to the organization's future.
2 Be a summary emanating from the marketing audit.
3 Be brief, interesting and concise.
4 Focus on key factors only.
5 List differential strengths and weaknesses *vis-à-vis* competitors, focusing on competitive advantage.
6 List key external opportunities and threats only.
7 Identify and pin down the real issues. It should not be a list of unrelated points.
8 The reader should be able to grasp instantly the main thrust of the business, even to the point of being able to write marketing objectives.
9 Follow the implied question 'Which means that ....?' to get the real implications.
10 Do not over-abbreviate.

Marketing planning – Principle 6(2)
Information is the foundation on which a marketing plan is built. From information (internal and external) comes intelligence.

Intelligence describes the marketing plan, which is the intellectualization of how managers perceive their own position in their markets relative to their competitors (with competitive advantage accurately defined, e.g. price leader, differentiation, niche), what objectives they want to achieve over some designated period of time, how they intend to achieve their objectives (strategies), what resources are required, and with what results (budget).

Marketing planning – Principle 7
Ensure all those responsible for marketing in SBUs have the necessary marketing knowledge and skills for the job. In particular, ensure they understand and know how to use the more important tools of marketing, such as:

• Information:

　　1　How to get it.
　　2　How to use it.

• Positioning:

　　1　Market segmentation.
　　2　Ansoff.
　　3　Porter.

• Product life cycle analysis – gap analysis.

• Portfolio management:

　　1　BCG matrix.
　　2　Directional policy matrix.

• 4 x Ps management:

　　1　Product.
　　2　Price.
　　3　Place.
　　4　Promotion.

Additionally, marketing personnel require communications and interpersonal skills.

Marketing planning – Principle 8

It is essential to have a set of written procedures and a well-argued common format for marketing planning. The purposes of such a system are:

1   To ensure all key issues are systematically considered.
2   To pull together the essential elements of the strategic planning of each SBU in a consistent manner.
3   To help corporate management to compare diverse businesses and to understand the condition of, and prospects for, the organization.

Marketing planning – Principle 9

Ensure that all objectives are prioritized according to their impact on the organization and their urgency and that resources are allocated accordingly. A suggested method for prioritization is given in Figure 13.2.

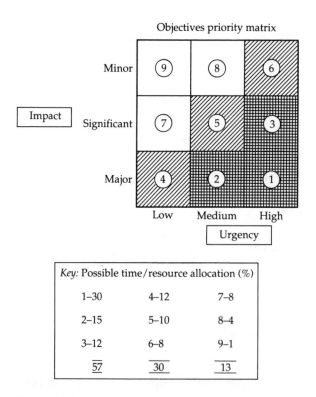

Figure 13.2

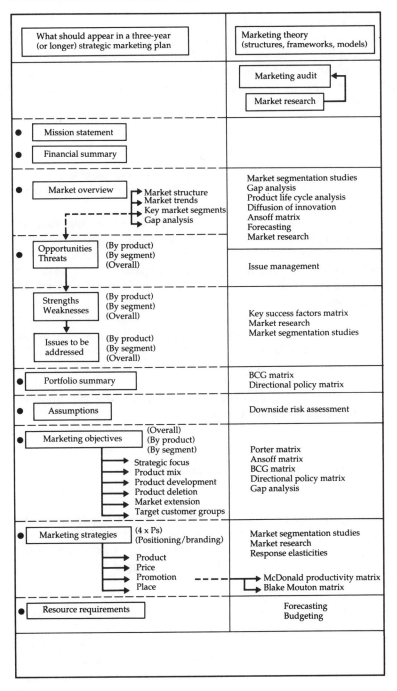

Figure 13.3

Marketing planning – Principle 10

Marketing planning will not be effective without the active support and participation of the culture leaders. But even with their support, the type of marketing planning has to be appropriate for the phase of the organizational lifeline. This phase should be measured before attempting to introduce marketing planning.

Conclusion

A summary of what appears in a strategic marketing plan and a list of the principal marketing tools/techniques/structures/frameworks which apply to each step is given in Figure 13.3.

It will be understood from the foregoing that marketing planning never has been just the simple step-by-step approach described so enthusiastically in most prescriptive texts and courses. The moment an organization embarks on the marketing planning path, it can expect to encounter a number of complex organizational, attitudinal, process and cognitive problems that are likely to block progress.

By being forewarned about these barriers, a company has a good chance of successfully using the step-by-step marketing planning system that follows in Part 2 of this chapter, and of doing excellent marketing planning that will bring all the claimed benefits, including a significant impact on the bottom line through the creation of competitive advantage. If the problems are ignored, however, marketing planning will remain the cinderella of business management.

Part 2: A marketing planning system

This marketing planning system comes in two sections. Section A takes you through a step-by-step approach to the preparation of a strategic marketing plan, and what actually appears in the marketing plan is given in Section B under the heading 'Strategic marketing plan documentation'.

Section A also takes you through the preparation of a 1-year marketing plan. What actually appears in a 1-year marketing plan is given in Section B under the heading 'The one-year marketing plan documentation' (p.318). Finally, Section A refers to the need for a headquarters consolidated plan of several SBU strategic marketing plans. A suggested format is given in B under the heading 'Example of format for a headquarters consolidated strategic plan' (p.325).

Section A

Let us first define a strategic business unit. It will:

- Have common segments and competitors for most of its products.
- Be a competitor in an external market.
- Be a discrete and identifiable unit.
- Have a manager who has control over most of the areas critical to success.

There are four main steps in the planning process (presented in diagrammatic form in Figure 13.4), which any strategic business unit (SBU) interested in protecting and developing its business must carry out:

1 *Analysis* – it must analyse both its market place and its own position within it, relative to the competition.
2 *Objectives* – it must construct from this analysis a realistic set of quantitative marketing and financial objectives, consistent with those set by the organization.
3 *Strategy* – it must determine the broad strategy that will accomplish these objectives in line with the organization's corporate strategy.
4 *Tactics* – it must draw together the analysis, the objectives and the strategy, using them as the foundation for detailed tactical action plans capable of implementing the strategy and achieving the agreed objectives.

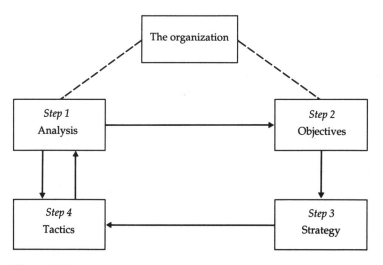

Figure 13.4

This process is formally expressed in two marketing plans, the strategic marketing plan and the tactical marketing plan, which should be written in accordance with the format provided in this system. It is designed for strategic business units (SBUs) to be able to take a logical and constructive approach to planning for success.

Two very important introductory points should be made about the marketing plan:

1 *Importance of different sections* – in the final analysis the strategic marketing plan is a plan for action, and this should be reflected in the finished document. The implementation part of the strategic plan is represented by the subsequent 1-year marketing plan.

2 *Length of analysis section* – to be able to produce an action-focused strategic marketing plan, a considerable amount of background information and statistics needs to be collected, collated and analysed. An analytical framework has been provided in the forms included in the database section of 'The strategic marketing plan documentation' (p.304), which each SBU should complete. However, the commentary given in the strategic marketing plan should provide the main findings of the analysis rather than a mass of raw data. It should compel concentration upon only that which is essential. The analysis section should therefore provide only a short background.

Basis of the system

Each business unit in the organization will have different levels of opportunity, depending on the prevailing business climate. Each business unit therefore needs to be managed in a way that is appropriate to its own unique circumstances. At the same time, however, the chief executive officer of the SBU must have every opportunity to see that the ways in which these business units are managed are consistent with the strategic aims of the organization. This system sets out the procedures, which, if adhered to, will assist in achieving these aims.

Section A sets out the marketing planning format and explains how each of the planning steps should be carried out. It explains simply and clearly what should be presented, and when, in both the 3-year marketing plan and the more detailed 1-year operational plan.

A glossary of planning terms is included at the end of the book (p.329). The marketing planning format is described in Figure 13.5. (Please note that for the sake of simplicity it has been assumed that the organization's year runs from January to December.) The following sections explain how each of the steps in the planning process should be completed.

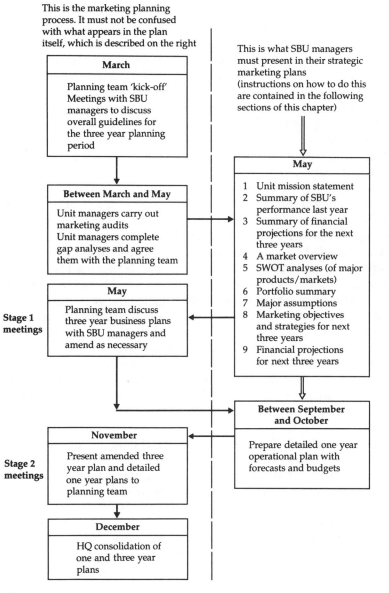

This is the marketing planning process. It must not be confused with what appears in the plan itself, which is described on the right

This is what SBU managers must present in their strategic marketing plans
(instructions on how to do this are contained in the following sections of this chapter)

March

Planning team 'kick-off' Meetings with SBU managers to discuss overall guidelines for the three year planning period

Between March and May

Unit managers carry out marketing audits
Unit managers complete gap analyses and agree them with the planning team

May

1 Unit mission statement
2 Summary of SBU's performance last year
3 Summary of financial projections for the next three years
4 A market overview
5 SWOT analyses (of major products/markets)
6 Portfolio summary
7 Major assumptions
8 Marketing objectives and strategies for next three years
9 Financial projections for next three years

Stage 1 meetings

May

Planning team discuss three year business plans with SBU managers and amend as necessary

Between September and October

Prepare detailed one year operational plan with forecasts and budgets

Stage 2 meetings

November

Present amended three year plan and detailed one year plans to planning team

December

HQ consolidation of one and three year plans

Figure 13.5

Marketing audit

Every market includes a wide variety of customer groups, not all of which will necessarily provide SBUs with opportunities for servicing profitably. In order to study those areas of the market that are potentially most favourable to the SBU's operations, it is necessary to divide the market into different market segments (hereafter just referred to as 'segments') and to analyse sales potential by type of product within each segment. All SBUs must therefore, analyse and evaluate the key segments in their market, plus any other segments which have been identified and selected as being of lesser importance to them.

It is appreciated that all the basic information required for this marketing audit may not be readily available. Nevertheless an analysis and evaluation of the SBUs' situation in each of the selected segments, i.e. a marketing audit, will provide the basis from which objectives can be set and plans prepared.

Each manager carrying out his audit should use internal sales data and the SBU marketing information system to complete his or her audit. It is helpful at this stage if the various SBU managers can issue any subordinates engaged in the audit with a market overview covering major industry and market trends. The audit will inevitably require considerably more data preparation than is required to be reproduced in the marketing plan itself. Therefore all managers should start a running reference file for their area of responsibility during the year; this file can also be used as a continual reference source and for verbal presentation of proposals.

It is essential to stress that the audit, which will be based on the running reference file, is not a marketing plan, and under no circumstances should voluminous documents relating to the audit appear in any business plans. The audit should be done between February and May each year.

The following sections (1–9) describe what should be presented in marketing plans. These should be completed by the end of May each year. These sections contain instructions. The actual documentation for the strategic marketing plans is provided in Section B.

1 SBU mission statement

This is the first item to appear in the marketing plan. The purpose of the mission statement is to ensure that the *raison d'être* of the SBU is clearly stated. Brief statements should be made to cover the following points:

(a) Role or contribution of the unit – e.g. profit-generator, service department, opportunity-seeker.
(b) Definition of business – e.g. the needs you satisfy or the benefits you provide. Do not be too specific (e.g. 'we sell grey fashion suits') or too general (e.g. 'we are in the clothing business').

(c) Distinctive competence – this should be a brief statement that applies only to your specific SBU. A statement that could equally apply to any competitor is unsatisfactory.

(d) Indications for future direction – a brief statement of the principal things you would give serious considerations to, e.g. move into a new segment.

Note: this is Form 1 in the strategic marketing plan documentation (p.304).

2   Summary of SBU's performance

This opening section is designed to give a bird's eye view of the SBU's total marketing activities. In addition to a quantitative summary of performance, as shown in Table 13.1, SBU managers should give a summary of reasons for good or bad performance. Use constant revenue (1–1) in order that the comparisons are meaningful. Make sure you use the same base-year values for any projections provided in later sections of this system.

Table 13.1

	Three years ago	*Two years ago*	*Last year*
Volume/turnover			
Gross profit (%)			
Gross margin (£000)			

Note: this is Form 2 in the strategic marketing plan documentation (p.305).

3   Summary of financial projections

This is the third item to appear in the marketing plan. Its purpose is to summarize for the person reading the plan, the financial implications over the full 3-year planning period. It should be presented as a simple diagram along the lines shown in Figure 13.6. This should be accompanied by a brief commentary. For example:

This 3-year business plan shows an increase in sales from £700,000 to £900,000 and an increase in contribution from £100,000 to £400,000. The purpose of this marketing plan is to show how these increases will be achieved.

There is a form, Form 3, in the strategic marketing plan documentation (p.306). In order to comply with this form, it is strongly recommended

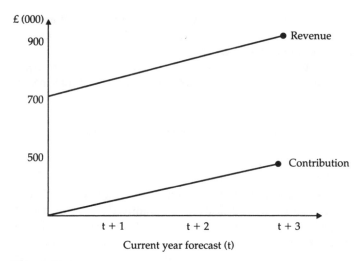

Figure 13.6

that Form 4, the strategic planning (gap analysis) form (p.307), is completed first. Please note that the 'objective' point should be (as a minimum) that point which will enable you to achieve the corporate objectives set for the SBU. Ideally, however, it should be set at a point that will make this SBU the best of its kind among comparable competitive SBUs. Note that the form for this is Form 4 (p.307).

4   Market overview

This section is intended to provide a brief picture of the market before descending to the particular details of individual market segments, which form the heart of the marketing plan.

This system is based upon the segmentation of markets, dividing these into homogeneous groups of customers, each having characteristics that can be exploited in marketing terms. This approach is taken because it is the one that is often the most useful for SBU managers to be able to develop their markets. The alternative, product-orientated approach is rarely appropriate, given the variation between different customer groups in the markets in which most organizations compete. The market segmentation approach is more useful in revealing both the weaknesses and the development opportunities than is an exclusively product-orientation.

While it is difficult to give precise instructions on how to present this section of the marketing plan, it should be possible (following completion of the marketing audit) to present a market overview that summarizes what managers consider to be the key changes in their markets.

In completing this section, SBU managers should consider the following:

- What are the major products, markets (or segments) which are likely to be able to provide the kind of business opportunities suitable for the organization.
- How are these changing, i.e. which are growing and which are declining?

This section should be brief and there should be some commentary by the SBU manager about what seems to be happening in the market. It is very helpful if SBU managers can present as much of this information as possible visually, i.e. bar charts or pie charts, product life cycles, etc.

There is a form, Form 5, in the strategic marketing plan documentation (p.308).

5 SWOT analyses of major products/market segments

To decide on marketing objectives and future strategy, it is first necessary to summarize the SBU's present position in its market(s). This was done in the previous section.

In respect of the major products/market segments highlighted in the previous section, the marketing audit must now be summarized in the form of a number of SWOT analyses. The word SWOT derives from the initial letters of the words strengths, weaknesses, opportunities and threats. In simple terms:

- What are the opportunities?
- What are the present and future threats to the SBU's business in each of the segments that have been identified as being of importance?
- What are the unit's differential strengths and weaknesses *vis-à-vis* competitors? In other words, why should potential customers in the target markets prefer to buy from your store(s) rather than from those of your competitors?

The market overview in Section 4 will have identified what you consider to be the major products/market segments on which you intend to focus. For presentation purposes it is helpful if you can present a brief SWOT for each of these key product/market segments. Each of these SWOTs should be brief and interesting to read. Complete SWOTs only for the key segments.

Section I concerns strengths and weaknesses. Section II is intended to indicate how the opportunities and threats section of the SWOT should be completed. Section III summarizes key issues to be addressed. Section

IV describes the setting of assumptions, marketing objectives and strategies for each major products/market segments. Section V summarizes the position of competitors.

I   Some important factors for success in this business (critical success factors). How would a competitor wishing to start retailing in this segment succeed? There are always relatively few factors that determine success. Factors such as product appeal, breadth of range, customer service, low price and so on, are often the most important factors.

You should now make a brief statement about your organization's strengths and weaknesses in relation to these most important factors for success that you have identified. To do this, you will probably wish to consider other retailers in the same segment in order to identify why you believe your organization can succeed, and what weaknesses must be addressed in the 3-year planning period.

These factors are called critical success factors. A layout such as that shown in Figure 13.7 is useful. You should then weight each factor out of 100, e.g. CSF 1 = 60; CSF 2 = 25; CSF 3 = 10; CSF 4 = 5. It is suggested that you score yourself and each competitor out of 10 on each of the CSFs, then multiply each score by the weight. This will give you an accurate reading of your position in each segment *vis-à-vis* your competitors. It will also highlight the key issues that should be addressed in the 3-year planning period.

II   Summary of outside influences and their implications (opportunities and threats). This should include a brief statement about how important environmental influences such as technology, government policies and regulations, the economy and so on, have affected this segment. There will obviously be some opportunities and some threats.

III   Key issues to be addressed. From I and II above will emerge a number of key issues to be addressed.

IV   Assumptions, marketing objectives, marketing strategies. Assumptions can now be made and objectives and strategies set. It should be stressed at this point that such assumptions, objectives and strategies relate only to each particular major products/market segments under consideration. These will guide your thinking when setting overall assumptions, marketing objectives and strategies later on.

There is a form, Form 6, in the strategic marketing plan documentation (p.309), which incorporates all the points made in I, II, III and IV above and should be completed for all major products/market segments under consideration.

V   Competitor analysis. Here you should summarize the findings of the audit in respect of major competitors only. For each competitor, you

Competitors Critical success factors	Weighting factor	Your organization	Competitor A	Competitor B	Competitor C
CSF 1					
CSF 2					
CSF 3					
CSF 4					
Total weighted score	100				

Figure 13.7

should indicate their sales within the particular product/market segment under consideration, their share now, and their expected share 3 years from now. The greater a competitor's influence over others, the greater their ability to implement their own independent strategies, hence the more successful they are. It is suggested that you should also classify each of your main competitors according to one of the classifications in the *Guide to Competitive Position Classification* below, i.e. leadership, strong, favourable, tenable, weak.

In addition, list their principal products or services. Next, list each major competitor's business direction and current strategies. Then, list their major strengths and weaknesses. The format shown in Figure 13.8 is useful, and there is a form, Form 7, in the strategic marketing plan documentation (p.310).

The following is a guide to competitive position classifications:

Leadership • Has major influence on performance or behaviour of others.

Strong • Has a wide choice of strategies.
• Able to adopt independent strategy without endangering short-term position.
• Has low vulnerability to competitors' action.

Competitor analysis					
Main competitor	*Products/ markets*	*Business direction and current objectives and strategies*	*Strengths*	*Weaknesses*	*Competitive position*

Figure 13.8

Favourable	• Exploits specific competitive strength, often in a product-market niche.
	• Has more than average opportunity to improve position; several strategies available.
Tenable	• Performance justifies continuation in business.
Weak	• Currently unsatisfactory performance; significant competitive weakness.
	• Inherently a short-term condition; must improve or withdraw.

The following list includes five business directions that are appropriate for almost any business. Select those that best summarize the competitor's strategy.

1   *Enter* – allocate resources to a new business area. Consideration should include building from prevailing company or division strengths, exploiting related opportunities and defending against perceived threats. May call for creation of a new retail format.

2 *Improve* – to apply strategies that will significantly improve the competitive position of the business. Often requires thoughtful product/market segmentation.
3 *Maintain* – to maintain one's competitive position. Aggressive strategies may be required, although a defensive posture may also be assumed. Product/market position is maintained, often in a niche.
4 *Harvest* – to relinquish intentionally competitive position, emphasizing short-term profit and cash flow but not necessarily at the risk of losing the business in the short term. Often entails consolidating or reducing various aspects of the business to create higher performance for that which remains.
5 *Exit* – to divest a business because of its weak competitive position or because the cost of staying in it is prohibitive and the risk associated with improving its position is too high.

6 Portfolio summary (summary of SWOTs)
All that remains is to summarize each of these SWOTs in a format that makes it easy to see at a glance the position and relative importance of each of these segments to the organization. This can be done by drawing a diagram in the form of a four-box matrix that will show each of the important product/market segments described earlier. A matrix is shown above as Figure 13.9. Some easy-to-follow instructions are given below on how to complete such a matrix. More detailed instructions are provided in Chapter 5.

The Portfolio matrix (referred to as the directional policy matrix in Chapter 5) enables you to assess which products or services or which groups of customers/segments will offer the best chance of commercial success. It will also help you to decide which products or services (or market segments) merit investment, both in terms of finance and managerial effort.

In this example, market segments are used, although it is possible to use products or services. We recommend that you follow the instructions given below. This is how you arrive at a portfolio matrix for your SBU.

1 List your market segments on a separate piece of paper and decide which ones are the most attractive. To arrive at these decisions you will no doubt take several factors into account:

(a) The size of the markets.
(b) Their actual or prospective growth.
(c) The prices you can charge.
(d) Profitability.

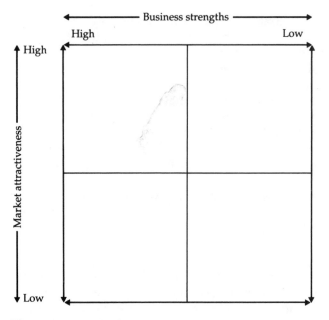

Figure 13.9

(e) The diversity of needs (which you can meet).
(f) The amount of competition in terms of quality and quantity.
(g) The supportiveness of the business environment.
(h) Technical developments, etc.

   Imagine that you have a measuring instrument, something like a thermometer but which measures not temperature but market attractiveness. The higher the reading, the more attractive the market. The instrument is shown in Figure 13.10. Estimate the position on the scale each of your markets would record (should such an instrument exist) and make a note of it as shown by the example above. You should use the methodology outlined in Chapter 5 and the example provided in Table 5.3.

2 Transfer this information on to the matrix in Figure 13.9, writing the markets on the left of the matrix.

3 Still using the matrix, draw a dotted line horizontally across from the top left-hand market, as shown in Figure 13.11.

4 Now ask yourself how well your SBU is equipped to deal with this most attractive market. A whole series of questions needs to be asked to establish the company's business strengths, for example:

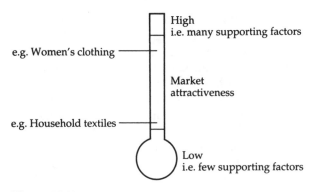

Figure 13.10

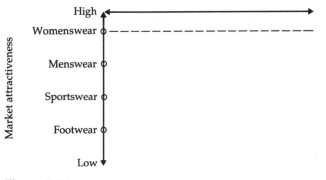

Figure 13.11

(a) Are we big enough?
(b) Can we grow?
(c) How large is our market share?
(d) Do we have the right products?
(e) How well are we known in this market?
(f) What image do we have?
(g) Do we have the right technical skills?
(h) Can we adapt to changes?
(i) Do we have the right supplier here?
(j) How close are we to this market?
(k) How do we compare with competitors?

The outcome of such an analysis will enable you to arrive at a conclusion about the 'fitness' of your unit, and you will be able to choose a point on the horizontal scale of the matrix to represent this.

The left of the scale represents many unit strengths, the right few unit strengths. Please note that the analysis completed in the previous section (Section 5 on SWOT analyses) should be used as input to this exercise, since you have already completed the necessary quantification. Draw a vertical line from this point on the scale, as shown in Figure 13.12, so that it intersects with the horizontal line. (Be certain, however, to use the quantitative method outlined in Chapter 5.)

5   Now redraw the circles, this time making the diameter of each circle proportional to that segment's share of your total sales turnover. (Please note that to be technically correct you should take the square root of the volume.

6   Now indicate where these circles will be in 3 years' time and their estimated size. (The matrix may therefore have to show segments not currently served.) Please note that there are two ways of doing this. First, in deciding on market or segment attractiveness you can assume that you are at t.0, i.e. today, and that your forecast of attractiveness covers the next 3 years, i.e. t + 3. If this is your chosen method, then it will be clear that the circle can only move horizontally along the axis, as all that will change is your business strength.

The second way of doing it shows the current attractiveness position on the vertical axis, based on the past 3 years, i.e. t − 3 to t.0, and then forecasts how that attractiveness position will change during the next 3 years, i.e. t.0 to t+ 3. In such a case the circles can move both vertically and horizontally. This is the method used in the

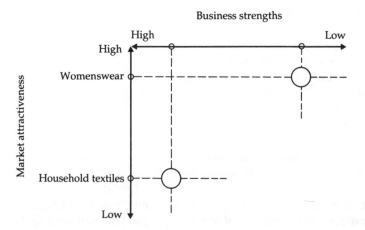

Figure 13.12

example provided (Figure 13.13), but it is entirely up to you which method you use. It is essential to be creative in your use of the matrix. Be prepared to change the name on the axes and to experiment with both products and markets.

There is a form, Form 8, in the strategic marketing plan documentation (p.311).

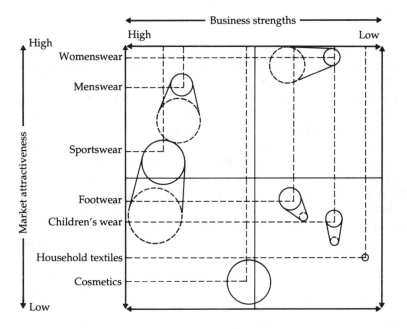

Figure 13.13

7 Assumptions
Each SBU must highlight the assumptions that are critical to the fulfilment of the planned marketing objectives and strategies.

Key planning assumptions deal in the main with outside features and anticipated changes that would have a significant influence on the achievement of marketing objectives. These might include such things as market growth rate, your organization's costs, capital investment and so on.

Assumptions should be few in number and relate only to key issues such as market growth rate, your organization's costs, capital investment and so on, i.e. issues such as those identified in the SWOT analyses. If it is possible for a plan to be implemented irrespective of the assumptions made, then those assumptions are not necessary and should be removed.

You should find that the more detailed lists of assumptions made for each of the principal product/market segments analysed in the SWOT stage (Section 5) will be helpful in deciding what the macro assumptions should be.

There is a form, Form 9, in the strategic marketing plan documentation (p.312).

8 Setting objectives and strategies

Following identification and statement of key strengths, weaknesses, opportunities and threats, and the explicit statement of assumptions about conditions affecting the business, the process of *setting marketing objectives* is made easier, since they will be a realistic statement of what the SBU desires to achieve as a result of market-centred analysis. As in the case of the objective setting for other functional areas of the business, this is the most important step in the whole process, as it is a commitment on an SBU-wide basis to a particular course of action that will determine the scheduling and costing out of subsequent actions.

An objective is what the unit wants to achieve. A strategy is how it plans to achieve it. Thus there are objectives and strategies at all levels in marketing. For example, there can be advertising objectives and strategies, pricing objectives and strategies, and so on.

However, the important point about marketing objectives is that they should be about products and markets only, since it is only by selling something to someone that the SBU's financial goals can be achieved. Advertising, pricing and other elements of the marketing mix are other means (the strategies) by which the SBU can succeed in doing this. Thus, pricing objectives, sales promotion objectives, advertising objectives and so on should not be confused with marketing objectives.

If profits and cash flows are to be maximized, each SBU must consider carefully how its current customer needs are changing and how its products offered need to change accordingly. Since change is inevitable, it is necessary for SBUs to consider the two main dimensions of commercial growth, i.e. product development and market development.

Marketing objectives are concerned with the following:

- Selling existing products to existing segments.
- Developing new products for existing segments.

- Extending existing products to new segments.
- Developing new products for new segments.

Marketing objectives should be quantitative, and should be expressed where possible in terms of values, volumes, and market shares. General directional terms such as 'maximize', 'minimize', 'penetrate' should be avoided, unless quantification is included.

Marketing objectives should cover the full 3-year planning horizon and should be acompanied by broad strategies (discussed in the following section) and broad revenue and cost projections for the full 3-year period. The 1-year marketing plan should contain specific objectives for the first year of the 3-year planning cycle, and the corresponding strategies that will be used to achieve these objectives. The 1-year and the 3-year plans should be separate documents. At this stage a detailed 1-year plan is not required.

At this point it is worth stressing that the key document in the annual planning round is the 3-year strategic plan. The 1-year plan represents the specific actions that should be undertaken in the first year of the strategic plan.

Marketing strategies should state in broad terms how the marketing objectives are to be achieved, as follows:

- The specific product policies (the range, technical specifications, additions, deletions, etc.).
- The pricing policies to be followed for product groups in particular market segments.
- The customer service levels to be provided for specific market segments (such as store staffing levels).
- The policies for communicating with customers under each of the main headings, such as window displays, advertising, sales promotion, etc., as appropriate.

Guidelines for setting marketing objectives and strategies are given in Chapter 6. However, the following summarizes some of the marketing objectives and strategies that are available to SBU managers.

Objectives include:

1 Market penetration.
2 Introduction of new products to existing markets.
3 Introduction of existing products to new markets (domestic).
4 Introduction of existing products to new markets (international).
5 Introduction of new products to new markets.

Strategies include:

1   Changing product mix/positioning.
2   Changing product design, performance, quality or features.
3   Changing advertising or promotion.
4   Changing pricing policy/stance.
5   Changing staffing levels and improving productivity.
6   Improving supply chain management.
7   Improving administrative productivity.
8   Changing sourcing.
9   Withdrawing from markets.
10   Changing stock levels.
11   Standardization of design, consolidation of production, change of sourcing.

9   Guidelines for setting marketing objectives and strategies

Completing a portfolio matrix (which you have done in Section 7) for each major product/market segment within each unit translates the characteristics of the business into visible and easily understood positions *vis-à-vis* each other. Additionally, each product/market segment's position on the matrix suggests broad goals which are usually appropriate for business in that position, athough unit managers should also consider alternative goals in the light of the special circumstances prevailing at the time.

The four categories on the matrix are:

• Star.
• Cash cow.
• Dog.
• Wildcat/problem child/question mark.

These are the original terms coined by the Boston Consulting Group, and they have been retained here for the directional policy matrix. You may prefer to use your own terms, although it should be stressed that it isn't necessary to attach any particular names to each of the quadrants. Each of these is considered in turn.

Star products enjoy competitive positions in markets/segments characterized by high growth rates, and are good for continuing attractiveness. The obvious objective for such products is to maintain growth rates at least at the market growth rate, thus maintaining market share and market leadership, or to grow faster than the market, thus increasing market share.

Three principal factors should be considered:

1   Possible geographical expansion.
2   Possible product line expansion.
3   Possible product line differentiation.

These could be achieved by means of internal development, acquisition, or joint ventures. The main point is that in attractive marketing situations like this, an aggressive marketing posture is required, together with a very tight budgeting and control process to ensure that capital resources are efficiently utlized.

Cash cow products enjoy competitive positions in markets/segments that are not considered attractive in the longer term. Here the thrust should be towards maintaining a profitable position, with greater emphasis on present earnings rather than on aggressive growth.

The most successful product lines should be maintained, while less successful ones should be considered for pruning. Marketing effort should be focused on differentiating products to maintain share of key segments of the market. Discretionary marketing expenditure should be limited, especially when unchallenged by competitors or when products have matured. Comparative prices should be stabilized, except when a temporary aggressive stance is necessary to maintain market share.

Dogs have a poor position in unattractive markets, but are 'bad' only if objectives are not appropriate to the company's position in the market segment. Generally, where immediate divestment is not warranted, these products should be managed for cash. Product lines should be aggressively pruned, while all marketing expenditure should be minimized, with prices maintained or, where possible, raised.

However, a distinction needs to be made between genuine 'dogs' and 'cash dogs'. **Genuine 'dogs'** should generally be managed as outlined above. **'Cash dogs'**, i.e. products close to the 'cash cow' quadrant, should generally be managed differently. For example, the reality of low growth should be acknowledged and the temptation to grow the product at its previous high rates of growth should be resisted. It should not be viewed as a 'marketing' problem, which will be likely to lead to high advertising, promotion, inventory costs and lower profitability. Growth segments should be identified and exploited where possible. Product quality should be emphasized to avoid 'commodity' competition. Productivity should be systematically improved. Finally, the attention of talented managers should be focused on 'cash dogs'.

Wildcats/problem children/question marks. With these it is necessary to decide whether to invest for future market leadership or to manage for present earnings. Both objectives are feasible, but it must be remembered that managing these products for cash today is usually inconsistent with market share growth, and it is usually necessary to select the most promising wildcats and invest in them only.

Further marketing and other functional guidelines that operating unit managers should consider when setting marketing objectives and corresponding strategies are given in Chapter 6. It should be stressed, however, that there can be no automatic policy for a particular product or market, and SBU managers should consider three or more options before deciding on 'the best' for recommendation. Above all, SBU managers must evaluate the most attractive opportunities and assess the chances for success in the most realistic manner possible. This applies particularly to new business opportunities, which would normally be expected to build on existing strengths, particularly in marketing, and can be subsequently expanded or supplemented.

The forms included in the database provide both an analytical framework and a summary of marketing objectives that are relevant to all strategic business unit managers. The forms are the following:

Form 10 (p.313)   Market segment sales value, showing, across a 5-year period, total market demand, the business unit's own sales and the market share these represent for the various market segments.

Form 11 (p.314)   Market segment gross profits, showing, across a 5-year period, the business unit's sales value, gross profit, and gross margin for the various market segments.

Form 12 (p.315)   Product group analysis, showing, across a 5-year period, the business unit's sales value, gross profit, and gross margin for different product groups.

Form 13 (p.316)   Summary (in words) of main marketing objectives and strategies.

Financial projections for 3 years

Finally, SBU managers should provide financial projections for the full 3-year planning period under all the principal standard revenue and cost headings as specified by your organization. See Form 14, in the strategic marketing plan documentation, p. 317. The tactical 1-year marketing plan should be kept separate from the 3-year strategic plan and should not be completed until the planning team has approved the strategic plan in May each year.

The **tactical 1-year marketing plan** should begin with the development of specific sub-objectives for products and segments, supported by more detailed strategy and action statements. Include budgets and targets and a consolidated budget, reflecting the marketing objectives and strategies; in turn the objectives, strategies and programmes must reflect the agreed budgets and sales forecasts. Their main purpose is to delineate the major steps required in implementation, to assign accountability to focus on the main decision points, and to specify required allocation of resources and their timing.

If the procedures in this system are followed, a hierarchy of objectives will be built up in such a way that every item of budgeted expenditure can be related back to the initial financial objectives (this is known as task-related budgeting). Thus, when, say, advertising has been identified as a means of achieving an objective in a particular market, i.e. advertising is a strategy to be used, all advertising expenditure against items appearing in the budget can be related back specifically to a main objective. The essential feature of this is that budgets are set against both the marketing objectives and the sub-objectives for each element of the marketing mix.

The principal advantage is that this method allows operating units to build up and demonstrate an increasingly clear picture of their markets. In addition, this method of budgeting allows every item of expenditure to be fully accounted for as part of an objective approach. It also ensures that when changes have to be made during the period to which the plan relates, such changes can be made in a way that causes the least damage to the SBU's long-term objectives.

Because of the varying nature of strategic business units, it is impossible to provide a standard format for all SBUs. There is, however, a minimum amount of information which should be provided to accompany the financial documentation between September and October. There is no need to supply market background information, as this should have been completed in the 3-year strategic marketing plan.

The suggested format for the 1-year marketing plan is as follows:

1(a) *Overall objectives* (see Form 1 in 1-year marketing plan documentation, p.318) – these should cover the following:

Volume or value	Last year	Current year estimate	Budget next year
Gross margins	Last year	Current year estimate	Budget next year

Against each there should be a few words of commentary/explanation.

1(b) *Overall strategies*, e.g. new customer segements, new products, advertising, sales promotion, selling, customer service, pricing. For a list of marketing strategies, see Chapter 6. See also Form 2 in 1-year marketing plan documentation, p.319.

2(a) *Sub-objectives* (see Form 3 in 1-year marketing plan documentation (p.320)) – more detailed objectives should be provided for products or markets or segments or major customers, as appropriate.

2(b) *Strategies* – the means by which sub-objectives will be achieved should be stated.

2(c) *Action/tactics* – the details, timing, responsibility and cost should also be stated.

3   *Summary of marketing activities and costs* (see Form 4 in 1-year marketing plan documentation, p.321).

4   *Contingency plan* (see Form 5 in 1-year marketing plan documentation, p.322) – it is important to include a contingency plan, which should address the following questions:

(a) What are the critical assumptions on which the 1-year plan is based?

(b) What would the financial consequences, i.e. the effect on the operating income, be if these assumptions did not come true?

(c) How will these assumptions be managed?

(d) What action will you take to ensure that the adverse financial effects of an unfulfulled assumption are mitigated, so that you end up with the same forecast profit at the end of the year?

To measure the risk, assess the negative or downside, asking what can go wrong with each assumption that would change the outcome. For example, if a sales growth rate of 5 per cent is a key assumption, what lower growth rate would have to occur before a substantially different management decision would be taken?

5   *Operating result and financial ratio* (see Form 6 in 1-year marketing plan documentation, p.323). Note: this form is provided only as an example, for clearly all organizations will have their own formats. They should include:

- Net revenue.
- Gross margin.
- Adjustments.
- Marketing costs.
- Store costs.
- Administrative costs.
- Buying department costs.

- Interest.
- Operating result.
- ROS.
- ROI.

6   *Key activity planner* (see Form 7 in 1-year marketing plan documen-
     tation, p.324) – finally, you should summarize the key activities and
     indicate the start and finish. This should help you considerably
     with monitoring the progress of your annual plan.
7   *Other* – there may be other information you wish to provide, such
     as sales call plans.

The author is frequently asked how several SBU strategic marketing
plans should be consolidated by senior headquarters marketing personnel. A suggested format for this task is provided in Section B under the
heading 'Example of format for a headquarters consolidated strategic
plan' (p.325).

Timetable
The main steps and timing for the annual round of strategic and operational planning are described in the following pages. The planning
process is in two separate stages, which are interrelated to provide a
review point before the detailed quantification of plans. 'Stage 1'
comprises the statement of key and critical objectives for the full 3-year
planning period, to be reviewed before the more detailed quantification
of the tactical 1-year plan in 'Stage 2' by 30 November for subsequent
consolidation into the company plans.

The planning team's 'kick-off' meeting (to be completed by 31 March)
will give the team a chance to outline expectations for the following
planning cycle. The main purpose of the meeting is to give the planning
team the opportunity to explain corporate policy, report progress during
the previous planning cycle, and give a broad indication of what is
expected from each SBU during the forthcoming cycle. The team's
review will include an appraisal of performance against plan, as well as
a variance analysis. The briefing will give guidance under some of the
following headings (as appropriate).

1   Financial:
    (a) Gross margins.
    (b) Operating profits.
    (c) Debtors.
    (d) Creditors.
    (e) Cash flow

2 Manpower and organization:
   (a) Organization.
   (b) Succession.
   (c) Training.
   (d) Remuneration.

3 Export strategy

4 Marketing:
   (a) Product development.
   (b) Target markets.
   (c) Market segments.
   (d) Volumes.
   (e) Market shares.
   (f) Pricing.
   (g) Promotion.
   (h) Market research.
   (i) Quality control.
   (j) Customer service.

This meeting comes before the SBUs engage in the mainstream planning activity, and is the principal means by which it can be ensured that plans do not become stale and repetitive through over-bureaucratization. Marketing creativity will be the keynote of this meeting.

Top-down and bottom-up planning
A cornerstone of the marketing planning philosophy is that there should be widespread understanding at all levels in the organization of the key objectives that have to be achieved, and of the key means of achieving them. This way, the actions and decisions that are taken by managers will be disciplined by clear objectives that hang logically together as part of a rational purpose. The only way this will happen is if the planning system is firmly based on market-centred analysis emanating from the SBUs themselves. Therefore, after the planning team's 'kick-off' meetings, audits should be carried out by all managers in the SBUs down to a level that will be determined by SBU managers. Each manager will also do SWOT analyses and set tentative 3-year objectives and strategies, together with proposed budgets for initial consideration by superior managers. In this way each superior will be responsible for synthesizing the work of those managers reporting to them.

The important steps in the annual planning cycle, listed below, are depicted schematically in Figure 13.14.

Figure 13.14 *Strategic and operational planning cycle*

Activity	Deadline
• Planning team's 'kick-off' meetings with SBU managers to discuss guidelines for the 3-year planning period	31 March
• Prepare marketing audits, SWOT analyses, proposed marketing objectives, strategies and budgets (cover full 3-year planning horizon)	31 May
• 'Stage 1' meetings: presentation to planning team for review	31 May
• Prepare short-term (1-year) operational plans and budgets, and final 3-year SBU managers' consolidated marketing plans	31 October
• 'Stage 2' meetings: presentation to planning team	31 November
• Final consolidation of the marketing plans	31 December

Section B(1) – The strategic marketing plan documentation

Form 1

Unit mission statement

This is the first item to appear in the business plan.

The purpose of the mission statement is to ensure that the *raison d'etre* of the unit is clearly stated. There should be brief statements covering the following points:

1 *Role or contribution of the unit*
For example,   Profit-generator
Service department
Opportunity-seeker

2 *Definition of the business*
For example, the needs you satisfy or the benefits you provide. Don't be too specific or too general.

3 *Distinctive competence*
This should be a brief statement that applies only to your specific unit. A statement that could equally apply to any competitor is unsatisfactory.

4 *Indications for future direction*
A brief statement of the principal things you would give serious consideration to (e.g. move into a new segment).

Form 2

Summary of SBU's performance

This opening section is designed to give a bird's eye view of the SBU's total marketing activities.

In addition to a quantative summary of performance, as follows, SBU managers should give a summary of reasons for good or bad performance.

Use constant revenue in order that comparisons are meaningful.

Make sure you use the same base year values for any projections in later sections of this system.

	3 years ago	2 years ago	Last year
Volume/turnover			
Gross profit (%)			
Gross margin (£000)			

Summary of reasons for good or bad performance

Form 3

Summary of Financial projections

This is the third item to appear in the marketing plan. Its purpose is to summarize for the person reading the plan the financial results over the full 3-year planning period.

It should be presented as a simple diagram along the following lines:

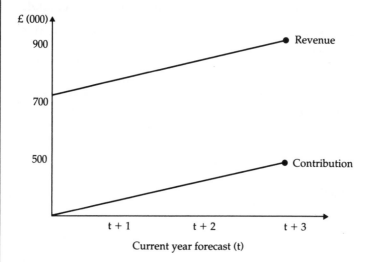

This should be accompanied by a brief commentary

For example:

'This 3-year business plan shows an increase in revenue from £700,000 to £900,000 and an increase in contribution from £100,000 to £400,000. The purpose of this business plan is to show how these increases will be achieved.'

Strategic planning exercise (gap analysis)

1 *Objective*

(a) Start by plotting the sales position you wish to achieve at the end of the planning period, point E

(b) Next plot the forecast position, Point A

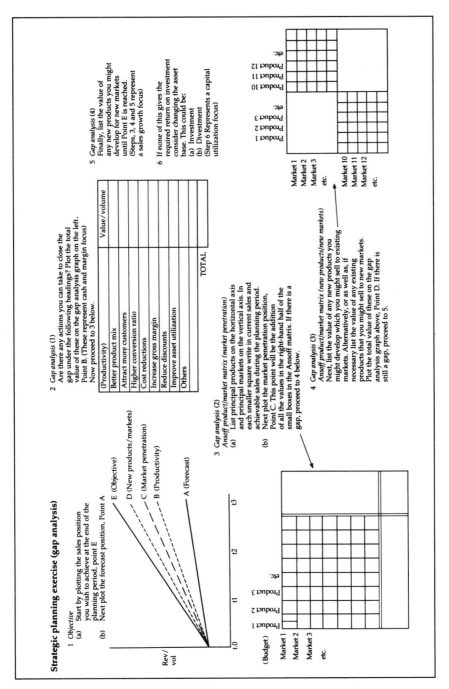

E (Objective)
D (New products/markets)
C (Market penetration)
B (Productivity)
A (Forecast)

Rev/vol

t.0   t1   t2   t3

(Budget) Product 1 Product 2 Product 3 etc.
Market 1
Market 2
Market 3
etc.

2 *Gap analysis (1)*

Are there any actions you can take to close the gap under the following headings? Plot the total value of these on the gap analysis graph on the left, Point B. (These represent cash and margin focus)

Now proceed to 3 below.

(Productivity)	Value/volume
Better product mix	
Attract more customers	
Higher conversion ratio	
Cost reductions	
Increase gross margin	
Reduce discounts	
Improve asset utilization	
Others	
TOTAL	

3 *Gap analysis (2)*

Ansoff product/market matrix (market penetration)

(a) List principal products on the horizontal axis and principal markets on the vertical axis. In each smaller square write in current sales and achievable sales during the planning period.

(b) Next plot the market penetration position, Point C. This point will be the addition of all the values in the right-hand half of the small boxes in the Ansoff matrix. If there is a gap, proceed to 4 below.

4 *Gap analysis (3)*

Ansoff product/market matrix (new products/new markets)

Next, list the value of any new products you might develop which you might sell to existing markets. Alternatively, or as well as, if necessary list the value of any existing products that you might sell to new markets. Plot the total value of these on the gap analysis graph above, Point D. If there is still a gap, proceed to 5.

Market 1
Market 2
Market 3
etc.
Market 10
Market 11
Market 12
etc.

Product 1 Product 2 Product 3 etc. Product 10 Product 11 Product 12 etc.

5 *Gap analysis (4)*

Finally, list the value of any new products you might develop for new markets until Point E is reached. (Steps, 3, 4 and 5 represent a sales growth focus)

6 If none of this gives the required return on investment consider changing the asset base. This could be:

(a) Investment

(b) Divestment

(Step 6 Represents a capital utilization focus)

Form 4

Form 5

Market Overview

Form 6

Strategic planning (SWOT analysis)

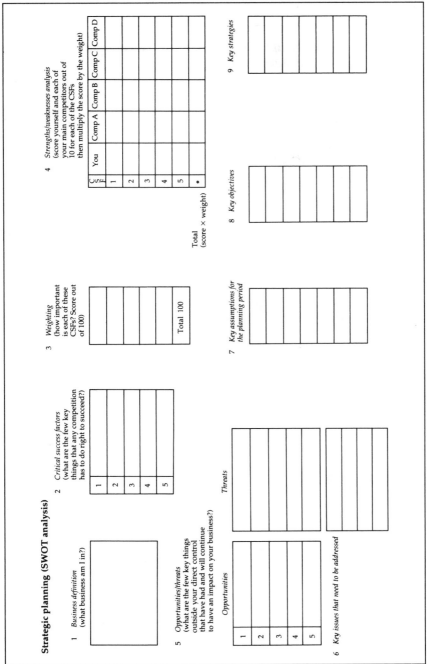

1 *Business definition*
(what business am I in?)

2 *Critical success factors*
(what are the few key
things that any competition
has to do right to succeed?)

1	
2	
3	
4	
5	

3 *Weighting*
(how important
is each of these
CSFs? Score out
of 100)

Total 100

4 *Strengths/weaknesses analysis*
(score yourself and each of
your main competitors out of
10 for each of the CSFs
then multiply the score by the weight)

CSF	You	Comp A	Comp B	Comp C	Comp D
1					
2					
3					
4					
5					
*					

Total
(score × weight)

5 *Opportunities/threats*
(what are the few key things
outside your direct control
that have had and will continue
to have an impact on your business?)

Opportunities

1	
2	
3	
4	
5	

Threats

6 *Key issues that need to be addressed*

7 *Key assumptions for
the planning period*

8 *Key objectives*

9 *Key strategies*

Form 7

Note: this form should be completed for each product market segment under consideration

Main competitor	Products/ markets and current objectives and strategies	Business direction	Strengths	Weaknesses	Competitive position

Form 8

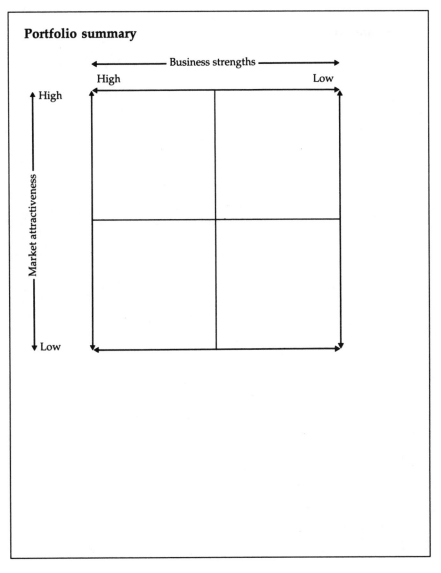

Portfolio summary

Form 9

Assumptions

Form 10

Database and summary of marketing objectives
Market segment sales values

Sales values	Last year (t–1) Total company market segment sales share	Current year (t+0) Total company market segment sales share	Next year (t+1) Total company market segment sales share	(t+2) Total company market segment sales share	(t+3) Total company market segment sales share
Key market segments (list)					
Total					

Form 11

Database and summary of marketing objectives
Market segment gross profits

Sales values	Last year (t–1)			Current year (t+0)			Next year (t+1)			(t+2)			(t+3)		
Key market segments (list)	Total company *market segment sales*		*share*	Total company *market segment sales*		*share*	Total company *market segment sales*		*share*	Total company *market segment sales*		*share*	Total company *market segment sales*		*share*
Total															

Form 12

Product group analysis

Product groups	Last year (t−1)		Current year (t+0)		Next year (t+1)		(t+2)		(t+3)	
	Sales value	Gross profit	Gross margin(%)	Sales value	Gross profit	Gross margin (%)	Sales value	Gross profit	Gross margin (%)	Sales value	Gross profit	Gross margin (%)	Sales value	Gross profit	Gross margin (%)
Total										

Form 13

Summary (in words) of main marketing objectives and strategies.

Form 14

Financial projections for 3 years

Form 1
Section B(2) – The one year marketing plan documentation

Overall objectives

Product/ market/ segment	Volume			Value			Gross margin			Commentary
	t-1	t.0	t+1	t-1	t.0	t+1	t-1	t.0	t+1	

Form 2

Overall strategies

	Strategies	Cost
1		
2		
3		
4		
5		
6		
7		
8		
9		
10		

Comments

Form 3

Sub-objectives, strategies, actions, responsibilities, timing, cost					
Product/ market/ segment	Objective	Strategies	Action	Responsibility	Timing	Cost

Total ____

Form 4

	t-1	*t.0*	*t+1*	*Comments*
Central costs:				
Depreciation				
Salaries				
Postage/telephones/stationery				
Legal and professional				
Training				
Data processing				
Advertising				
Sales promotion				
Travelling				
Buying and merchandising				
Printing				
Meetings/conferences				
Market research				
Internal costs				
Other (specify)				
Store costs:				
Rent				
Rates				
Heating/light/power				
Salaries				
Depreciation				
Packaging				
Display costs				
Total				

Form 5

Suggested downside risk assessment format

Key assumption	Basis of assumption	What event would have to happen to make this strategy unattractive?	Risk of such an event occurring (%) High P(7–10) Medium P(4–6) Low P(0–3)	Impact if event occurs	Trigger point for action	Actual contingency action proposed

Form 6

	t-1	*t.0*	*t+1*

Net revenue
Gross margin
Adjustments
Central costs:
  Marketing
  Buying and merchandising
  Administration
  Systems
  Distribution costs
Store costs:
  Rent
  Rates
  Heat/light/power
  Salaries
  Depreciation
  Packaging
  Display costs			

Operating result			
Other interest and financial costs			
Result after financial costs			
Net result			

Form 7

Key activity planner

Date/activity	Jan				Feb				March				April				May				June				July				Aug				Sept				Oct				Nov				Dec			
	1	2	3	4	1	2	3	4	1	2	3	4	1	2	3	4	1	2	3	4	1	2	3	4	1	2	3	4	1	2	3	4	1	2	3	4	1	2	3	4	1	2	3	4	1	2	3	4

Section B(3) – Example of format for a headquarters consolidated strategic plan

Directional statement

1 *Role/contribution* – this should be a brief statement about the company's role or contribution. Usually it will specify a minimum growth rate in turnover and profit, but it could also encapsulate roles such as opportunity-seeking, service and so on.

2 *Definition of business* – this statement should describe the needs that the company is fulfilling, or the benefits that it is providing for its markets.

3 *Distinctive competence* – all companies should have a distinctive competence. It does not have to be unique, but it must be substantial and sustainable. Distinctive competence can reside in integrity, unique/specialist product range, store siting, international coverage, reputation and so on.

4 *Indications for future direction* – this section should indicate guidelines for future growth. For example, does the company wish to expand internationally, or to acquire new skills and resources? The purpose of this section is to indicate the boundaries of future business activities.

Summary of main features of the plan

- Here draw a portfolio matrix indicating the current and proposed relative position of each of the strategic business units. Alternatively, this can appear later in the plan (see page 326).
- Include a few words summarizing growth in turnover, profit, margins, etc.
- Draw a graph indicating simply the total long-term plan. At least two lines are necessary – turnover and profit.

Financial history (past 5 years)

Include a bar chart showing relevant financial history, and, at the very least, include turnover and profit for the past 5 years.

Major changes and events since the previous plan

Here describe briefly major changes and events (such as divesting a subsidiary) which occured during the previous year.

Market characteristics

Here, it might be considered useful to provide a table listing strategic business units, alongside relevant market characteristics. See Table 13.2.

Table 13.2

	SBU1	SBU2	SBU3	SBU4
Market size				
Market growth				
Competitive intensity				
Relative market share				
etc.				

Competitive characteristics

Here, it might be considered useful to list the critical success factors by strategic business unit and rate each unit against major competitors. See Table 13.3.

Table 13.3

Critical success factors/competitors	Our company	Competitor 1	Competitor 2
CSF 1			
CSF 2			
CSF 3			
CSF 4			
CSF 5			

Key strategic issues

This is an extremely important section, as its purpose is to list (possibly by strategic business unit) the key issues facing the company. In essence, this really consists of stating the strengths, weaknesses, opportunities and threats, and indicating how they will be either built on or dealt with. Key strategic issues might consist of technology, regulation, competitive moves, institutional changes and so on.

Strategic objectives by strategic business

This is a summary of the objectives of each SBU. It should obviously be tailored to the specific circumstances of each company. See Table 13.4. Alternatively, or additionally, put a portfolio matrix indicating the current and proposed relative position of each of the strategic business units.

Table 13.4

Objectives Strategic business unit	Market share		Relative market share		Real growth		Key statistics				etc.
							Sales per employee		Contribution per employee		
	Now	+5 years	Now	+5 years	+5 years	p.a.	Now	+5 years	Now	+5 years	
SBU 1											
SBU 2											
SBU 3											
SBU 4											
SBU 5											

Financial goals (next 5 years)

Here, draw a bar chart (or a number of bar charts) showing the relevant financial goals. At the very least show turnover and profit by SBU for the next 5 years.

Appendices

Include whatever detailed appendices are appropriate. Try not to rob the total plan of focus by including too much detail.

Glossary of terms

Assumptions The major assumptions on which the marketing plan is based.

Benefit A perceived or stated relationship between a product feature and the need the feature is designed to satisfy. See also *Differential advantage* and *Feature*.

Business plan A plan commonly intermediate between a company's strategic plan and its annual marketing plan. The purpose of the business plan is to establish the broad business objectives and strategies to be pursued by the business unit or centre over a time period of as many as 5 years. In this respect, business plans are similar to strategic plans which concern themselves with equally long time-frames. Business plans are like strategic plans in one other respect: usually they deal with such strategic considerations as new product development, product acquisition, and new market development to achieve desired financial goals. Business plans also require extensive marketing input for their formulation and in this respect, they share characteristics in common with marketing plans. However, business plans generally do not include action programmes – a feature typical of marketing plans – but simply spell out intentions and directions. For example, if new product development was among the strategies pursued, this would be stated along with appropriate supporting rationale. However, the statement of this strategy would not be accompanied by a new product development plan.

Charter A statement of the chief function or responsibilty of an operating unit within an organization made up of several operating units. See also *Mission*.

Core strategy A term used in marketing to denote the predominant elements of the marketing mix, selected by marketing management to achieve the optimum match between the benefits customers seek and those the product offers. This process of selection is sometimes referred to as `making the differential advantage operational'.

Differential advantage A benefit or cluster of benefits offered to a sizeable group of customers which they value (and are willing to pay for) and which they cannot obtain elsewhere. See also *Feature* and *Benefit*.

Distribution A term used in marketing to refer to the means by which a product or service is made physically available to customers. Distribution encompasses such activities as warehousing, transportation, inventory control, order processing, etc. Because distribution is the means of increasing a product's availability, it is also a tool which can be used by marketing management to improve the match between benefits sought by customers and those offered by the organization.

Experience effect It is a proven fact that most value-added cost components of a product decline steadily with experience and can be reduced significantly as the scale of operation increases. In turn this cost (and therefore price advantage) is a significant factor in increasing the company's market share.

Feature A characteristic or property of a product or service such as reliability, price, convenience, safety, and quality. These features may or may not satisfy customer needs. To the extent that they do, they can be translated into benefits. See also *Benefit* and *Differential advantage*.

Gap In marketing terms, the difference between a product's present or projected performance and the level sought. Typically, the gaps in marketing management are those relating to return on investment, cash generation or use, return on sales, and market share.

Gap analysis The process of determining gaps between a product's present or projected performance and the level of performance sought. See also *Gap*.

Growth/share matrix A term synonymous with 'product portfolio' which in essence is a means of displaying graphically the amount of 'experience' or market share a product has and comparing this share with the rate of growth of the relevant market segment. With the matrix, managers can decide, for example, whether they should invest in getting more 'experience' – that is, fight for bigger market share – or perhaps get out of the market altogether. These choices are among a number of strategic alternatives available to the manager – strategic in the sense that they not only affect marketing strategy but determine use of capital within the organization. See also *Experience effect*.

Marketing audit A situational analysis of the company's current marketing capability. See also *Situational analysis*.

Marketing mix The 'tools' or means available to an organization to improve the match between benefits sought by customers and those offered by the organization so as to obtain a differential advantage. Among these tools are product, price, promotion and distribution service. See also *Differential advantage*.

Marketing objectives A statement of the targets or goals to be pursued and achieved within the period covered in the marketing plan. Depending on the scope and orientation of the plan – whether, for example, the plan is designed primarily to spell out short-term marketing intentions or to identify broad business directions and needs – the objectives stated may encompass such important measures of business performance as profit, growth and market share. With respect to profit, market share, sales volume, market development or penetration and other broader considerations are sometimes referred to as 'primary' marketing objectives. More commonly, they are referred to as 'strategic' or 'business' objectives since they pertain to the operation of the business as a whole. In turn, objectives set for specific marketing sub-functions or activities are referred to as 'programme' objectives to distinguish them from the broader business or strategic objectives they are meant to serve.

Marketing plan Contains a mission statement, SWOT analysis, assumption, marketing objectives, marketing strategies and programmes. Note that the objectives, strategies and policies are established for each level of the business.

Market segment A group of actual or potential customers who can be expected to respond in approximately the same way to a given offer; a finer more detailed breakdown of a market.

Market segmentation A critical aspect of marketing planning and one designed to convert product differences into a cost differential that can be maintained over the profit's life cycle. See also *Product life cycle.*

Market share The percentage of the market represented by a firm's sales in relation to total sales. Some marketing theorists argue that the term is misleading since it suggests that the dimensions of the market are known and assumes that the size of the market is represented by the amount of goods sold in it. All that is known, these theorists point out, and correctly, is the volume sold; in actuality, the market may be considerably larger.

Mission A definite task with which one is charged; the chief function of an institution or organization. In essence it is a vision of what the company is or is striving to become. The basic issue is: 'What is our business and what should it be?' In marketing planning, the mission statement is the starting point in the planning process, since it sets the broad parameters within which marketing objectives are established, strategies developed, and programmes implemented. Some companies, usually those with several operating units or divisions make a distinction between 'mission' and 'charter'. In these instances, the term 'mission' is used to denote the broader purpose of the organization as reflected in corporate policies or assigned by the senior management of the company; the term 'charter', in comparison, is used to denote the purpose or reason for being of individual units with prime responsibility for a specific functional or product-marketing area.

Objective   A statement or description of a desired future result that cannot be predicted in advance but which is believed, by those setting the objective, to be achievable through their efforts within a given time period; a quantitative target or goal to be achieved in the future through one's efforts, which can be used to measure performance. To be of value, objectives should be specific in time and scope and attainable given the financial, technical and human resources available. According to this definition, general statements of hopes or desire are not true 'objectives'. See also *Marketing objectives*.

Planning   The process of pre-determining a course or courses of action based on assumptions about future conditions or trends which can be imagined but not predicted with any certainty.

Policies   Guidelines adopted in implementing the strategies selected. In essence, a policy is a summary statement of objectives and strategies.

Positioning   The process of selecting, delineating and matching the segment of the market with which a product will be most compatible.

Product   A term used in marketing to denote not only the product itself – its inherent properties and characteristics – but also service, availability, price, and other factors which may be as important in differentiating the product from those of competitors as the inherent characteristics of the product itself. See also *Marketing mix*.

Product life cycle   A term used in marketing to refer to the pattern of growth and decline in sales revenue of a product over time. This pattern is typically divided into stages: introduction, growth, maturity, saturation and decline. With time, competition among firms tends to reduce all products in the market to commodities – products which can only be marginally differentiated from each other – with the result that pioneering companies – those first to enter the market – face the choice of becoming limited volume, high-priced, high-cost speciality producers or high-volume, low-cost producers of standard products.

Product portfolio   A theory about the alternative uses of capital by business organizations formulated originally by Bruce Henderson of the Boston Consulting Group, a leading firm in the area of corporate strategy consulting. This theory or approach to marketing strategy formulation has gained wide acceptance among managers of diversified companies, who were first attracted by the intuitively appealing notion that long-run corporate performance is more than the sum of the contributions of individual profit centres or product strategies. Other factors which account for the theory's appeal are: (a) its usefulness in developing specific marketing strategies designed to achieve a balanced mix of products that will produce maximum return from scarce cash and managerial resources; and (b) the fact that the theory employs a simple matrix representation useful in portraying and communicating a product's position in the market place. See also *Growth/share matrix*.

Programme   A term used in marketing planning to denote the steps or tasks to be undertaken by marketing, field sales and other functions within an organization to implement the chosen strategies and to accomplish the objectives set forth in the marketing plan. Typically, description of programmes include a statement of objectives as well as a definition of the persons or units responsible and a schedule for completion of the steps or tasks for which the person or unit is responsible. See also *Strategy statement* and *Marketing objectives*.

Relative market share   A firm's share of the market relative to its largest competitor. See also *Market share*.

Resources   Broadly speaking, anyone or anything through which something is produced or accomplished; in marketing planning, a term used to denote the unique capabilities or skills that an organization brings to a market or business problem or opportunity.

Situational analysis   The second step in the marketing planning process (the first being the definition of mission), and reviews the business environment at large (with particular attention to economic, market and competitive aspects) as well as the company's own internal operation. The purpose of the situational analysis is to identify marketing problems and opportunities, both those stemming from the organization's internal strengths and limitations, and those external to the organization and caused by changes in economic conditions and trends, competition, customer expectations, industry relations, government regulations and, increasingly, social perceptions and trends. The output of the full analysis is summarized in key-point form under the heading SWOT (strengths, weaknesses, opportunities and threats) analysis; this summary then becomes part of the marketing plan. The outcome of the situational analysis includes a set of assumptions about future conditions as well as an estimate or forecast of potential market demand during the period covered by the marketing plan. Based on these estimates and assumptions, marketing objectives are established and strategies and programme formulated.

Strategy statement   A description of the broad course of action to be taken to achieve a specific marketing objective such as an increase in sales volume or a reduction in unit costs. The strategy statement is frequently referred to as the connecting link between marketing objectives and programmes – the actual concrete steps to be taken to achieve those objectives. See also *Programme*.

Target   Something aimed at; a person or group of persons to be made the object of an action or actions intended, usually to bring about an effect or change in the person or group of persons, e.g. our target is the canned food segment of the market.

Index